Vocational Preparation and Employment of Students with Physical and Multiple Disabilities

Vocational Preparation and Employment of Students with Physical and Multiple Disabilities

by

Jo-Ann Sowers, Ph.D.
and
Laurie Powers, Ph.D.
Oregon Research Institute
Eugene

·P·A·U·L·H·
BROOKES
PUBLISHING C?

Baltimore • London • Toronto • Sydney

Paul H. Brookes Publishing Co.
P.O. Box 10624
Baltimore, Maryland 21285-0624

Typeset by Brushwood Graphics, Inc., Baltimore, Maryland.
Manufactured in the United States of America by
The Maple Press Company, York, Pennsylvania.

The writing of this book was partially supported by a grant (G008730431) from the
Department of Education.

Library of Congress Cataloging-in-Publication Data

Sowers, Jo-Ann.
    Vocational preparation and employment of students with physical and multiple
    disabilities /   Jo-Ann Sowers and Laurie Powers.
        p.   cm.
    Includes bibliographical references and index.
    ISBN 1-55766-066-2
    1. Handicapped children—Vocational education.   2.   Physically
    handicapped children—Vocational education.   3.   Handicapped—
    Employment.   4.   Physically handicapped—Employment.   I.   Powers,
    Laurie.   II.   Title.
    LC4019.7.S69   1991
    371.91—dc20   90-24249
                                                                              CIP

Contents

Foreword

*V*ocational Preparation and Employment of Students with Physical and Multiple Disabilities represents a major step forward in the field of vocational education. Author Jo-Ann Sowers was one of the pioneers in establishing the first supported employment programs at the University of Washington. Until that time, persons with severe disabilities were seen to be unfit or incapable of employment in real work settings. The Washington food service program and succeeding demonstrations established the fact that persons with more challenging needs could also work effectively in the mainstream. Thus, the supported employment movement was born. The new question became not whether the individual was capable of being employed, but what kind of support services were needed to ensure successful work performance. Throughout the past decade, both individual and group placement models have been developed within the rubric of supported employment. The present volume eloquently reviews these historical trends and leaves the reader with the flavor of their accomplishments.

Yet, after a decade of supported employment, its assumptions and goals have not been completely met. Supported employment entails a principle of zero-rejection, that all persons, regardless of the severity of their disabilities, can be gainfully employed. Recent studies by Paul Wehman show that persons with mild and moderate mental retardation are the primary recipients of this service. Issues facing adults with severe/profound mental retardation, behavior disorders, and physical impairments have barely been addressed by this vocational model. It is within this context of addressing unserved populations that the Sowers and Powers book is so critical and timely.

Persons with physical impairments pose particular challenges in the employment arena. Often their production rates are low. There may be difficulties in transporting them to and from work. Also, chronic medical needs may present barriers to performing in the workplace. The power of this volume emerges in the way that it conceptually and practically takes on and dispenses with these obstacles to employment. It makes a total commitment to the social integration of employees with physical disabilities at the workplace. The employee works side by side with nondisabled co-workers who often become friends and supportive colleagues.

As might be expected from two fine social scientists, Sowers and Powers extend the technology of applied behavior analysis in its most creative directions. At the task and personal level, they advance innovative strategies for designing job tasks. Even more impressive is the manner in which their job creation strategies offer new roles for the worker with physical disabilities. Finally, the book advances thoughtful solutions to job-related problems like bowel/bladder control, wheelchair mobility, and behavioral disturbances.

Vocational Preparation and Employment of Students with Physical and Multiple Disabilities is a well written and accessible volume. Its tables, figures, and recording sheets give the reader a true sense of the vocational training process. It also serves as a document of what can be done with this population. It can therefore be said to serve as a historical landmark and as an inspiration to future educators and consumers.

Robert Gaylord-Ross, Ph.D.
Vanderbilt University

Author's note: *Word of the death of Dr. Robert Gaylord-Ross arrived as this book was going to press. Robert was one of the most productive and genuinely nice people in our field. He will be sorely missed as a colleague and friend.*

Jo-Ann Sowers, Ph.D.

Preface

A large portion of the credit for this book should be given to a young man named Kelly. Several years ago the first author was asked by Kelly's teacher what she should do to prepare Kelly for the transition from school to work. Kelly, who was 16 years old at the time, experiences cerebral palsy and mental retardation, uses a power wheelchair, has limited functional use of his hands, and uses speech but is difficult to understand. After reviewing the available vocational preparation literature and speaking with other professionals around the country, it was clear that few attempts had been made to address the unique challenges that staff encounter in preparing students like Kelly for the transition from school to work.

This book reflects our efforts over the past 6 years to address these challenges. We have had the opportunity to work directly or in a consultative role with over 100 students with physical and multiple disabilities, in over 20 different school districts and with these districts' staff. We also began and operated a supported employment program, Alternative Work Concepts (Alternatives), for adults with physical and multiple disabilities. Many of the students with whom we were involved when they were in school have made the transition from school into this program. This has provided us with the chance to see the long-term impact of the vocational preparation strategies utilized with them. Alternatives has also provided supported employment opportunities to adults, most of whom were recently deinstitutionalized, who have physical and multiple disabilities. Case descriptions of some of the students and adults with whom we have worked are provided between chapters of this book.

This book was written primarily for school staff who are involved in the vocational preparation of students with physical and multiple disabilities. This includes teachers, vocational trainers, occupational therapists, physical therapists, and speech therapists. We have attempted to make the book as practically oriented as possible and to provide sufficient detail that will permit staff to utilize the strategies and practices described.

Although the book focuses on school program and vocational preparation issues, it should also be of use to adult service programs. The information related to supported employment models, work-related issues, training techniques, and job design strategies will be particularly relevant to adult service programs.

Acknowledgments

Most importantly, we would like to express our appreciation to the students and adults with disabilities who have given us the opportunity to learn from them. We would also like to thank their parents, who have been our greatest supporters in advocating for and implementing programs to prepare their young adults to work in nonsheltered settings.

The dedication and effort of the staff who were willing to take on the challenge of getting their students with significant physical and multiple disabilities into community work experiences and placing them into paid, nonsheltered employment is greatly appreciated.

Finally, there are a few people who have been particularly instrumental in supporting and contributing to our efforts. We would like to give special thanks to Jacque Gerdes, Ryam Nearing, Chris Jenkins, Diana Roberts, Linda Crites, Penny Reed, and Sandy Hall.

1 An Overview of Vocational Preparation and Employment

Since the mid-1970s, great strides have been made in the availability of employment opportunities for persons with severe disabilities. Before this time it was assumed that these individuals had little capacity beyond sheltered employment. Reflecting this view, school programs saw their responsibility to be no more than providing students with prevocational skill training that would prepare them for their entrance into a sheltered program. It now has been demonstrated that the vocational capacity of persons with severe disabilities is far greater than previously thought and that they can work in community settings if provided with systematic training and ongoing support (Rhodes & Valenta, 1985; Rusch & Mithaug, 1980; Sowers, Thompson, & Connis, 1979; Vogelsberg, 1990). In addition, the belief that all individuals, regardless of the severity of their disability, have the right to work in these settings has been accepted by increasing numbers of professionals, parents, and consumers. These factors have culminated in the advent of the supported employment movement, which represents the most significant systems change in vocational services since the 1920s when these services were first mandated. Through supported employment the adult vocational service system for persons with developmental disabilities is shifting from one that is primarily sheltered to one that is integrated and community-based (Bellamy, Rhodes, Mank, & Albin, 1988; Rusch & Hughes, 1990; Wehman, Kregel, & Shafer, 1990; Wehman & Moon, 1988). Reflecting these changes, school programs now see vocational preparation as one of their most important responsibilities (and in some cases *the* most important), and a significant portion of the secondary special education program resources of many districts are devoted to it (Bates, 1989; Hutchins & Renzaglia, 1990; McDonnell, Hardman, & Hightower, 1989; Pumpian, West & Shepard, 1988; Wehman, Moon, Everson, Wood, & Barcus, 1988). Along with the realization of the importance of school programs in preparing students for the transition from school to community employment, much attention has been devoted to identifying strategies that schools can utilize to achieve this outcome. A few of these strategies include training those tasks that are available in the local job market, training critical work-related skills, providing this training in real businesses, and careful coordination with adult services agencies to insure students' successful transition. These "best practices" have been implemented on a widespread basis with the assistance of federal and state sponsored in-service training and technical assistance projects, as well as through the publication and dissemination of texts and training materials.

Most of the efforts to identify practices that schools should use to prepare students vocationally have focused on students with cognitive disabilities (i.e., mental retardation) (McDonnell et al., 1989; Pumpian et al., 1988; Wehman, Moon, et al., 1988). Little attention has been given to the unique challenges that schools face in preparing students who experience physical and multiple disabilities vocationally (Sowers, Jenkins, & Powers, 1988; Sowers & Powers, 1989; Wehman, Wood, Everson, Goodwyn, & Conley, 1988; Wood, 1988). These are students who experience a physical disability such as cerebral palsy, spina bifida, or muscular dystrophy. Many of these students also experience cognitive disabilities as well as other concomitant disabilities including limited vision, limited hearing, and communication difficulties. Identifying the types of tasks that students with multiple disabilities can be trained to perform is one challenge faced when developing a vocational program for them. Another is attempting to provide these students, who may require more training and supervision than others, with community-based work experiences, given the limited resources of most districts. Other challenges include identifying strategies that can effectively overcome employment barriers encountered by these students, such as using the bathroom, getting into and around employment sites, eating and drinking while at work, and communicating with co-workers.

The philosophical foundation of the supported employment movement is the belief that all persons, regardless of the nature or severity of their disabilities, should have the opportunity to work in integrated settings (Moon, Inge, Wehman, Brooke, & Barcus, 1990; Rusch & Hughes, 1990). If this goal is to be realized for students with physical and multiple disabilities, those practices that schools can use to meet these students' vocational preparation challenges must be identified and implemented. Through the work of these authors and the efforts of others, it is clear that although the "best practices" that have been identified for vocationally preparing students with cognitive disabilities have application to students with physical and multiple disabilities, they need to be modified and adapted (Sowers et al. 1988; Wehman, Wood, et al., 1990; Wood, 1988). In this chapter, a description of each of the current vocational preparation best practices and how they can be applied to students with physical and multiple disabilities is presented, along with an overview of the phases of vocational preparation that should be implemented by school programs. A brief description of the traditional adult service and supported employment approaches and their implications for persons with physical and multiple disabilities is also provided.

VOCATIONAL PREPARATION BEST PRACTICES

There are nine strategies that have been widely acknowledged as critical components of successful vocational preparation programs for students with disabilities (McDonnell et al., 1989; Pumpian et al., 1988; Wilcox, McDonnell, Bellamy, & Rose, 1988). These are:

1. Identify and train jobs and tasks that reflect the local community job market.
2. Train work-related skills that are critical to job success.
3. Train students in community settings.
4. Use systematic instructional procedures to train students.
5. Identify adaptive strategies that will increase student independence.
6. Reconceptualize staff roles and organizational structures.
7. Involve parents in the vocational preparation of their children.
8. Establish paid employment for students before they leave school.
9. Coordinate and collaborate with adult service programs.

These practices and the manner in which they need to be implemented to meet the unique challenges of students with physical and multiple disabilities are addressed in this section.

Identify and Train Jobs and Tasks that Reflect the Local Community Job Market

Traditionally, prevocational curricula served as the core of vocational programs for students with disabilities (Brown, Branston, Hamre-Nietupski, Pumpian, Certo, & Gruenewald, 1979). This approach is based on the assumption that students must master a set of prerequisite skills (e.g., color identification, size discrimination, staying on task, following directions) before they will be able to learn actual work tasks. The prevocational approach also assumes that there is a standard set of skills that is critical to all students in all programs.

Research and experience has demonstrated that the most effective and efficient means to prepare students to work in community businesses is to train them to perform the actual tasks that are performed in these businesses (Brown et al., 1979; Wehman, Moon, et al., 1988). This approach recognizes that students can learn to wipe tables or photocopy a piece of paper without first learning colors or counting to ten. This approach is also based on the reality that different business sectors in the community offer students different future employment opportunities and that students should be trained to perform those jobs and skills that specifically reflect their own community's businesses and industries. For example, if students live in a city where there are a lot of electronic assembly jobs, then it would be appropriate to train these types of tasks. However, training these tasks to students who live in a city with few of these job opportunities would contribute little to their future employment. This community-referencing approach obviates the utility of a standard skills curriculum and requires that school programs become knowledgeable of their community's business sector and employment market.

Of course, when identifying which tasks to train, the ability of the students to learn these tasks and the feasibility of placing them in jobs that involve the performance of these tasks must be weighed (Wilcox et al., 1988). Food service and janitorial tasks are often trained to students with cognitive disabilities. This is true because there is typically an abundance of these jobs in many communities, the cognitive requirements of the tasks involved are minimal, and the students are physically able to perform them.

Students who experience physical and multiple disabilities present a particular challenge to staff when attempting to identify the types of tasks to train. Physically demanding tasks like those involved in food service and janitorial jobs are not ones that most of these students will be able to perform. On the other hand, sedentary jobs frequently require more sophisticated cognitive and academic skills than many of these students possess or can learn.

The lack of attempts by the adult service system to place individuals with these disabilities into community jobs has provided school programs with little guidance in identifying the types of jobs that have future employment potential for their students. These authors as well as others who have made the first attempts to place individuals with physical and multiple disabilities have identified a pool of tasks which may serve as the starting point for districts in identifying tasks to train to their students (Sowers et al., 1988; Wehman, Wood, et al., 1988). This list includes such tasks as simple computer data entry and typing, phone answering, photocopying, filing, and light delivery (a complete list of these tasks is provided in Chapter 2).

Train Work-Related Skills Critical to Job Success

Research and experience has shown that persons with disabilities lose their jobs more frequently due to work-related difficulties than to task-performance difficulties (McDonnell et al., 1989; Wilcox et al., 1988). As with tasks, there is no standard list of work-related skills that should be taught to all students. The skills that are critical to job success will depend on the type of work setting and job into which a student will be placed. For example, social skills will be more important if a student's job will involve interacting with customers than if it does not. However, there have been a number of work-related skills that have been identified as important across a variety of jobs and work sites. Examples of these include good grooming, the ability to sequence between tasks (when the person completes one task, he or she goes on to the next one on the assignment list without prompting), good attendance and punctuality, taking instructions and feedback from supervisors in a positive manner, being able to interact and socialize with co-workers, and the ability to get to and from work (Rusch & Mithaug, 1980; Rusch, Schutz, & Agran, 1982; Wehman, 1981).

The skills identified above should be part of the vocational preparation of students with physical and multiple disabilities. However, there are a number of other work-related issues that frequently need to be addressed for these students. These include mobility, communication, bathroom use, and eating and drinking. Students who use a wheelchair need to learn (or an alternative or support strategies devised) to maneuver their chairs on and off buses, to negotiate curbcuts, to open doors, and to move around a business. Alternative communication strategies need to be identified and trained to students who are unable to speak or who speak with difficulty. These students may need to learn how to transfer themselves as independently as possible when using the bathroom or have arrangements made to provide the needed transferring assistance. Many students with physical and multiple disabilities have difficulty eating and drinking. Thus, strategies that they can utilize to eat and drink as independently as possible at a job site also need to be identified.

Train Students in Community Settings

Most if not all vocational training was traditionally provided to students with severe disabilities in the classroom. The shortcomings of this approach were realized when students failed to generalize what they had learned in the classroom to community employment settings (Wilcox & Bellamy, 1982; Wacker & Berg, 1986). Research and experience have demonstrated that the extent to which students generalize skills is directly related to how similar the learning setting is to the setting in which they will then be expected to perform the trained skills. It is virtually impossible to simulate the environments of real work settings in a classroom. Consequently, school programs have begun to provide students with work experiences in community businesses (McDonnell et al., 1989).

School districts face a particular challenge when attempting to provide community-based work experience opportunities to students with physical and multiple disabilities (Baumgart & VanWalleghem, 1986). Problems that are frequently encountered include transportation and the staff ratios necessary to supervise these students while ensuring that they are able to profit from their work experiences. One solution is for administrators to demonstrate their commitment to vocational preparation by designating additional resources to it. However, given the limited resources that are available in most districts, other strategies are needed. For example, placing a student who requires a large amount of support with one or two other students who have fewer support needs is one simple strategy. Using sites in close proximity to the school building is another strategy that can be used to help alleviate transportation difficulties.

Use Systematic Instructional Procedures to Train Students

A fairly comprehensive and well researched technology exists for training persons with cognitive disabilities (Bellamy, Horner, & Inman, 1979; Mank & Horner, 1988; Moon et al. 1990; Rusch & Mithaug, 1980). In particular, the strategies for assisting students to learn new tasks and work-related skills have been identified (e.g., task analysis, prompting, and reinforcement procedures). A substantial degree of progress has also been made in identifying strategies to assist students to generalize and maintain learned skills (Wacker & Berg, 1986).

The discriminations required by tasks typically cause the greatest performance difficulties for students with cognitive disabilities. However, a student with a physical disability such as cerebral palsy may also experience a great deal of difficulty in attempting to execute the movements required by tasks. Behavioral techniques used for discrimination training can also be used for teaching these movements to students with motor control difficulties (Rice, McDonald, & Denney, 1968; Orelove & Sobsey, 1987). However, these techniques may need to be modified for this purpose. For example, physical assistance may not be a prompting strategy that is effective when training students with athetoid cerebral palsy because they reflectively resist physical manipulation. In addition, strategies may need to be employed with which many trainers are not familiar. For example, providing students with athetoid and spastic cerebral palsy with relaxation instructions can assist them in executing movements required by tasks (Inman, 1979; Nielson & McCaughey, 1979).

Identify Adaptive Strategies that Will Increase Student Independence

It often is not feasible for a student with a severe disability to learn to perform a task as it is currently designed and performed by other individuals. However, there are frequently alternative or adaptive strategies that can be used to allow a student to perform the task independently (York & Rainforth, 1987). For example, a student who is unable to "tell time" may be able to learn to use a picture of a clock face to independently initiate tasks and activities based on time (Sowers, Rusch, Connis, & Cummings, 1980). The practice of focusing on the functional outcomes of behaviors, as opposed to the form or manner in which a behavior is performed, has been a particularly important contribution to educational and vocational programs for students with severe disabilities (Campbell, 1989; Wilcox & Bellamy, 1982).

Task design and adaptations are especially important for students who may have difficulty performing a task because of physical limitation (Campbell,

1989). A major goal of school staff should be to identify those adaptations that will increase the ability of a student to perform tasks as independently and productively as possible. Staff often assume that adaptations must be "high tech" and expensive. In fact, the most useful adaptations are frequently the simplest and do not involve specialized equipment or devices (Sowers, 1990).

Reconceptualize Staff Roles and Organizational Structures of School Programs

Limited staff resources is probably the major challenge that districts face in providing students with community-based work experience. This is particularly true in districts where staff perceive their roles traditionally. Traditional school models maintain teachers in classrooms and related service staff in therapy rooms. To successfully implement a community-based model, staff must be willing to reconceptualize their roles, and administrative regulations must support these new roles (McDonnell et al., 1989; Wilcox & Bellamy, 1982).

The consultative as well as direct assistance of related service personnel at work experience sites is particularly critical for students with physical and multiple disabilities. To be of greatest assistance, these staff must be provided with training related to functional skill orientations in general, and vocational preparation issues and strategies in particular (Sowers, Hall, & Rainforth, 1990).

Involve Parents in Vocational Preparation of Their Children

The Education for All Handicapped Children Act (PL 94-142) mandated the involvement of parents in the education of children with disabilities. Unfortunately, this involvement is often restricted to participation in an annual Individualized Education Program (IEP) meeting. The extent to which parents can influence the employment opportunities and successes of their children has been widely acknowledged (McDonnell, Wilcox, Boles, & Bellamy, 1985; Sowers, 1989a). Many parents are reluctant to allow a de-emphasis of academic activities to permit time for vocational and functional training activities. School staff must educate parents about the importance of work in their child's future life and the need for early and ongoing vocational preparation. Some parents may also believe that community-based employment is not a feasible goal for their child. This is particularly true for parents of students with physical and multiple disabilities. Again, schools must take the responsibility for educating these parents about supported employment and the implications it can have for their children. Simply providing parents with the opportunity to observe their child at a community site working alongside nondisabled employees can go a long way in achieving this outcome. In addition, sharing with parents the employment successes of individuals who experience disabilities similar to their child's is another effective strategy for this purpose.

Establish Paid Employment for
Students Before They Depart School

Student placement into a job is the ultimate goal and measure of the success of school vocational programs. To ensure this outcome, school programs should attempt to obtain or work closely with adult service agencies to establish students in jobs before they leave school.

The schools should summarize the information that they collected throughout students' vocational preparation programs and utilize it to determine the type of job that should be sought for them, the type of work setting in which they are most likely to be successful, and the types and amounts of supports that they will require.

The goal of the school should be to arrange employment situations for students that are as normalized and integrated as possible. Students with severe disabilities and high support needs, including those with physical and multiple disabilities, are often provided only with the opportunity to work in group placement situations such enclaves or crews. There is a growing awareness of the need to identify strategies that will enable these students to work in more integrated situations, and a number of approaches for accomplishing this have been identified (Nisbet & Hagner, 1988). These include the use of co-workers as support agents, and work incentive programs that allow persons to assist in paying for their own support.

Coordinate and Collaborate with Adult Service Programs

In the past, the roles of the school and adult service systems were viewed as distinct and separate. The school program worked with students until they completed their school eligibility and then the adult program was expected to take over. Few attempts were made to systematically link these two systems. Today, the importance of careful planning and coordination between school and adult service agencies is widely acknowledged (Hardman & McDonnell, 1987; McDonnell & Hardman, 1985; Wehman, Moon, et al., 1988).

Communication and collaboration is important in the development of the vocational preparation program devised and provided to students. The adult service programs can make suggestions and recommendations about the type of tasks and jobs available in the local job market and the types of work-related skills that are important in these job areas. Providing adult programs with regular updates on the students who will be exiting the school programs, including their skills and support needs, will assist the adult programs to prepare to serve these individuals.

The need for careful planning and coordination when a student is nearing school departure and a permanent job situation is being considered is particularly critical, especially for students with physical and multiple disabilities for whom new and innovative employment and support arrangements may be needed. At the present time, few adult service employment programs have experience working with individuals with physical and multiple disabilities. Those who have served these individuals have rarely attempted to do so outside of a sheltered setting. Consequently, the school program may need to strongly encourage and work with adult service programs to convince them to serve these students and to do so in community settings. School staff should assist in educating and training the adult program staff in strategies and procedures that may be unique to working with these individuals.

Summary

Most school districts have implemented the current best practices in their vocational programs for students with cognitive disabilities. Students with physical and multiple disabilities, however, frequently have not been included in these programs in part due to an uncertainty about how to do so. Here an overview of the manner in which these practices can be adapted in order to provided students with multiple and physical disabilities with the opportunity to gain vocational preparation comparable to other students has been presented.

PHASES OF VOCATIONAL PREPARATION

Vocational preparation is often perceived to be an activity that occurs only when a student begins high school. In fact, to be most effective, it should be viewed as a longitudinal process, beginning when students are in elementary school, proceeding through middle school and high school, and culminating in a paid job before the student leaves school (Wehman, Wood, et al., 1988). A brief description of the activities that will contribute to a student's future employment at each of these junctures is provided in this section.

Elementary School

Elementary school teachers can contribute to the future employment success of students with physical and multiple disabilities in many ways. Probably the most important of these is instilling in students the expectation that they can work and a belief in the importance of work. One means to achieve this outcome is to actually begin providing students with the opportunities to perform work tasks and chores. A teacher can develop a list of classroom chores and duties that are assigned to students on a rotating basis. This list might include such things as cleaning the erasers, taking the class attendance to the front office, and getting the teacher's mail from the mail room. Teachers can also organize special work projects that will teach students work tasks and skills. For example, a weekly or monthly newsletter aimed at describing class activities for parents could be produced. Students could assist in writing the newsletter using a computer, as well as photocopying, folding, and stapling it.

The elementary years are also a good time to have adults who experience disabilities visit the classroom to discuss their lives and work. These individuals will serve as important role models to students and help establish the belief that despite their disabilities they can work and earn a living.

Teachers should also begin to discuss work with parents during the elementary years. Many parents of students with physical and multiple disabilities hold little hope that their children will be able to work as adults. This view can greatly influence their general perception of their child's competence and their hopefulness for their child's future. Perhaps the most important thing that teachers can do for parents at this stage is to simply provide them with descriptions of individuals with disabilities similar to their own child's who are working in community settings. Teachers should also discuss with parents the importance of early and ongoing vocational preparation. These discussions will set the stage for gaining the support of parents for the inclusion of vocational objectives in their child's program during the middle and high school years.

Middle School

Vocational instruction should begin in earnest in the middle school years. Students should have the opportunity to perform tasks identified as applicable to the local community job market, and to perform them in real work settings. During the middle school years, offices and other work areas in school buildings can serve as excellent work experience sites. Students should have a regular schedule of work and specific task assignments to perform during these periods. Although the amount of a student's day that should be devoted to work will depend on a number of factors, one or two periods per day is a suggested amount during the middle school years. The emphasis of the middle school training should be on building the students' and their parents' belief in their ability to work, assessing what types of tasks the student is able to perform most independently and his or her task preferences, identifying the types of adaptations that will assist them to perform these tasks, and beginning to teach students these critical work-related skills.

High School

During the early high school years, intensive training should be provided that allows students to become as independent and productive as possible when performing tasks and work-related behaviors. For some students this may involve identifying a small number of tasks that they demonstrate a particular capacity for performing during the middle school years for the focus of training. Students should have the opportunity to participate in out-of-school work experience and to learn to ride the public bus to and from these sites. Staff will continue to attempt to identify adaptations that will assist students in becoming as independent and productive as possible. In addition, the amount of a student's program that is devoted to vocational activities should be increased to several hours a day. For students who remain in school past 18 years of age, the vast majority of their program should be devoted to vocational activities (McDonnell et al., 1989).

When students are no more than 1 or 2 years from school completion, attention should turn to attempting to create a paid employment situation for them. In fact, during this time students may spend most or all of their day at a paid job. The school's role is to provide training and follow-up support to the students at their work sites.

Summary

Schools should not wait until students enter high school to begin providing them with experiences that will contribute to their future employment. Teachers at the elementary and middle school levels can make a significant contribution to the vocational preparation of students. To be most effective, staff from all levels should have a shared vision of the importance of vocational preparation and should coordinate their efforts in providing these services.

ADULT EMPLOYMENT SERVICES AND MODELS

The focus of this book is the role of schools in preparing students with physical and multiple disabilities for the transition from school to work. Within the framework of the new vocational preparation and supported employment models, schools are responsible for placing students into paid employment before they leave school or for working closely with an adult program that will do this for the student. Consequently, it is critical that school staff understand supported employment approaches and models. A brief review of the adult service system in both the traditional and supported employment models is provided in this section. In addition, specific attention is given to discussing why persons with physical and multiple disabilities have not been included in these programs as well as describing programs that have included these persons and demonstrated their employment capacity.

Traditional Service System

Attempts to address the difficulties that individuals with disabilities encounter in gaining employment occurred more than 100 years ago. However, the real drive behind these efforts occurred with the passage of the Vocational Rehabilitation Act in 1920. This act mandated that states provide services to their residents with disabilities that would assist them in gaining employment. The traditional adult service vocational system, which evolved over the subsequent decades, offered individuals three employment options (Bellamy, Rhodes, Bourbeau, & Mank, 1986). The first option was competitive employment, which was only offered to persons who could be placed into an existing job in a regular business, learn to perform this job independently and to high productivity standards, and do so with little or no assistance. An individual being considered for competitive employment also had to be able to perform a wide variety of work-related skills thought to be necessary for job success (e.g., time telling) and not exhibit behaviors that might be deemed "inappropriate."

The second employment option available to persons with disabilities in the traditional system was sheltered workshops. The major purpose of sheltered workshops was to prepare individuals for competitive employment. Sheltered workshops were also supposed to provide a person a place to work and earn money while waiting to move on to competitive employment.

The third option was a work activity center. These programs typically focused on teaching "prevocational skills," such as eye-hand and fine-motor coordination, staying on task, and basic self-help skills. These skills were thought to be necessary before a person could work in a sheltered workshop or in a competitive employment placement.

Because the traditional employment service system was based on the belief that a person could be considered for nonsheltered employment only when she or he demonstrated the ability to function independently at a work site with little or no training, the focus of the system was to prepare persons to meet this requirement. In fact, the traditional system was characterized and rationalized as a flow-through model (Bellamy et al., 1986). It was assumed that a person would begin in a work activity center, move on to a sheltered workshop, and finally into competitive employment.

In the late 1970s, evaluations of the traditional system illustrated that it was not achieving its goals (U.S. Department of Labor, 1979). Relatively few persons moved out of sheltered workshops into competitive employment or from work activity centers to sheltered workshops. In addition, the low wages offered by these programs also cast doubt on their utility.

In addition to the evidence related to the existing service system, there was a growing belief in the right of persons with disabilities to participate in community settings and activities (Wolfensberger, 1972). There was also a developing technology of vocational training based on behavioral principles, which was found to be highly effective for persons with mental retardation. In response to these events, attempts were made to develop an alternative model that would better assist in moving individuals into competitive employment (Rusch & Mithaug, 1980; Wehman, 1981). These new competitive employment programs typically included a brief, intensive preplacement training period that targeted only the most critical skills and behaviors. Individuals were then placed in a job and provided with on-the-job training. A key feature of these programs was the use of systematic, behavioral instructional techniques to train tasks and work-related behaviors. In addition, ongoing support was provided to help insure job maintenance.

These new competitive employment programs proved to be highly successful in attaining competitive employment for many individuals with developmental disabilities (Hill, Wehman, Kregel, Bank, & Metzler, 1987; Sowers, Thompson, & Connis, 1979; Wehman & Kregel, 1985). However, this approach still relied on the same basic assumption as the traditional system—that only those individuals who could function independently at work sites with relatively little ongoing assistance and support could work in community settings. The new programs were more effective in assisting individuals to achieve this outcome. However, there remained a large number of persons, particularly those with severe disabilities, for whom these programs were not effective. At the same time, the belief continued to grow that all individuals, including those with the most severe disabilities, should have the opportunity to work in integrated settings. The challenge faced by the rehabilitation field was to determine how to achieve this outcome given the reality that many of these individuals required substantial levels of support. It was clear that there was a need for a reconceptualization of the existing service system and the assumptions upon which it was built.

Supported Employment

Supported employment is an attempt to reconceptualize the traditional employment service delivery system and to identify models that will open nonsheltered employment opportunities to all persons with disabilities, regardless of the severity of their disabilities (Bellamy et al., 1986; Rusch & Hughes, 1990; Wehman & Moon, 1988). At the heart of supported employment is the rejection of the assumption that a person can work in a regular business only if she or he can function independently and without ongoing support. While the focus of the earlier systems was on identifying techniques that were effective for training persons to function independently, the focus of supported employment has shifted to identifying strategies by which ongoing support can be given to persons who may not be able to achieve full independence in the work environment.

There are several major approaches to supported employment that have been developed to provide individuals who experience disabilities with the opportunity to work in nonsheltered settings. One model is the *Individual Placement Model*, which is quite similar to the competitive employment programs described earlier. However, the supported employment individual placement programs typically do not include a preplacement training component. Rather, individuals are placed directly into jobs and all training occurs on the job. The expectation is that the individual will be able to work independently with routine but relatively minimal ongoing assistance. A second model is the *Enclave*. Using an enclave approach, a group of eight or less individuals with disabilities are placed at a business (Rhodes & Valenta, 1985). Some enclaves are arranged so that the individuals work as a team in the same area while other enclaves are structured so that the individuals work in different locations in a company. Typically, a program staff person provides the enclave members with ongoing supervision (Moon et al., 1990). A third model is the *Mobile Crew*. Here a group of individuals (eight or less) perform janitorial and/or cleaning duties for a number of different businesses (Bourbeau, 1985). Transportation between sites and supervision of the crew is provided by a program staff person.

Small businesses offer a fourth approach frequently identified as a supported employment model (Bellamy et al., 1986). A business is established by a program and a small number of persons with disabilities (no more than eight can be involved in order to meet the federal supported employment guidelines) work at one location to produce a product or provide a service. In fact, this approach is very similar to the traditional sheltered employment approach and provides very limited opportunities to service recipients for integration with persons without disabilities. To attempt to overcome these limitations nondisabled persons can be hired as co-workers in these programs. The extent to which this actually occurs in programs using this approach, however, is not clear. Even when this does occur the model is still seriously limited with regard to the extent that it provides individuals with disabilities the opportunity to gain "normalized" employment.

As suggested earlier, the individual placement approach is clearly superior to the group placement models. This approach provides the most normal employment situation and the greatest opportunity for integration to persons with disabilities. This is also the approach that has been most widely utilized by supported employment programs (Wehman, Kregel, & Shafer, 1990). However, persons with the most significant disabilities are typically the ones who are employed using a group placement approach. Given the amount of money programs are provided for supported employment, most are unable to provide the high level of support needed by these persons at an individual site. When a number of individuals with high support needs are grouped together, one or two staff can provide the required assistance and support to the members of the group. The financial reasons for using group approaches is understandable. However, from a values perspective, it is not appropriate that persons who have more significant disabilities should have restricted employment opportunities because of financial constraints.

There is the recognition that new and innovative strategies and approaches must be identified that will allow these persons to have the same opportunities as others and to be placed individually. In fact, there have been two alternative strategies identified that are beginning to be used (Nisbet & Hagner, 1988). The first strategy offers an alternative to the commonly held belief that training and support can only be provided by program staff. This strategy advocates for the use of co-workers at a work site to provide training and ongoing support. Depending on the site, the co-workers at the site, and the individual with the disabilities, it may be possible for a co-worker or co-workers to provide initial skill training or ongoing support after initial training has been conducted by a program staff person.

A second strategy that is beginning to be used is to have the person with the disability assist in paying for his or her own training and support, the cost of which is beyond that provided to the program in fee-for-services. Two work incentive programs offered through the Social Security Administration make this a viable approach. The first is called a Plan for Achieving Self-Support (PASS) and the second an Impairment-Related Work Expense (IRWE). Both of these programs permit individuals to deduct expenses incurred in gaining and maintaining employment when calculating their earnings in relation to the amount of SSI and SSDI income and benefits for which they are eligible. By deducting the amount of these expenses the person will likely lose less SSI and SSDI income, thus maintaining a higher overall level of income. Expenses that can be conducted under these programs include job coach services, attendant care needed at a job site, equipment and job site modifications, and transportation costs.

Although the supported employment movement has made great strides in changing the existing vocational service system and in opening up job opportunities for persons with disabilities, it really is only in its infancy. There are still many more persons with disabilities who remain in sheltered programs or who receive no employment services than there are those who work in community settings. In fact, the extent to which supported employment has actually reached those for whom it was first intended, those with severe disabilities, has been limited. Persons who experience physical and multiple disabilities in particular have rarely been included in supported employment programs (Wehman, Wood, et al., 1988). In the next section, a number of reasons for this lack of inclusion and descriptions of a few programs that have begun to attempt to do so will be provided.

Supported Employment for Persons with Physical and Multiple Disabilities

The supported employment movement has revolutionized employment services for persons with disabilities. For the first time these individuals are being given the opportunity to work in regular businesses next to persons without disabilities and to earn a meaningful wage. However, in 1990 there have still been few attempts to provide these opportunities to persons who experience physical and multiple disabilities. A survey of 27 states involved in statewide supported employment implementation, conducted by Wehman et al. (1990), showed that 70.2% of all persons in supported employment programs experienced mental retardation, while only 2.1% of these service recipients experienced cerebral palsy. Certainly the lower incidence rates of the latter account for some of this discrepancy. However, there are a number of other contributing factors. To a large extent, supported employment is being implemented by programs moving existing clients out of their sheltered programs and into community jobs (Bellamy et al., 1986). In most cases, persons with cerebral palsy have not been included even in these sheltered programs and thus are not part of the conversion process. A survey conducted in Oregon in 1983 showed that 61% of persons with cerebral palsy were receiving no vocational services (State of Oregon Developmental Disabilities Program, 1983). In fact, a substantial number of these individuals still lived in state institutions at the time of the survey. Those who remained in their communities were often not offered services by the local vocational providers because of their high support and assistance needs and because they were deemed not capable of profiting from such services. This lack of inclusion in traditional sheltered programs not only resulted in their not participating in the conversion to the supported employment process, but also in program staff having little experience or knowledge of how to work with persons with physical and multiple disabilities. In addition, most of the research and demonstration projects in the past that have identified vocational training strategies and techniques upon which the supported employment approaches have been based were also focused on those individuals served in programs. Again, few of these individuals experienced physical and multiple disabilities. Finally, and perhaps a factor that is as important as any, are the contingencies under which programs and funding agencies operate that encourage the provision of services to the persons who can be placed with the greatest ease and the least cost. This fact has contributed to the general concern regarding the extent to which supported employment is being provided to persons with severe disabilities. Certainly, persons with physical and multiple disabilities are not "easy" to place and in comparison to a person with mild or moderate mental retardation will take more effort and money (Sowers, 1990).

There have been a few attempts to demonstrate that persons with physical and multiple disabilities can work in community settings and to identify the strategies that can be used to achieve these objectives. The national United Cerebral Palsy Association has conducted a federally funded supported employment demonstration project focusing on persons who experience cerebral palsy. This project was conducted in several states across the nation, and through it 75 persons have been employed during a 3-year period. All of these persons were placed into individual jobs (Callahan, 1990; Everson et al., 1990). The Elliot Bay Employment Program in Seattle, Washington has also made a commitment to placing persons with physical disabilities into individual jobs. Through a locally funded model project this program has successfully placed 16 persons (Cooper & Mank, 1989).

Both the United Cerebral Palsy and Elliot Bay programs have provided excellent demonstrations that persons with very significant physical disabilities can work in community settings. However, the majority of the persons served by these programs experience mild cognitive disabilities, if any. One of the few programs that has attempted to provide individual placement opportunities to persons who experience both significant physical and multiple disabilities is Alternative Work Concepts (Alternatives) based in Eugene and Portland, Oregon (Sowers, 1989b). This program is funded only through the regular supported employment fees-for-service provided to other service programs in the state. At present (September, 1990), Alternatives provides supported employment to 13 persons with physical and multiple disabilities; 9 have been at the same job site for at least 1 year. Of these persons, 4 were students who made their transitions from local school programs into Alternatives. The remaining individuals are adults who were placed after leaving the state institution.

Two major approaches are used to provide the individuals served by Alternatives with individual employment opportunities. The first approach is similar to the individual placement model commonly used with other persons. However, the specific strategies utilized have been tailored to meet the unique challenges of the individuals served. These strategies include:

1. *Creating jobs.* It is often difficult to find existing positions that persons with significant physical and multiple disabilities can feasibly learn to perform. An alternative strategy is to create jobs for them from those tasks they are most adept at performing and that the employees at a company have difficulty completing given their other job duties.
2. *Using subminimum wage certificates.* Many persons with physical and multiple disabilities will produce at significantly lower productivity levels. To decrease the disincentive to employers to hire these individuals, a business can be assisted to obtain a certificate from the Department of Labor that allows it to pay a person based on his or her productivity.
3. *Providing longer periods of training.* A person with a physical and multiple disability may not be able to learn to perform a job in a few weeks or even a couple of months. However, if the resources are allocated to allow a trainer to remain with the person for 3 or 4 months, he or she may be able to achieve independence. Although initially costly, the long-term benefits (both from a financial and quality-of-life perspective) is well worth it.
4. *Using co-workers to assist in providing support.* Co-workers at a site can often be recruited to assist in the initial training or with ongoing support, thus reducing the need for program staff time at the site.
5. *Using adaptations to reduce the difficulty of the tasks.* Redesigning and adapting tasks can significantly reduce the difficulty of tasks and, thus, increase the ability of the person to perform them.

Some of the individuals served by Alternatives have exceptionally severe disabilities. Even with the use of all of the strategies described above it is not feasible that these persons would be able to be employed without very significant levels of support. In order to provide these individuals with the opportunity to also work in nongroup settings, the program is utilizing an approach called the Co-worker Support Model. This model involves placing a person with a disability and a person without a disability at a work site as a team that performs the assigned tasks and duties together. The person who does not experience the disability is not a trainer, but rather is a colleague and co-worker to the person with the disability. This person also assists the person with the disability with his or her personal care needs. At present, the businesses where the teams work contract with Alternatives for the work performed. The person with the disability is paid half of the revenue received from the site each month or based on his or her productivity, whichever is higher (the highest level of productivity achieved by any of the individuals with disabilities who have been placed using this approach is 20%). By combining fees-for-service and contract monies, the program is able to afford to provide one-to-one support.

Summary

Although few, the programs described here demonstrate that persons with physical and multiple disabilities can work in community settings, and with the use of innovative strategies and approaches individual placements are possible. There is a clear need for additional attention to be given by researchers and program developers to identifying supported employment approaches aimed at the unique employment challenges encountered by these individuals and for in-service and technical assistance projects to encourage and assist programs and staff to provide services to these persons.

CONCLUSION

The 1990s will hopefully be the time when the dream becomes a reality that all persons, regardless of the nature or severity of their disabilities, including those with severe physical and multiple disabilities, have the opportunity to work in fully integrated employment situations. For this to occur there must be a renewed commitment to this goal and attention focused on identifying strategies and approaches that can be used by school and adult service programs to meet the unique employment challenges faced by these individuals. This chapter has provided an overview of the strategies and approaches that these authors and others who have begun the initial work in this area have found effective in preparing students with physical and multiple disabilities for the transition from school to work and supported employment models that can be used to establish paid and independent placement opportunities for them.

REFERENCES

Bates, P. (1989). Vocational training for persons with profound disabilities. In F. Brown & D. H. Lehr (Eds.), *Persons with profound disabilities: Issues and practices* (pp. 265–294). Baltimore: Paul H. Brookes Publishing Co.

Baumgart, D., & Van Walleghem, J. (1986). Staffing strategies for implementing community-based instruction. *Journal of The Association for Persons with Severe Handicaps, 11*(2), 92–102.

Bellamy, G. T., Horner, R. H., & Inman, D. P. (1979). *Vocational habilitation of severely retarded adults: A direct service technology.* Baltimore: University Park Press.

Bellamy, G. T., Rhodes, L. E., Bourbeau, P. E., & Mank, D. M. (1986). Mental retardation services in sheltered workshops and day activity programs: Consumer benefits and policy alternatives. In F. R. Rusch (Ed.), *Competitive employment issues and strategies* (pp. 257–271). Baltimore: Paul H. Brookes Publishing Co.

Bellamy, G. T., Rhodes, L. E., Mank, D. M., & Albin, J. M. (1988). *Supported employment: A community implementation guide*. Baltimore: Paul H. Brookes Publishing Co.

Bourbeau, P. E. (1985). Mobile work crews: An approach to achieve long-term supported employment. In P. McCarthy, J. Everson, S. Moon, & M. Barcus (Eds.), *School-to-work transition for youth with severe disabilities* (pp. 151–166). Richmond, VA: Virginia Commonwealth University, Rehabilitation Research and Training Center.

Brown, L., Branston, M. B., Hamre-Nietupski, A., Pumpian, I., Certo, N., & Gruenewald, L. (1979). A strategy for developing chronological age-appropriate and functional curricular content for severely handicapped adolescents and young adults. *Journal of Special Education, 13*, 81–90.

Callahan, M. (1990). National demonstration project on supported employment. *The Networker, 3*(2). Washington, DC: United Cerebral Palsy Association, Inc.

Campbell, P. H. (1989). Dysfunction in posture and movement in individuals with profound disabilities: Issues and practices. In F. Brown & D. H. Lehr (Eds.), *Persons with profound disabilities: Issues and practices* (pp. 163–190). Baltimore: Paul H. Brookes Publishing Co.

Cooper, A., & Mank, D. (1989). Integrated employment for people with severe physical disabilities: Case studies and support issues. *American Rehabilitation*, Autumn, 16–23.

Everson, J., Callahan, M., Hollohan, J., Gradel, C., Cohen, R., Button, C., Franklin, K., & Brady, F. (1990). *Getting the job done: Supported employment for persons with severe physical disabilities*. Washington, DC: United Cerebral Palsy Association.

Hardman, M., & McDonnell, J. (1987). Implementing federal transition initiatives for youths with severe handicaps: The Utah Community-Based Transition Project. *Exceptional Children, 53*, 493–499.

Hill, M., Wehman, P., Kregel, J., Bank, P. D., & Metzler, H. M. D. (1987). Employment outcomes for people with moderate and severe disabilities: An eight-year longitudinal analysis of supported competitive employment. *Journal of The Association for Persons with Severe Handicaps, 12*, 182–189.

Hutchins, M. P., & Renzaglia, A. (1990). Developing a longitudinal vocational training program. In F. Rusch (Ed.), *Supported employment: Models, methods and issues*. Sycamore, IL: Sycamore Publishing Co.

Inman, D. P. (1979). Gaining control over tension in spastic muscles. In G. Hammerlynch (Ed.), *Behavioral systems for the developmentally disabled: II: Institutional, clinic, and community environments* (pp. 160–189). New York: Brunner-Mazel.

Mank, D. M., & Horner, R. H. (1988). Instructional programming in vocational education. In R. Gaylord-Ross (Ed.), *Vocational education for persons with handicaps* (pp. 142–173). Mountain View, CA: Mayfield Publishing Co.

McDonnell, S., & Hardman, M. (1985). Planning the transition of severely handicapped youth from school to adult services: A framework for high school programs. *Education and Training of the Mentally Retarded, 20*, 275–286.

McDonnell, J., Hardman, M., & Hightower, J. (1989). Employment preparation of high school students with severe handicaps. *Mental Retardation, 27* (6), 395–405.

McDonnell, J., Wilcox, B., Boles, S. M., & Bellamy, G. T. (1985). Transition issues facing youth with severe handicaps: Parents' perspective. *Journal of The Association for Persons with Severe Handicaps, 10*, 61–65.

Moon, M. S., Inge, K. J., Wehman, P., Brooke, V., & Barcus, J. M. (1990). *Helping persons with severe mental retardation get and keep employment*. Baltimore: Paul H. Brookes Publishing Co.

Nielson, P., & McCaughey, J. (1979). Self-regulation of spasm and spasticity in cerebral palsy. *Journal of Neurology, Neurosurgery and Psychiatry, 45,* 1223–1135.

Nisbet, J., & Hagner, D. (1988). Natural supports in the workplace: A reexamination of supported employment. *Journal of The Association for Persons with Severe Handicaps, 13* (4), 260–267.

Orelove, F. P., & Sobsey, D. (1987). Curriculum and instructional programming. In F. P. Orelove & D. Sobsey (Eds.), *Educating children with multiple disabilities: A transdisciplinary approach* (pp. 157–188). Baltimore: Paul H. Brookes Publishing Co.

Pumpian, I., West, E., & Shepard, H. (1988). Vocational education of persons with severe handicaps. In R. Gaylord-Ross (Ed.), *Vocational education for persons with handicaps (pp. 355–386).* Mountain View,, CA: Mayfield Publishing Co.

Rhodes, L. E., & Valenta, L. (1985). Industry-based supported employment: An enclave approach. *Journal of The Association for Persons with Severe Handicaps, 10,* 12–20.

Rice, H., McDonald, B., & Denney, S. (1968). Operant conditioning techniques for use in the physical rehabilitation of the multiply handicapped retarded patient. *Physical Therapy, 48,* 342–346.

Rusch, F. R., & Hughes, C. (1990). Historical overview of supported employment. In F. R. Rusch (Ed.), *Supported employment: Models, methods and issues* (pp. 5–14). Sycamore, IL: Sycamore Publishing Co.

Rusch, F. R., & Mithaug, D. E. (1980). *Vocational training for mentally retarded adults.* Champaign, IL: Research Press.

Rusch, F. R., Schutz, R. P., & Agran, M. (1982). Validating entry-level survival skills for service occupations: Implications for curriculum development. *Journal of The Association for the Severely Handicapped, 1,* 32–41.

Sowers, J. (1989a). Critical parent roles in supported employment. In G. H. S. Singer & L. K. Irvin (Eds.), *Support for caregiving families: Enabling positive adaptation to disability* (pp. 269–282). Baltimore: Paul H. Brookes Publishing Co.

Sowers, J. (1989b). Supported employment of persons with physical and multiple disabilities. *The Advance: The Association for Persons in Supported Employment Newsletter, 1*(4).

Sowers, J. (1990). Special issues on employment for persons with physical disabilities and related technology. *Journal of Vocational Rehabilitation.*

Sowers, J., Hall, S., & Rainforth, B. (1990). Related services personnel in supported employment: Roles and training needs. *Rehabilitation Education.*

Sowers, J., Jenkins, C., & Powers, L. (1988). Vocational education of persons with physical handicaps. In R. Gaylord-Ross (Ed.), *Vocational education for persons with handicaps.* Mountain View, CA: Mayfield Publishing Co.

Sowers, J., & Powers, L. (1989). Preparing students with cerebral palsy and mental retardation for the transition from school to community-based employment. *Career Development for Exceptional Individuals, 12,* 25–35.

Sowers, J., Rusch, F. R., Connis, R. T., & Cummings, L. E. (1980). Teaching mentally retarded adults to time manage in a vocational setting. *Journal of Applied Behavior Analysis, 13*(4).

Sowers, J., Thompson, L., & Connis, R. (1979). The food service vocational training program. In G. T. Bellamy, G. O'Connor, & O. C. Karan (Eds.), *Vocational rehabilitation of severely handicapped persons: Contemporary service strategies.* Baltimore: University Park Press.

State of Oregon Program for Developmental Disabilities. (1983). *Survey report: Services to persons with cerebral palsy.* Salem: State of Oregon Program for Developmental Disabilities Office, Mental Health Division, Department of Human Resources.

U.S. Department of Labor. (1979, March). *Study of handicapped clients in sheltered workshops* (Vol. II). Washington, DC: Author.

Vocational Rehabilitation Act of 1920 (P.L. 236).

Vogelsberg, R. T. (1990). Supported employment in Pennsylvania. In F. R. Rusch (Ed.), *Supported employment: Models, methods and issues.* Sycamore, IL: Sycamore Publishing Co.

Wacker, D. P., & Berg, W. K. (1986). Generalizing and maintaining work behavior. In F. R. Rusch (Ed.), *Competitive employment issues and strategies* (pp. 129–140). Baltimore: Paul H. Brookes Publishing Co.

Wehman, P. (1981). *Competitive employment: New horizons for severely disabled individuals.* Baltimore: Paul H. Brookes Publishing Co.

Wehman, P., Hill, J. W., & Koehler, F. (1979). Placement of developmentally disabled individuals into competitive employment: Three case studies. *Education and Training of the Mentally Retarded, 14,* 269–276.

Wehman, P., & Kregel, J. (1985). A supported work approach to competitive employment of individuals with moderate and severe handicaps. *Journal of the Association for Persons with Severe Handicaps, 10,* 3–11.

Wehman, P., Kregel, J., & Shafer, M. (1990). *Emerging trends in the national supported employment initiative: A preliminary analysis of twenty-seven states.* Richmond, VA: Virginia Commonwealth University, Rehabilitation Research and Training Center.

Wehman, P., & Moon, M. S. (1988). *Vocational rehabilitation and supported employment.* Baltimore: Paul H. Brookes Publishing Co.

Wehman, P., Moon, M. S., Everson, J. M., Wood, W., & Barcus, J. M. (1988). *Transition from school to work.* Baltimore: Paul H. Brookes Publishing Co.

Wehman, P., Wood, W., Everson, J. M., Goodwyn, R., & Conley, S. (1988). *Vocational education for multihandicapped youth with cerebral palsy.* Baltimore: Paul H. Brookes Publishing Co.

Wilcox, B., & Bellamy, G. T. (1982). *Design of high school programs for severely handicapped students.* Baltimore: Paul H. Brookes Publishing Co.

Wilcox, B., McDonnell, J. J., Bellamy, G. T., & Rose, H. (1988). Preparing for supported employment: The role of secondary special education. In G. T. Bellamy, L. E. Rhodes, D. M. Mank, & J. M. Albin (Eds.), *Supported employment: A community implementation guide* (pp. 183–208). Baltimore: Paul H. Brookes Publishing Co.

Wolfensberger, W. (1972). *Normalization: The principle of normalization in human services.* Toronto: National Institute on Mental Retardation.

Wood, W., (1988). Supported employment for persons with physical disabilities. In P. Wehman & M. S. Moon (Eds.), *Vocational rehabilitation and supported employment* (pp. 341–364). Baltimore: Paul H. Brookes Publishing Co.

York, J., & Rainforth, B. (1987). Developing instructional adaptations. In F. P. Orelove & D. Sobsey, *Educating children with multiple disabilities: A transdisciplinary approach.* Baltimore: Paul H. Brookes Publishing Co.

ANGEL

Angel completed high school 2 years ago and is now 23 years of age. She uses a power wheelchair for traveling distances, but can use a manual chair for shorter distances, which she propels with one hand and her feet. Angel has some functional use of one hand. She can speak, but with a great deal of difficulty.

During school, Angel had the opportunity to learn a variety of clerical tasks at community work experience sites. She learned to photocopy, staple, type, do simple computer data entry, do postage meter work, use a hole punch, and do simple filing. When Angel first began the work experience program, she had a great deal of difficulty executing many of the movements required by these tasks. With systematic instruction she learned to make many of these movements. Assistive devices were also identified that permitted her to work more independently and productively. Work attendance, drool management, safe power wheel chair use, and bus riding were among the work-related skills trained.

During her last year of school, a job was created for Angel at a credit union. She has been employed on a part-time basis there for 2 years. Her task assignments include typing and laminating new membership cards, photocopying, filing, cleaning up and stocking the customer area, tearing up misprinted checks, and collating information packets for new members. These were tasks the credit union indicated that their current employees had difficulty completing, given their other job duties, and

ANGEL
(continued)

tasks for which they wanted to create a position for Angel to perform. Angel is paid based on her productivity, which is approximately 50%, and her base wage is $4.25 per hour.

A number of simple job adaptations were utilized to assist Angel to perform her tasks. Because the photocopy machine was on a table that was too high for her to reach, a shorter table was purchased. A work area was set-up for Angel, which includes a typing table and a desk on which all her work materials are kept. The jig shown in the picture was built to assist her place the card into the laminating sleeve. Another jig was created to help her more easily tear checks with one hand. She also uses a simple jig that allows her to staple papers with the use of only one hand. An electric typewriter with a correcting key was also purchased for her.

A job coach remained with Angel for 4 months before beginning to fade. Today, a job coach checks in on Angel 2 or 3 times a week.

The credit union encourages employee cohesiveness by holding frequent celebrations (for birthdays, showers) and other events (picnics) that take place during evenings and on weekends. Angel is included and participates in all of these social activities.

2   *Identifying Tasks to Train to Students*

One of the major issues that school programs encounter when attempting to organize vocational preparation programs for students with disabilities is the targeting of tasks that will be trained. In the past, task selection has been commonly guided by a belief in the importance of prerequisite skills and general work behaviors (Bellamy, Rose, Wilson, & Clark, 1982; Mithaug, Mar, & Stewart, 1978). Specifically, it was believed that individuals should learn a set of basic skills generic across all or most vocational tasks before learning and performing real work. Examples of these prerequisite skills are eye-hand coordination, match-to-sample, attention to task, and sequencing. Based on this model of vocational preparation, tasks that in theory provided students with the best opportunity to learn these prerequisite skills were identified and trained.

It is now understood that the most efficient and effective way to prepare students with severe developmental disabilities for community employment is to identify the specific types of tasks that they will perform in their future jobs and then to teach these tasks (Brown, Nietupski, & Hamre-Nietupski, 1976; Falvey, 1986; Gaylord-Ross & Holvoet, 1985; Hutchins & Renzaglia, 1990; Pumpian, West, & Shepard, 1988; Renzaglia & Hutchins, 1988; Wilcox, McDonnell, Bellamy, & Rose, 1988).

The foundation of this new approach is the behavioral principle of generalization (Berg, Wacker, & Flynn 1990; Stokes & Baer, 1977). This principle reflects the fact that the more similar the task trained is to the task a person does at a later date, the greater the effect of the training on the individual's performance. An analogy of the contrast between the traditional, prerequisite skills model and this new approach is the difference between a liberal arts education and a vocational trade school training. On the one hand, the person who receives a liberal arts education has learned a great deal of interesting information; however his or her education will probably not have included skills related to any specific job and he or she may need additional training in order to become employed. On the other hand, the person who receives a degree in refrigeration repair is prepared to get a job repairing refrigeration systems. In general, the more important it is that a student obtain the best job possible after completing a training program (in this case, high school), the greater the need for identifying and teaching specific tasks.

Bench works (i.e., small parts assembly) has been one of the most common tasks trained to students with severe disabilities (Mithaug & Stewart, 1978). Because these tasks are performed in many sheltered programs, bench works were appropriately selected when the majority of adults with severe disabilities were employed in these settings. Along with the availability of community employment opportunities for persons with disabilities, many districts have begun to train students in other skills (Bellamy et al., 1982; Pumpian et al., 1988).

Students who experience physical *and* cognitive disabilities (and, in many cases, sensory and other disabilities) present a great challenge with respect to identifying tasks to train them. To some extent, this challenge derives from the fact that, given the multiple nature of their disabilities, it is difficult for staff to imagine what jobs or tasks these students could perform in a community business. This perspective is understandable given the few demonstrations of the vocational competence of these individuals (Callahan, 1990; Sowers & Powers, 1989; Wehman, Wood, Everson, Goodwyn, & Conley, 1988).

The purpose of this chapter is to address the issues that surround the selection of vocational tasks for students with physical and multiple disabilities. Specifically, guidelines of a task selection process are provided for developing a pool of tasks for students in a district and for selecting tasks from this pool to train individual students.

TASK IDENTIFICATION FACTORS

As indicated, training the specific tasks that a student will perform when placed into a paid community job is a more effective and efficient means to ensure his or her future successful employment than is training general and "prerequisite" skills (Brown et al., 1976; Falvey, 1986; Orelove & Sobsey, 1987). However, the dilemma for staff is how to identify what jobs or tasks the student is likely to perform as an adult. In fact, the factors that should be taken into account when identifying and selecting tasks are the same as those used for and by anyone attempting to determine what career training path to pursue. Specifically, there are three questions that should be posed when selecting a task to train to a student:

1. When the student completes training, what job or task areas will offer the greatest number of employment opportunities in his or her community?
2. What tasks does the student have the greatest ability and capacity to learn to perform?

3. What tasks involve the type of activities that the student enjoys per-
    forming?

Job Availability

It would be of little use to a student to learn a particular task if there are few or
no job openings available that involve the performance of that task. The more
openings and opportunities available in a job area, the more likely the training
in that area and related tasks will pay off for the student (Gaylord-Ross, Forte,
& Gaylord-Ross, 1986; Pumpian et al., 1988; Sowers, Lundervold, Swanson,
& Budd, 1980; Wehman, Wood, et al., 1988; Wehman, Moon, Everson, Wood,
& Barcus, 1988; Wilcox et al., 1988). The number and availability of different
types of jobs can vary dramatically among local communities. For example, the
types of jobs available in a small, rural community will likely be different from
those in a large, urban city. Consequently, it is important for districts to obtain
information about the business sector and employment trends in their local
communities (Hutchins & Renzaglia, 1990; Wehman et al., 1988; Weisgerber,
Dahl, & Appleby, 1981).

Employment trends, in terms of the number of openings in different job
types, change over time. Although there may be a large number of a certain
type of job available in a community at the present time, this may not be the
case when a student wishes to obtain a job in 2 or 3 years. On the other hand,
the availability of another type of job may dramatically increase. Consequently,
it is important for districts to continue to assess changes in the employment
sector rather than to simply train the same tasks that were identified in the past
(Weisgerber et al., 1981).

Student Ability and Capacity to Perform the Task

Tasks that a student has a high likelihood of being able to successfully perform
should be selected (Gaylord-Ross, 1986). To some degree, this is an easy determination to make. It is obvious that most students with physical disabilities will
not be well suited to performing tasks that involve heavy lifting and other physically demanding duties (Wehman, et al., 1988). However, after clearly inappropriate tasks have been eliminated, the decision regarding a student's capacity to perform a particular task becomes more difficult. In fact, it is difficult to
determine how well a student is able to perform a task until he or she is given a
chance to try it (Gaylord-Ross, 1986; Menchetti & Flynn, 1990). In many
cases, it may seem completely impossible that students with severe physical
and multiple disabilities could learn to perform certain tasks. However, when
provided with the opportunity, job design modifications, and systematic training, these students frequently prove otherwise (Sowers, Jenkins, & Powers,
1988; Wehman et al., 1988).

It is true that many students with severe disabilities may require some
level of ongoing assistance while performing any task. Consequently, the ques-

tion that must be posed is not what task(s) a student could perform independently, but what task(s) she or he is likely to require the *least amount of support* to perform.

Task Preference

Without question, one of the most important factors that must be weighed when selecting the tasks or jobs to train a student is the extent to which she or he enjoys them (Gaylord-Ross, 1986; Miller & Schloss, 1982). As with most individuals, a prime determinant of job or task preference is frequently related to how competently the person can perform it. On the one hand, we all like to do things at which we are good. On the other hand, most of us also wish to be at least minimally challenged by the tasks that we perform. Consequently, the goal is to identify those tasks that a student can perform to his or her highest level of independence and productivity, but that still provide some degree of challenge.

TASK SELECTION PROCESS

The three criteria for task identification are fairly straightforward and are ones that most school staff, parents, students, and any individuals who have attempted to make career training decisions for themselves or others would agree are critical. The challenge is how to identify the tasks that meet these same criteria for a particular student with physical and multiple disabilities. As with all individuals who seek career and vocational guidance, the answers to these questions are typically not simple, nor are they easily obtained in a short period of time. There is not one list of tasks that is the best across students with different disabilities, abilities, and interests; there is not one list that is common across communities; and there is not one list that continues to be appropriate from year to year. In other words, task identification must be seen as a dynamic, ongoing, and individualized process. There are three steps recommended for task identification:

1. Develop a task pool for students who are served by the program, based on the local employment market.
2. Select tasks to be trained to individual students.
3. Continue to refine task selection based on job market changes as well as student performance and interest.

Developing a Task Pool

As has been emphasized, task selection must be done on an individual student basis. However, there is a useful function for identifying a list of tasks (i.e., a task pool) that fit a substantial number of job development opportunities in the local community and that may be appropriate for one or more of the students in the school program who have physical and multiple disabilities (Sowers et al.,

1988; Wilcox et al., 1988). The specific tasks that will be selected and trained to individual students can then be selected from the task pool.

To provide a starting point for staff in the development of a task pool for the students in their district, a comprehensive list or pool of tasks has been identified by the authors (Table 1). This list targets tasks that are part of entry-level positions, and for which employers do not typically require a person to have formal secondary education or training. The list also targets tasks with low physical demands, particularly in terms of strength.

The list provided here must be used only as a starting point in the creation of a district's own task pool. To accomplish this, a district should first attempt to identify the tasks on the list for which there are a significant number of jobs in the local community. One of the best strategies for this purpose is to obtain information from the city and/or county employment division (Miller & Schloss, 1982). These government offices maintain statistics on the number of individuals currently employed in different job classifications and industries. They also typically have forecasted employment trends, which are particularly useful for school districts that are preparing students for future employment. Talking with agencies that are in the business of assisting individuals to obtain employment is also extremely informative. These agencies should include those that work with individuals who experience disabilities as well as agencies that work with nondisabled individuals. It is particularly useful to actually visit businesses in the community in order to obtain information about the types of tasks that occur there (Hutchins & Renzaglia, 1990; Stainback, Stainback, Nietupski, & Hamre-Nietupski, 1986; Weisgerber et al., 1981). It is important to do this as regularly as possible since the tasks that are done in businesses change over time. This is particularly true with the increasing development and use of technology in businesses. For example, most businesses today have pho-tocopy machines that collate papers automatically, thus eliminating a task that used to be done manually. If possible, an attempt should be made to visit one or two companies that represent a particular type of business. For example, staff would want to visit a couple of banks, doctor's offices, real estate offices, direct mail services, and so on. After obtaining employment statistics, input from other agencies, and conducting a business survey, district staff should be able to eliminate tasks for which there are few local jobs available and highlight those that have particularly good employment outlooks.

The second activity in developing a task pool is to further eliminate from and highlight tasks on the list based on the characteristics of the students in the district's program. Again, it must be remembered that task selection must be done on an individual student basis. However, it may be clear that there are a number of tasks on the list that are not appropriate for training to any of the students served by a particular district. For example, if all of the district's students experience very severe cognitive disabilities, word processing may be a task that could reasonably be eliminated from the pool.

Table 1.   Generic task pool for students with physical/multiple disabilities

Tasks	Examples/descriptions
Typing	Type membership cards at banks, associations, clubs, libraries. Type file folder labels. Type addresses on mailing labels or envelopes.
Computer Data Entry	Input customer, patient, client information for businesses and medical offices, and billing, inventory information for same. Input mailing list information for associations and commercial businesses.
Word Processing	Word process memos and letters. This occurs in almost any office. It requires ability to read cursive writing.
Filing	Place papers in individual file folders, placing folders in file drawers, and retrieving files. Complexity varies depending on file system. Some companies/agencies maintain card file systems (rather than file folders).
Phone Answering	In small, informal offices one person may answer phone and then tell co-workers they have a call. Larger and more formal offices will include putting callers on hold and transferring calls. Typically will require taking messages (usually written, but potentially recording messages).
Photocopying	Few businesses are without a photocopy machine. The type of copying done varies among companies. Some only need copies of single page documents; others need large documents and books or manuals. In most cases the person who photocopies is also responsible for collating (if it is not done by the machine) and stapling.
Collating/Stapling	Companies that perform a large amount of photocopying or have materials printed elsewhere may hire persons to collate and staple. Examples include print shops, direct mail businesses, associations.
Mail Preparation	Includes folding letters, stuffing envelopes, placing labels and stamps on envelopes, running a postage meter machine.
Packaging	Packaging products in manufacturing or distribution businesses. Type of product and packaging process will vary greatly.
Unpackage/Price	Most stores require merchandise received from distributors to be unpackaged (in some cases repackaged for sale) and a price tag or label placed on it. Pricing may be done by hand or with price gun. May also include placing the items on shelves.

(continued)

Table 1.   (continued)

Tasks	Examples/descriptions
Delivery	Deliver food for a restaurant, items from central supply or pharmacy to floors in hospital, fax messages that come in on central machine, documents from one office to other offices (e.g., legal documents from law office to courthouse).
Assembly/Light	Electronics assembly is a common type of light manufacturing task. There are hundreds of other products assembled in large and small businesses in most communities.
Light Cleaning	Most offices desire some light clean-up and straightening in addition to the more heavy cleaning done by a janitorial service. For example, banks need to have someone straighten up the lobby a couple of times a day.
Microfilming	Microfilming is becoming less prevalent due to the advent of computers. However, some businesses still employ microfilming for recordkeeping. Some banks microfilm checks. Hospitals and government offices also typically maintain microfilm records.

Again, it is important that the task pool not be viewed in a static fashion. The local job market will change. In addition, staff will get to know the local market better in terms of job availability and the feasibility of placement success in specific tasks as they begin to place students into jobs. The characteristics of the students in the district and the type of tasks that may be feasible for them will also change. All of this information should be fed back into the task pool and used to modify it.

Identifying Tasks for Individual Students

The task pool serves as the basis upon which the specific tasks that will be trained to individual students are selected. Selecting tasks from the task pool will insure that the tasks trained to students are those for which there are a significant number of job development and creation possibilities in the local community.

The primary goal when selecting tasks to train to individual students is to attempt to identify and provide training in those tasks that a student, given his or her unique abilities and disabilities, will be able to learn to perform with the highest degree of independence and productivity. It is particularly important for staff to keep in mind the "highest degree" aspect of this goal and activity. Most students with severe physical and multiple disabilities may require at least some ongoing support on certain tasks, and many may require a great deal of support for any task. If the aim was to identify only those tasks that these students could learn to perform totally independently and to meet regular productivity standards, the list would be very short for most students and nonexistent for many.

As with the development of the task pool, the process of determining which tasks to train to a student should be viewed as a dynamic and ongoing one. As the student has the opportunity to receive training on tasks, staff will gain insight into those tasks to which the student is best suited, the amount and type of training and design strategies required, and the student's task preferences.

Number of Tasks to Train

Is it better for students to receive a little training in a large number of different tasks or a large amount of training in a small number of tasks? This is an issue for which there is no definitive answer, and about which professionals continue to debate and disagree (Bellamy et al., 1982; Renzaglia & Hutchins, 1988; Wilcox et al., 1988). On one hand, the student who has learned a number of tasks may have more options when a job is being sought or created. However, this may be the case only if it can be assumed that the student actually acquired some degree of competence in performing these tasks. In fact, it will take a significant period of systematic instruction and practice for many individuals with more severe disabilities to begin to learn the steps and skills required by a task. If the tasks that are being trained to such a student are frequently changed, this instruction and progress will not be possible. Another factor that argues for training a few tasks more intensely is the perception of the student about his or her vocational abilities. Students, like all of us, want to feel a sense of accomplishment and competency. If these feelings can be associated with work, then the student will be more motivated to be employed. When a student is moved from task to task, she or he will always be in the state of trying to learn a new task, and may never get to the point of feeling particularly competent performing it. The answer to this question is to attempt to strike a balance between the two approaches. Students should have the opportunity to learn to be as competent as possible in at least a few tasks. If possible, these should be tasks to which they are best suited and for which the greatest amount of effort will be made to find them a permanent job. Students should also have the chance to at least gain some exposure to and experience performing as wide a range of tasks as time permits. The actual number of tasks that a student can receive significant amounts of experience and training on and the number that a student can receive some exposure to will vary from student to student and will depend on the resources of the district.

Task Selection Phases

The process of selecting tasks can be organized into two major phases, distinguished by the primary goal of each. The first phase should occur when a student is just beginning his or her vocational preparation, hopefully during the middle school years. During this time the primary goal is to provide the student with the opportunity to try out as many different tasks as possible, in order to determine ones to which she or he is best suited in terms of skills and preferences. A second important goal is to build a strong sense in the student that work is a reinforcing and important activity (Gaylord-Ross, Siegel, Park, & Wilson, 1988; Wehman et al., 1990).

The goal of the second phase is to attempt to increase and refine a student's independence and productivity in performing those tasks that appear to be most suitable for him or her during the try-out or job-exploration phase. For example, Steve is a student with 3 remaining years of school eligibility. It appeared that Steve had the greatest potential for independent performance in delivery-related tasks and as a photocopy assistant (he was particularly adept, with the use of a jig, at stapling). Steve also seemed to really enjoy these tasks. Consequently, it was decided to provide him with as many opportunities as possible to perform these tasks in the following 2 years (hopefully Steve would be placed on a job during the 3rd and final year in school) in order to allow him to receive additional training and to refine his skills.

It should be recognized that if a student has already achieved a significant degree of competence at a particular task, she or he should be given the opportunity to learn other tasks (Wilcox et al., 1988). For example, stapling is also a strength of Denise. In fact, with a jig she can staple completely independently and has reached her maximal level of productivity doing so. Consequently, she would gain little by continuing to be placed into work experiences where her major task is stapling. Of course, it is important to give her some ongoing practice to permit her to maintain this skill. Consequently, it was decided to focus her training on other tasks, but to continue to attempt to include at least a small amount of stapling in the work experiences in which she will be involved in the future.

CONCLUSION

The purpose of this chapter has been to provide school personnel with guidance in identifying the vocational tasks to train to students with physical and multiple disabilities. An attempt has been made to provide some suggestions that should help in this regard. It would certainly make all of our jobs easier if we could provide or suggest a neatly packaged assessment instrument or system that would identify the tasks to train to these students. Such instruments and systems have proved of little use for students with severe developmental disabilities, when the goal of training is to prepare them to work and live in community settings (Karan & Schalock, 1983). The best system for identifying a career path (the vocational tasks) to train to students is really very similar to the one that most persons without disabilities use. Over the years we have the opportunity to experience a number of different tasks and jobs. During this time we eliminate the ones that are clearly not our strengths, the ones in which we have little interest, and in most cases the ones that offer few job opportunities, and we begin to focus on those that we are good at, enjoy, and for which there are jobs available. The role of the school program is to also provide this opportunity to students with the most severe disabilities.

REFERENCES

Bellamy, G. T., Rose, H., Wilson, D. J., & Clark, J. Y. (1982). Strategies for vocational preparation. In B. Wilcox & G. T. Bellamy (Eds.), *Design of high school programs for severely handicapped students* (pp. 139–152). Baltimore: Paul H. Brookes Publishing Co.

Berg, W., Wacker, D., & Flynn, T. (1990). Teaching generalization and maintenance of work behavior. In F. R. Rusch (Ed.), *Supported employment: Models, methods and issues* (pp. 145–160). Sycamore, IL: Sycamore Publishing Co.

Brown, L., Nietupski, J., & Hamre-Nietupski, S. (1976). The criterion of ultimate functioning. In M. A. Thomas (Ed.), *Hey, don't forget about me!* (pp. 2–15). Reston, VA: CEC Information Center.

Callahan, M. (1990). National demonstration project on supported employment. *The Networker, 3*(2). Washington, DC: United Cerebral Palsy Association, Inc.

Chadsey-Rusch, J., & Rusch, F. (1988). Ecology of the workplace. In R. Gaylord-Ross (Ed.), *Vocational education for persons with handicaps* (pp. 234–236). Mountain View, CA: Mayfield Publishing Co.

Falvey, M. A. (1986). *Community-based curriculum: Instructional strategies for students with severe handicaps.* Baltimore: Paul H. Brookes Publishing Co.

Gaylord-Ross, R. (1986). Dimensions of supported employment assessment. *Career Development for Exceptional Individuals, 9,* 129–134.

Gaylord-Ross, C., Forte, J., & Gaylord-Ross, R. (1986). The community classroom: Technological vocational training for students with serious handicaps. *Career Development for Exceptional Individuals, 9,* 24–33.

Gaylord-Ross, R. J., & Holvoet, J. F. (1985). *Strategies for educating students with severe handicaps.* Boston: Little, Brown.

Gaylord-Ross, R., Siegel, S., Park, H. S., & Wilson, W. (1988). Secondary vocational training. In R. Gaylord-Ross (Ed.), *Vocational education for persons with handicaps* (pp. 174–204). Mountain View, CA: Mayfield Publishing Co.

Hutchins, M. P., & Renzaglia, A. (1990). Developing a longitudinal vocational training program. In F. R. Rusch (Ed.), *Supported employment: Models, methods and issues* (pp. 365–380). Sycamore, IL: Sycamore Publishing Co.

Karan, O. C., & Schalock, R. (1983). Assessing vocational and community living skills: An ecological model. In O. C. Karan & W. I. Gardner (Eds.), *Habilitation practices with developmentally disabled persons presenting emotional and behavioral disorders* (pp. 121–173). Madison: Research and Training Center in Mental Retardation, University of Wisconsin–Madison.

Menchetti, B., & Flynn, C. (1990). Vocational evaluation. In F. R. Rusch (Ed.), *Supported employment: Models, methods and issues* (pp. 111–130). Sycamore, IL: Sycamore Publishing Co.

Miller, S., & Schloss, P. (1982). *Career-vocational education for handicapped youth.* Rockville, MD: Aspen Systems.

Mithaug, D., Mar, D., & Stewart, J. (1978). *Prevocational assessment and curriculum guide.* Seattle: Exceptional Education.

Mithaug, D. E., & Stewart, J. E. (1978). *Match-Sort-Assemble: A prevocational program for handicapped children and adults.* Seattle: Exceptional Education.

Orelove, F. P., & Sobsey, D. (1987). *Educating children with multiple disabilities: A transdisciplinary approach* (pp. 157–182). Baltimore: Paul H. Brookes Publishing Co.

Pumpian, I., West, E., & Shepard, H. (1988). Vocational education of persons with severe handicaps. In R. Gaylord-Ross (Ed.), *Vocational education for persons with handicaps (pp. 355–386).* Mountain View, CA: Mayfield Publishing Co.

Renzaglia, A., & Hutchins, M. (1988). A community-referenced approach to preparing persons with disabilities for employment. In P. Wehman & M. S. Moon (Eds.), *Vocational rehabilitation and supported employment* (pp. 91–110). Baltimore: Paul H. Brookes Publishing Co.

Sowers, J., Jenkins, C. & Powers, L. (1988). Vocational education of persons with physical handicaps. In R. Gaylord-Ross (Ed.), Vocational education for persons with handicaps (pp. 387–416). Mountain View, CA: Mayfield Publishing Co.

Sowers, J., Lundervold, D., Swanson, M., & Budd, C. (1980) *Competitive employment training for mentally retarded adults: A systematic approach.* Eugene, OR: University of Oregon, Specialized Training Program.

Sowers, J., & Powers, L. (1989). Preparing students with cerebral palsy and mental retardation for the transition from school to community-based employment. *Career Development for Exceptional Individuals, 12*(1), 25–35.

Sowers, J., Thompson, L., & Connis, R. (1979). The food service vocational training program. In G. T. Bellamy, G. O'Connor, & O. C. Karan (Eds.), *Vocational rehabilitation of severely handicapped persons: Contemporary service strategies* (pp. 181–206). Baltimore: University Park Press.

Stainback, W., Stainback, S., Nietupski, J., & Hamre-Nietupski, S. (1986). Establishing effective community-based training stations. In F. R. Rusch (Ed.), *Competitive employment issues and strategies* (pp. 103–113). Baltimore: Paul H. Brookes Publishing Co.

Stokes, T. F. & Baer, D. M. (1977). An impact technology of generalization. *Journal of Applied Behavior Analysis, 10,* 349–367.

Wehman, P., Hill, J., & Koehler, F. (1979). Placement of developmentally disabled individuals into competitive employment: Three case studies. *Education and Training of the Mentally Retarded, 14,* 269–276.

Wehman, P., Moon, M. S., Everson, J. M., Wood, W., & Barcus, J. M. (1988). *Transition from school to work.* Baltimore: Paul H. Brookes Publishing Co.

Wehman, P., Wood, W., Everson, J. M., Goodwyn, R., & Conley, S. (1988). *Vocational education for multihandicapped youth with cerebral palsy.* Baltimore: Paul H. Brookes Publishing Co.

Weisgerber, R., Dahl, P., & Appleby, J. (1981). *Training the handicapped for productive employment.* Rockville, MD: Aspen Systems.

Wilcox, B., McDonnell, J. J., Bellamy, G. T., & Rose, H. (1988). Preparing for supported employment: The role of secondary special education. In G. T. Bellamy, L. E. Rhodes, D. M. Mank, & J. M. Albin (Eds.), *Supported employment: A community implementation guide* (pp. 183–208). Baltimore: Paul H. Brookes Publishing Co.

PATTY

Patty, who is 36 years of age, utilizes a power wheelchair and has limited functional use of her hands. Until 4 years ago, Patty lived in an institutional setting and her only vocational experience was performing simulated sorting tasks. She now lives in a small group home and works as a photocopy assistant for a large company. This job was created for Patty by Alternative Work Concepts when she first moved out of the nursing home to Eugene.

Patty's job was created using a Support Co-worker Model. The company contracts with Alternative Work Concepts for the work performed. Patty and a support co-worker perform the photocopying as a team for 4 hours a day. The support co-worker does not experience a disability and is an employee of Alternatives, as is Patty. Patty is then paid half of the contracted dollars received from the company (approximately $300 per month). Patty's primary job duty is to staple the copies that are made by her co-worker. Patty is able to do this task fairly independently using the jig shown in the picture.

Patty's co-worker assists her with personal needs, including using the rest room. A lift was purchased by the Division of Vocational Rehabilitation and placed at the site to permit the co-worker to transfer Patty without the need for a second person. Before the lift was available, another Alternative's staff person would come to the site to assist with the lift.

3

Critical Work-Related Issues

Research and experience have demonstrated the effect that work-related skills can have on the employment of individuals with disabilities. In fact, individuals more frequently lose jobs because of difficulties in these areas than because of work performance deficits (Chadsey-Rusch, 1986; Greenspan & Shoultz, 1981; Hanley-Maxwell, Rusch, Chadsey-Rusch, & Renzaglia, 1986). A number of work-related skills have been identified as particularly important contributors to the ease with which persons with mental retardation can be placed and maintained in community jobs. These include grooming, attendance, and social behaviors (Renzaglia & Hutchins, 1988; Rusch & Mithaug, 1980; Sowers, Thompson, & Connis, 1979; Wehman, 1981). These work-related behaviors are also important to the job success of persons with physical and multiple disabilities. In addition, there are a number of other work-related issues that may serve as employment challenges to these persons, including bathroom use, eating and drinking, communication, mobility, and drooling (Sowers, Jenkins, & Powers, 1988; Wehman, Wood, Everson, Goodwyn, & Conley, 1988). In fact, these issues may serve as the major barriers to employment for these individuals. Students may be able to perform a number of work tasks, but if they require assistance using the bathroom, eating, and getting to work it may be concluded that it is not feasible for them to work in community settings or that they can only be placed in a group situation such as an enclave. Consequently, school programs should focus a significant amount of effort on identifying and implementing interventions that will permit students to function as independently as possible in each of these areas. School programs typically do attempt to identify adaptive strategies that students can use to perform these skills and provide skill training. However, in most cases the strategies and interventions are based on what will work for the student in the classroom. The requirements that will exist in future employment situations may demand different skills and strategies. To increase the likelihood that students will be provided with opportunities to work in community sites, school programs must understand the requirements of community work sites (including the lower availability of assistance and support) and attempt to identify and implement adaptive and training interventions that will allow their students to meet these requirements and to function with as little assistance as possible.

In this chapter, the requirements that exist in community employment sites related to each of the five work-related skills (bathroom use, eating and drinking, communication, mobility, and drooling) and adaptive and training strategies that can be used to allow students to meet these requirements will be described. A brief discussion of issues and strategies pertinent to grooming, attendance, and social skill training will also be provided.

BATHROOM USE

Some students with multiple and physical disabilities experience bladder or bowel incontinence (Bigge, 1982; Lindemann, 1981; Orelove & Sobsey, 1987). For obvious reasons, these difficulties have a potential negative impact upon a student's future employment. Employers may be very hesitant to hire a person who has toileting accidents. In addition, co-workers' perceptions of an individual who has accidents may be negative. Finally, persons who have frequent accidents will require assistance to clean up and change clothes, decreasing the level of independence that they can achieve at the job site. A student may also require assistance during bathroom use. In this section, a variety of strategies that can be used to assist students who experience incontinence or who require assistance using the bathroom are described.

Bladder and Bowel Control

There are a number of reasons why a student with physical and multiple disabilities may experience incontinence (Orelove & Sobsey, 1987). Due to their disabilities, some individuals may actually have a decreased ability to sense and recognize the physiological cues associated with a full bladder or bowel. This is frequently the case for persons who have spina bifida or a spinal cord injury (Lindemann, 1981). It is typically less true of persons with cerebral palsy. However, a student who is not verbal and relies on the assistance of others to use the bathroom is particularly susceptible to incontinence problems. The student may have to wait too long and be unable to maintain control by the time he or she gets the attention of a teacher or parent, communicates the need, is taken to the bathroom, and then is transferred to the toilet or provided with a bedpan or urinal. After frequent accidents the student, parents, and staff may become discouraged and assume that continence is either not possible or not worth the trouble. Without practice and encouragement the student may no longer attend to the physiological cues that signal the need to go to the bathroom. It is likely that this phenomenon is the reason why many students with cerebral palsy experience incontinence.

Bladder Control Strategies   In this section a number of strategies that can be used to assist an individual who experiences bladder control difficulties are described.

1. Assistance, Support, and Training   As suggested earlier, most incontinence problems experienced by students with cerebral palsy can be attributed to the fact that they have not been given the opportunity and encouragement to be continent (Bigge, 1982; Orelove & Sobsey, 1987). Staff and parents may indicate that they have attempted to train a student to be continent on many occasions, but with little success. However, these attempts have not always been systematic. Because incontinence greatly increases the difficulty of community-based employment, it is critical that significant effort be devoted to assisting students to gain bladder control.

In some cases, simply providing a student with a reliable method for quickly communicating the desire to use the bathroom and encouraging the student to use the method when she or he senses the need to do so will be sufficient to achieve continence. If a student is not verbal and cannot walk or move his or her wheelchair quickly to a person who is to provide help, some type of signal device can be arranged. One strategy that can be used is to mount a small light on the back of the individual's chair where it can be easily seen. The light is connected to a switch placed on the arm of the wheelchair or another location that is accessible to the student. When the student needs to use the bathroom, he or she activates the switch to turn on the light. An auditory cue (e.g., beep, buzz) activated by a switch could also be used. Of course, an electronic communication device may be an excellent way for some students to express their need to use the bathroom. Students who have a means to communicate their desire to use the bathroom, but do not use it, may be able to be toilet trained (Foxx & Azrin, 1973). A person with expertise in toilet training should be consulted before initiating such a program. To be successful the program must be carefully designed and systematically carried out. Many students will be able to learn to recognize that their bladders are full and initiate using the bathroom. Even if this cannot be achieved, staff should determine how frequently a student needs to go to the bathroom to avoid accidents. This information can then be used to provide the student with a bathroom schedule.

2. Protective Pants   If a student is unable to maintain consistent continence, protective pants is one alternative to ensure that an accident does not occur at work. There are protective pants on the market that are excellent in terms of their absorbency and their effectiveness in reducing skin irritation and breakdown.

However, these pants will need to be changed within a fairly short period of time after wetting. If possible, students should be taught to change their own pants. However, this will not be feasible for most students. Consequently, when considering the use of protective pants, staff must recognize that this may ne-cessitate the need for someone to be available at the student's future job site to assist in changing him or her. Consequently, protective pants should only be considered after every effort has been made to train the student to control his or her bladder or because it is not feasible for a student to learn to do so because of the particular disability.

3. *Condom Catheter* A male who experiences bladder control prob-lems can use a condom catheter, which is a condom-like device that is placed over the penis, with a tube connecting the condom to a leg bag (Bigge, 1982; Orelove & Sobsey, 1987). The danger of skin breakdown when using this de-vice will vary from person to person. The condom must fit properly to avoid leakage or backflow (Jones, 1985). Individuals with skin resistive to breakdown may be able to wear the condom for several hours daily. If an individual works full-time, it may be necessary to empty the leg bag while at work. Students who have fairly good use of their hands can be taught to do this. Again, condom catheters should not be used until systematic attempts have been made to assist students to learn to control their bladder or to at least establish a toileting sched-ule for them.

4. *Intermittent Catheterization* Another available option is intermit-tent catheterization (Orelove & Sobsey, 1987; Stauffer, 1983). A catheter (a small tube) is inserted into the urethra to the bladder in order to drain the urine from it. The frequency that this procedure must be performed varies from per-son to person. A student may be able to perform the catheterization independ-ently, if he or she can sit on the toilet without assistance and has fairly good hand control. Intermittent catheterization is typically only recommended for persons with spina bifida or a spinal cord injury. Students who use this pro-cedure will frequently experience some leakages between their scheduled catheter times. Consequently they will need to use protective pants.

Many students with spina bifida can learn to self-catherize and change their protective pants. However, a challenge frequently encountered by staff is to get them to do these things without prompting and monitoring. The student may not stay with the schedule of catherization, not perform a thorough catheterization, or not change his or her protective pants. The most obvious sign that a student is not following a bladder management protocol is that he or she smells of urine. Of course, this can have detrimental effects on a student's employment. It is not uncommon for staff to assume that students with spina bifida should follow a bladder management program after simply being trained how to do so. In many cases, this does not occur and the response is to "nag" and provide negative feedback to the student. Given the general difficulties that many students with spina bifida have related to organization and self-manage-ment and the fact that bladder management is not particularly reinforcing in itself, it is critical that a systematic and positive program be outlined and imple-mented. This may involve staff and parents being willing to prompt the student and to provide reinforcement at a very high level during the first few months while the student is learning the management program. This prompting and feedback would then be slowly decreased. If the student begins to have difficulties following the program during this fading, staff and parents should again begin providing additional assistance and support in a positive fashion and avoid becoming frustrated with the student. Nagging and negative feedback usually only result in the student becoming resistive to cooperating with the program.

5. *Surgical Intervention*   A procedure technically named an ileal conduit has commonly been performed for students with spina bifida (Bigge, 1982; Orelove & Sobsey, 1987). This procedure involves disconnecting the ureters from the bladder and implanting them in the small bowel which is then led to the abdomen, where a small hole is formed. A pouch is then attached to this hole through which urine passes into the pouch. There are a number of different bag systems that can be used. The one that best meets the needs of the student should be determined by a medical specialist who has expertise in this area. The urine collection bag will probably need to be emptied while the student is at work. If possible the students should be taught how to do this. Again, a specialist should be sought who can assist in describing the bag changing procedures and provide suggestions for training the student.

Strategies for Dealing with Bowel Control Problems   Bowel control accidents are particularly problematic in community-based employment settings. Several strategies for decreasing these accidents are described in this section.

1. *Bowel Evacuation*   The most effective strategy for dealing with bowel incontinence problems is to insure that the individual's bowels are empty before he or she leaves home (Bigge, 1982; Orelove & Sobsey, 1987). To initially facilitate this, a student may need to be assisted with the use of digital stimulation of the bowel, suppositories, laxatives, or enemas (Jones, 1985). A standard routine should be established for the person when one of these procedures is used. For example, after getting up in the morning, Steve eats breakfast, watches television for 15 minutes, and then has a bowel movement. By establishing such a routine, the student may eventually begin to have a bowel movement without the assistance of these other procedures. A physician with experience in bowel control and management issues for individuals with neuromuscular disabilities should select the specific technique that is used and prescribe the specific program for doing so.

2. *Diet Regulation*   It is also extremely important that the eating schedule and diet of a person with bowel control problems be regulated (Orelove & Sobsey, 1987). The time of day when meals are consumed should be kept as regular as possible, since variations will affect when a bowel movement occurs. Foods that increase the likelihood of a loose bowel should be avoided at meals consumed prior to or at work or school (Orelove & Sobsey, 1987).

3. *Protective Pants*   If an individual experiences bowel accidents, pro-

tective pants can be used at work. With the use of bowel evacuation procedures and diet regulations, major bowel accidents should not be a concern for students. However, some students, particularly those who do not have any physiological control of their bowels, may still frequently have some bowel discharge. These students will also need to use protective pants. If possible these students should learn to routinely check their pants to determine if they are in need of changing and to change them.

4. Surgical Intervention   Students with spina bifida frequently have had an ileostomy or colostomy (Bigge, 1982; Orelove & Sobsey, 1987). These procedures involve bringing either the small or large intestine to the abdominal wall, where a hole is created through which fecal matter is discharged into an attached bag. These students will have a special diet that needs to be followed and of which the vocational staff and adult service program should be aware. A medical specialist should be consulted to gain specific information about how these systems should be managed.

Incontinence is a complex issue, and the strategy that is most appropriate will depend on a number of factors, including the reason for the incontinence, the frequency of accidents, the student's personal preference, the potential health-related side effects of a strategy, and the supports that will be available at a work site. When attempting to select a strategy, input should be gained from a health professional who has expertise in dealing with incontinence, especially one who has worked with individuals with disabilities.

Bathroom Assistance

If an individual uses a wheelchair, the bathroom at the job site needs to be wheelchair accessible. During the initial work experience or job analysis, the width of the door and its ease of opening, the size of toilet stalls, and the presence of rails should be noted. If there are accessibility difficulties, the employer's willingness to make modifications should be explored and assistance should be provided to make these. Title V of the Rehabilitation Act requires employers who are federal agencies, have federal contracts, or receive federal financial assistance to make reasonable accommodations for employees with disabilities. Bathroom accessibility is considered a "reasonable accommodation." The new Americans with Disabilities Act (ADA) expanded this regulation to employers who receive no federal assistance. In addition, the Division of Vocational Rehabilitation should pay for bathroom modification costs, if these will permit a student to gain employment.

Strategies for Increasing Bathroom Independence   Many students who use wheelchairs may have difficulty getting from their chair to the toilet. The purpose of this section is to identify a number of strategies that may be employed to allow an individual to use the bathroom as independently as possible.

1. Transfer Instructions   Many individuals can learn to transfer themselves to the toilet. Instruction and practice should focus on insuring that the student can do so safely (Bigge, 1982). Of course, the ease of transferring is affected by the size and design (e.g., the presence of transfer bars, the height of the toilet) of the bathroom that the student will use at the job site.

School staff should evaluate a student's ability to use bathrooms and toilets that have different dimensions and characteristics in order to identify those that she or he can and cannot use. This information will then need to be considered when seeking an employment site for the student.

2. *Clothing*   Students who have either use of only one hand or limited control of both hands may have some difficulty getting their pants unbuttoned or unzipped (and rebuttoned and rezipped). The family or residential provider should be requested to provide the student with clothes that are easily manipulated, such as pants that are held up by an elastic waist band (Orelove & Sobsey, 1987). Pants that are fastened with velcro can be purchased through special clothing companies. Someone with sewing skills can also alter pants by removing the zipper and buttons and replacing them with velcro.

3. *Portable Urinal for Males*   One strategy to avoid the need for transferring is to have the student learn to use a portable urinal (Bigge, 1982). This option, however, is best for males, and of course can only be used for urinating. There are portable urinals for females, but they are extremely difficult to use without spillage. If a man has some functional use of his hands and fairly good upper body control, he can be taught to independently use a portable urinal. This instruction includes opening the pants, positioning the portable urinal, holding it in place, and emptying and washing it out.

Parents should be asked to provide students with pants and underwear with a fly-front opening. Again, if the student has difficulty zipping and buttoning, velcro can be used. If a student cannot learn to independently use a urinal, another person will need to provide assistance. However, this is a much less difficult procedure than is required in transferring.

4. *Bathroom Equipment*   As indicated, the ease with which a student is able to independently transfer may be affected by the height of the toilet seat and the presence of bars. If a particular work site does not have a raised toilet seat, a portable raised seat can be installed on the toilet. These can be rented on a short-term basis or purchased. Costs will vary depending on the chair purchased. However, most are in the $100–$200 range. There are many different types and designs. The toilet and the needs of the student will determine which should be selected. Transfer bars can be purchased and installed with little expense and trouble. A mechanical lift can also be purchased and placed at a site to enable a student to be transferred by one person, although these lifts are expensive (usually at least $1000).

5. *Bedpan*   A bedpan can be used by a female for urinating or by both sexes for a bowel movement. However, it is extremely difficult for a person to use a bedpan while in a wheelchair. A person usually needs to be placed on a

bed or mat when using a bedpan. This will frequently not be feasible at an employment site.

Summary

While the student is in school, every attempt should be made to identify and train the strategy that enables him or her to avoid toileting accidents and use bathrooms with the least amount of assistance. The strategies that the student can use, the type of bathroom facilities and the equipment needed, and the amount and type of support required will then need to be considered when planning for the placement of the student at a permanent job site.

COMMUNICATION

The amount and type of communication that is required at a job will depend on the specific tasks that a person performs as well as the employment setting. Individuals should at least have some means to communicate basic needs such as the desire to use the bathroom, that they feel ill, and the need for assistance related to their tasks. In addition, the opportunity to interact socially with non-disabled co-workers is one of the major advantages of community-based employment (Chadsey-Rusch, 1986). Consequently, in order to take advantage of these opportunities, students must have the means to communicate during times established for social interaction (i.e., breaks).

Communication Strategies

There are four major strategies that can be used by a person to communicate: verbal communication, gestures and signs, communication boards and books, and electronic devices. This section reviews each of the options that should be considered for use by a student for communication purposes at a job site, as well as the utility of each of these options for communication of basic needs during on-task and social periods.

Verbal Communication Employers and co-workers are most comfortable verbally communicating with an employee. Consequently, whenever possible, verbal communication should be used by a person with a disability at a work site. Obviously, if a person is able to speak fairly clearly, verbal communication should be the mode selected for use at the work site (Musselwhite & St. Louis, 1982). As Orelove and Sobsey (1987) have suggested, verbal communication is preferable because it is portable, rapid, and precise.

Verbal communication should also be considered for students who are difficult to understand. With training, the person may be able to learn to articulate a few words clearly enough to be understood. For example, John was taught to say bathroom, help, sick, and a small number of task-specific words clearly enough so that co-workers and supervisors could interpret his intended message. He was able to communicate these needs verbally more quickly than if he used a communication board or device. Speed of communication is extremely important in employment settings during on-task periods.

Break periods are typically the time when more complex and novel communications occur, which are those that will be more difficult for co-workers to understand if an individual does not speak clearly. However, during break time co-workers may have more time to communicate with an individual. Thus, it may be appropriate for other communication systems to be used during breaks (e.g., a communication board or device).

Gestures and Signs   The use of formal sign language as the primary mode of communication is, in most cases, not a feasible option for persons who have limited use of their hands (Sailor & Guess, 1983). Signing in the formal sense also has limited utility in an employment setting, since few co-workers or supervisors have been trained in sign language. However, if a student is unable to speak clearly, the use of a few signs to communicate basic needs may be possible. This may be particularly true if the student works with a small number of co-workers, who can be trained to recognize the signs.

It is, of course, not necessary for a person to use a formal sign system to communicate what she or he needs. In fact, an informal gesture may be more easily understood by lay persons and more functional in its expression (Orelove & Sobsey, 1987). For example, co-workers would quickly understand that pointing to the stapler meant that it was out of staplers. Gestures are particularly effective when used in conjunction with a verbal statement. Thus, a person who can speak but is difficult to understand might be taught to say key words as clearly as possible, and to make a gesture or sign at the same time. However, it may be difficult for a student to use gestures for social communication purposes during break times. Again, other options, such as communication boards, books, or electronic devices, may be used during this time.

Communication Boards and Books   Communication boards and books contain pictures, symbols, words, letters, or numbers that a person can point to and thereby express a message (Allaire & Miller, 1983; Mirenda, 1985; Orelove & Sobsey, 1987). The size, shape, and configuration of the board or book that is most useful will depend on a student's cognitive, sensory, and physical characteristics, as well as the specific communication purpose for which it will be used. This option can be a very efficient and effective means of communication for persons who are unable to speak.

When a communication board or book is used by a student for expressing basic information, it is important to make sure that the board is accessible to him or her. A board or book that is kept in a pouch in the back of a wheelchair cannot be easily obtained by the student when she or he needs to communicate. Boards are instead frequently affixed to a lapboard for purposes of accessibility. However, lapboards should be avoided in vocational settings, as they typically make it difficult for a person to move around a work area and to interface with the equipment and materials involved in task performance. In addition, lapboards accentuate the "disabled" appearance of the person.

One of the most useful types of communication boards for employment situations is a small card with only the most critical messages. The individual can keep the card wedged between his or her legs or in a small pouch on the side of the chair. When a message needs to be communicated, the card can be placed on the lap or on a table. The student can then point to the words or symbols on it. The card can also be affixed to the wheelchair arm, or on the work tables, walls, or equipment in the work area.

Communication boards and books can be an effective way for persons with disabilities to communicate with co-workers in a more in-depth fashion at lunch or break times. In fact, this may be the best mode for individuals who can speak or use gestures to express basic information during on-task periods, but who cannot use these means effectively for more in-depth social communication purposes. When used for social communication purposes, a larger board or book with more symbols will probably be needed. This board or book could be placed on a table in the break room by the student or by a co-worker. The number of symbols included in the book should reflect the vocabulary that the individual actually uses. If a person has a large expressive repertoire, the board or book should reflect this. However, if the expressive repertoire of the student is more limited, many additional symbols will serve little purpose and will increase the difficulty in using the book.

Electronic Communication Device   The advances in electronic communication devices hold great promise for persons with disabilities (Bigge, 1982; Capozzi & Mineo, 1984; Orelove & Sobsey, 1987). Many of these devices are similar in general configuration to communication boards—a flat surface is divided into squares and a letter, number, symbol, or message appears in each square. There are two major ways in which a person can operate an electronic device. Some devices are operated by the user touching the square corresponding to the information to be communicated. Other devices are operated via a light-scanning method. A light appears in each square, one at a time, and when the light appears in the square with the information that the person wishes to communicate, she or he activates a switch. The type and location of the switch depends on the need of the user. There are some devices that look much like computer or calculator keyboards, where letters and numbers are on keys and the person "types" what is to be communicated.

Devices also vary in terms of how information is output (i.e., how others receive the information). Some devices print the message out on a sheet of paper in the same fashion as a computer printer, while other devices print messages on a screen or monitor. Finally, some devices allow voice output (i.e., the device speaks the message).

Electronic devices have a great potential for enhancing the ability of persons to communicate. However, the practical utility of these devices may be limited for employment purposes. The major reason for this is their lack of portability. Most devices must be carried on a lapboard or placed on a table for the person to be able to use them. As suggested before, lapboards both serve as obstacles when a person is performing tasks and increase the "disabled" appearance of the person. It may be possible to place the device on a table at the person's work station, if she or he typically remains in one area throughout the work period. However, the size of the device will determine the feasibility of this solution. Every attempt should be made to purchase the smallest device that the student can use. However, the smaller the device, and thus the size of the keys or squares, the more control the student must have in order to be able to operate it.

An electronic device may be of greatest utility for social communication purposes. The device can be placed on a table in the break room and co-workers can take the time to communicate with the person. However, an attempt should still be made to use the smallest device possible. A large device may be intimidating to co-workers. It may also serve to create a physical barrier between the person and his or her co-workers.

Summary

The communication strategy selected for a student will depend on many factors, including his or her ability to speak clearly, to manipulate a device or board, the communication demands of the tasks performed, the amount of naturally occurring social interactions at the job site, the number of co-workers, and their level of interest and comfort in interacting with the person with the disability. In school programs, speech therapists typically have the responsibility for guiding the selection of a communication system for students. These individuals have much valuable knowledge. However, many speech therapists have no or little experience related to employment issues. They sometimes do not understand that the need to get work done must be weighed against a person's opportunity to communicate and that, in fact, the former frequently will outweigh the latter in importance in a real business setting. Consequently, every attempt should be made to educate speech therapists regarding employment issues and realities.

DRINKING AND EATING

Many individuals who experience physical and multiple disabilities have some difficulties eating and drinking (Bigge, 1982; Gallender, 1979; Morris & Weber, 1978; Orelove & Sobsey, 1987). Co-workers may be hesitant to sit with a person at break or lunch who is extremely messy. In addition, a person who cannot eat independently may require the presence of an attendant or adult program staff at the site for this purpose. This section discusses a number of very simple strategies that staff might consider using to assist students to more independently eat and drink at work. However, eating and drinking are very complex skills for persons with abnormal oral-motor patterns. Decisions about the specific eating and drinking techniques that are both the most effective and safe for a student to use require the input of a professional with expertise and knowledge in this area. Occupational and speech therapists are often excellent resources for assistance related to drinking and eating. The reader is also encouraged to review Orelove and Sobsey (1987) for a thorough description of mealtime skill training issues and techniques for students with physical disabilities.

Drinking

There are two major problems that a student may experience when drinking. First, the neurological disability of some individuals has an impact on their mouth and throat region, and they thus experience difficulty holding liquid in their mouth and/or swallowing (Gallender, 1979; Orelove & Sobsey, 1987). If this is the case, liquid may run out of their mouth when they attempt to drink. Second, some persons have difficulty getting the cup or glass to their mouth due to limited upper body control. There are a number of strategies that may be of assistance in alleviating each of these problems in an employment setting.

Strategies to Assist Students Who Have Difficulty Drinking One strategy that may be recommended for an individual who has difficulty swallowing is to teach the individual to take very small amounts of liquid into his or her mouth during each drink. This decreases the amount that can run back out of the mouth. Some individuals may be able to learn to do this using a regular drinking implement. However, this will be much easier for students if they are provided with a cup with a small opening, such as a commuter cup. A cutaway cup can be used for students who may gag or choke when they tip their head back. Cutting away part of the rim permits liquid to be obtained when the cup is tipped only slightly (Morris, 1978). Cups such as these also assist students who have difficulty getting the cup to their mouths without spillage.

Persons who have a great deal of difficulty getting the cup to their mouths should be taught to use a straw, if possible, so that the container can remain on a table. The cup or glass should be placed on a table that is at a height that does not require the student to lean forward, since leaning forward will only increase the likelihood that liquid will pour out of the mouth. There are also cup holders that can be attached to a wheelchair. However, when using these holders the student still must lift the cup to drink. These authors have successfully used an articulated arm that was designed for holding and positioning cameras for students who cannot lift cups and glasses when drinking. The device attaches to the wheelchair, a cupholder is attached to it with velcro, and the arm and cup positioned in front of the student's mouth so that he or she can drink with a straw independently. These devices can be purchased from full-service camera stores.

Eating

The same two major types of problems experienced when drinking may also be experienced by students when eating food. First, some students have difficulty chewing and swallowing food and, thus, food may fall out of their mouth while eating. Second, some students have difficulty getting the food to their mouth due to their limited hand control.

Strategies to Assist Students Who Have Difficulty Eating   One simple strategy that can be used with students who have eating difficulties is to teach them to take small bites and to swallow the food before taking another bite. Doing this will decrease the amount of food that can fall out of the mouth. A second strategy is to identify the foods that the student can chew and swallow with the least amount of difficulty. For example, a student may have difficulty chewing and swallowing peanut butter sandwiches. Those foods that are difficult for the student to eat neatly should be identified and the parent or residential program should be asked not to send these to work. If the person will buy lunch, she or he will need to be taught what foods are preferable for eating at work.

Some foods can be appropriately eaten with one's hands or fingers (i.e., finger foods such as sandwiches, raw vegetables, fruit, cookies, cheese bits, crackers). Other foods can only be appropriately eaten using a utensil. If a student is significantly more proficient at using one method, then those types of foods should be sent to work with the student or the student should be taught what type of foods to order.

If a student prefers the finger food technique it is helpful to have the parents or the residential program cut the food items into the size that is easiest to handle. This will also help insure that the student takes small amounts of food into the mouth at one time. If a student prefers to use a utensil for eating, there are special utensils available from medical supply stores that make handling less difficult.

Individuals who experience difficulty swallowing drink or food have a higher potential for choking than other persons (Dailey, 1983). Certain types of foods are most frequently associated with choking, such as hot dogs, candy, nuts, and grapes (Harris, Baker, Smith, & Harris, 1984). Soft foods that become compressed during swallowing and bread, especially with sticky spreads, often cause choking (Dailey, 1983; Orelove & Sobsey, 1987). It may be advisable for the person to not eat such problematic foods at his or her work site. The student's parents should be asked not to send these foods, and if possible the student should be taught what foods to avoid. The school program will also need to ensure that they pass on this information to the adult service program. If the student may choke while eating and no school or adult program staff will be there, co-workers will need to be recruited to be trained to assist the student if choking occurs.

Most employees need or want to drink and eat during their work breaks. If a student experiences difficulties eating or drinking, the school program should try a number of the strategies described here in order to find those that will allow him or her to eat and drink as independently, neatly, and safely as possible. Of course, some students may need a substantial amount of assistance when eating or drinking. When the time comes to consider a paid job, the person and his or her advocates should weigh the pros and cons of eating at the job site. For example, a full-time data entry position, which Steve would be able to do independently, was found for him. However, he required assistance when eating. Unfortunately, no assistance was available. Should he turn down the job and stay at home? An alternative solution might be for Steve to take a high-protein drink to work and use this for nutrition. Another option might be for him to work only part-time, which would allow him to eat before and after work.

Summary   Eating and drinking is an issue that is not often considered by schools in relation to a student's future employment. However, for students with physical and multiple disabilities, these issues can pose a major employment challenge. Schools should think of the eating and drinking programs and the strategies that are implemented with students not just with the thought of what works at school or even at home, but how the student will eat and drink at work when there may be less assistance, if any, available.

MOBILITY

Most students with severe physical and multiple disabilities experience some difficulty walking and in many cases they require a special mobility device (Bigge & O'Donnell, 1976; Sowers, Jenkins, & Powers, 1988; Wehman, Wood, et al., 1988). Due to the lack of accessible transportation and the widespread inaccessibility of many businesses, mobility can serve as one of the major barriers to employment.

There are, of course, a variety of different mobility modes available for persons with disabilities, including walking, canes, crutches, manual wheelchairs, electric wheelchairs, and electric carts. In many cases the type of option selected will be determined by the nature and severity of a student's physical disability. However, in many cases a student may be able to use more than one method of mobility. For example, John may need to use a power chair when going from the bus stop to the work site. However, he is better at driving a manual wheelchair than a power wheelchair inside the site, where he needs to maneuver around furniture and people.

In this section each of the possible modes of mobility (e.g., walking, crutches, wheelchair) is described. In addition, the different transportation options that may be available for a person to get to and from work (public bus, private van) are delineated, along with a description of the extent to which each type of mobility device affects the utilization of the transportation options. Finally, a number of issues that should be considered regarding a person getting around a work site are discussed.

Modes of Mobility

There are six major modes of mobility that can be used by a person with a disability: unassisted walking, canes and crutches, walkers, manual wheelchair, power wheelchairs, and power carts. Each of these is briefly discussed in this section.

Unassisted Walking   Some individuals with physical and multiple disabilities can walk without the aid of a special mobility device. Of the individuals who can walk unassisted, there is a great degree of variation in the distance that these individuals can walk before needing to rest. In addition, the steadiness of walking also varies greatly among individuals. The degree of endurance and steadiness are most directly affected by how much lower body control and strength a person has. However, upper body control and strength can also have an important impact on how far a person can walk and how steady he or she is when walking.

Canes and Crutches   As when walking unassisted, there is a great deal of variability among individuals in the distance that they can walk as well as their steadiness when using a cane or crutches. Since canes or crutches must be manipulated, a person using them must have good arm control.

Walker   Probably the most widely employed mobility device for persons with some use of their legs is the walker. Walkers provide the user with a substantial amount of support and stability, which increases steadiness and endurance. The walker requires less manipulation than canes or crutches, and thus less need for arm control.

There are dozens of different walker designs. One of the most important design variations is the presence or absence of wheels. Some walkers have wheels on the front and back, which allow users to simply push the walker as they would a grocery cart. However, the danger does exist that the person might lose control of the walker and fall. Other walkers have wheels only on the back legs, with rubber tips on the front. When walking the person slightly lifts the walker and pushes. Pushing down on the walker will result in it automatically stopping. While this design allows a person to move less quickly than the four-wheeled version, it is much more safe. Another walker design is the one with no wheels. To use this type of walker, the person lifts it up and forward for each step made. For many individuals, this can be a difficult type of walker to master. This is particularly true for persons with spastic or athetoid cerebral palsy. Some individuals with these forms of cerebral palsy have a tendency to lose control when they lift the walker up to move it, and may end up falling. This problem can be decreased if weights are added to the walker. Obviously, the weights should not be so heavy that the person has to struggle to lift the walker.

Manual Wheelchair   Persons with very limited use of their legs but fairly good use of one or both arms may be able to use a manual wheelchair. The distance that a person can propel the chair varies greatly. Persons who must propel the chair with only one arm typically cannot do so for long distances.

Learning to accurately manipulate the chair is also made much more difficult for persons who can use only one arm.

There are a large number of manual wheelchair designs from which to select. Probably the most important design factor is the amount of body support that the chair gives to the user. For the individual with little body control or strength, and for the person with leg or torso structural deformities, it is critical that a chair provide a high degree of support. In fact, a chair should be designed specifically for these individuals. On the other hand, the individual who has excellent upper body control and strength may be able to use a sports chair, which provides no support but is extremely lightweight. Due to the lightness of these sports chairs, they offer many advantages over conventional wheelchairs. They can be pushed faster and longer distances with little fatigue, and they also have more handling responsiveness. These chairs can be easily folded, picked up, and placed in a vehicle. On the down side, the chair's lightness increases the chances that it will turn over.

Motorized Wheelchair   One of the most important contributions to the quality of life of persons with severe physical disabilities is the motorized wheelchair. Persons with even the most limited body control can move about independently with the use of these chairs. In most cases, the person manipulates the chair via a hand-operated joystick device mounted on the lap or arm of the chair. However, different types of control devices can be mounted at different locations depending on the manner in which the person can best manipulate the chair. For example, for a person with no hand use, a control could be placed under the chin. The person would manipulate the chair by placing his or her chin on the control, and moving it forward, backward, or to the side.

A person using a motorized wheelchair can move rapidly and for long distances without experiencing fatigue. However, the battery that powers these chairs must typically be recharged after a few miles.

Unfortunately, motorized wheelchairs are too heavy to be lifted. Thus, a person using one of these chairs must have access to a wheelchair-accessible vehicle and cannot enter a building that has even a small step up or down unless a ramp is available.

Learning to accurately manipulate a motorized wheelchair can be difficult for some individuals, because the controls are extremely sensitive. The person must learn to precisely discriminate how much pressure to place on the control to make it go different speeds, which way to push the control to make it turn at different angles, as well as how to back up. Because of these factors, there is a higher likelihood that a person may run into things (furniture, office equipment), run off street curbs, or even inadvertently dart in front of a car. However, with very careful training, most individuals can learn to safely and independently use a motorized wheelchair.

Motorized Carts   In recent years, another type of mobility device has become available for persons with disabilities. These devices are basically small versions of golf carts—a swivel seat along with a steering wheel type control is situated on a base that has four small wheels. The seat provides no support for the user's body. Consequently, these devices are meant to be used by persons with good upper body control. As with the conventional motorized wheelchair, a user of a cart can drive long distances with no fatigue. However, carts also require recharging after a few miles. As with the motorized chairs, the cart can be difficult to learn to accurately and safely drive for many individuals.

Carts vary in terms of their design. One important characteristic that should be considered is whether the cart can be disassembled, and if so, whether this can be done easily. Second, the weight of the cart is important. Some carts are extremely heavy and cannot be easily lifted, while others are lighter. A cart that can be lifted and quickly disassembled opens up the possibility that a person can use a vehicle that is not wheelchair accessible.

Transportation: Getting to and from Work

Many sheltered programs provide transportation to and from work to their "clients." Today, with the move to community-based employment, it is no longer feasible for programs to offer this service. In general, transportation is one of the major difficulties facing supported employment programs and persons with disabilities who wish to work in community settings (Wehman, Wood, et al., 1988). Access to transportation is particularly problematic for persons who experience physical disabilities. School programs should become active in their support for wheelchair-accessible public transportation.

Consequently, simply getting to and from work may be one of the greatest challenges that a student with physical and multiple disabilities will encounter. This section describes different transportation options that may be available. Some of the issues, including the type of mobility device a student uses, which should be considered when selecting an option are discussed.

Public Buses that Are Not Wheelchair Accessible A student who walks unassisted with a cane, crutches, or a walker can use a regular public bus to get to and from work. The student, of course, will require instruction to use the bus correctly and safely (Moon, Inge, Wehman, Brooke, & Barcus, 1990; Rusch & Mithaug, 1980; Sowers, Rusch, & Hudson, 1979). The most difficult aspect of bus-riding for this student is getting on and off the bus. The person must be able to safely climb up and move down the steps at the entrance of the bus. If the trainer is uncertain about how well the student can climb steps, an assessment should be conducted. The assessment can be done at any stairwell that is similar to those on buses. The stairs should be fairly steep and have rails on both sides. If the person does have difficulty climbing the steps, training and practice should be provided until the person is independent and safe. Some bus companies allow schools to use a bus at the garage or will bring a bus to the school for training purposes.

Public Buses that Are Wheelchair Accessible   A person who uses a wheelchair will only be able to use wheelchair accessible buses. The most difficult aspect of riding the bus for a person in a wheelchair is getting on and off of it. Most bus companies will not permit drivers to assist persons to get on and off a bus, other than to put the safety strap in place. To be independent, the student will need to do the following: maneuver the chair onto the lift, lock the brakes on the chair, unlock the brakes, move to the area designated for wheelchairs, and lock the brakes. Again, the bus company should be requested to provide access to a bus at the garage for purposes of training. If the student is unable to perform any or all of the steps, attempts should be made to gain assistance from another rider or the driver.

Alternative Modes of Transportation   If there is no public transportation system available or the student cannot access it, other options must be considered (Wehman, Moon, Everson, Wood, & Barcus, 1988). These options include private van services, a program van, a relative's vehicle, a taxi, or riding with a co-worker.

Private Van Service   In some cities, there are private companies that own and operate wheelchair accessible vans. The cost of using these services is quite high. Due to the expense, the vans are typically used by persons for infrequent trips such as going to a doctor's appointment. Although these services are primarily targeted for individuals in wheelchairs, they are usually willing to transport other individuals.

Program Van   A vocational or residential program may have a vehicle that is used for transporting the individuals in their program. In some cases, the vehicle may be wheelchair accessible, and in other cases it will not be.

Relative's Vehicle   If a student lives at home, the family may be willing and able to provide transportation to work. The type of vehicle owned by the family and the type of mobility device used by the person will determine if this option is a possibility.

Taxi   Although expensive, using a taxi is another option. Many companies today have a few taxis that are wheelchair accessible.

Riding with a Co-worker   A final option for getting to and from work is to obtain a ride with a co-worker. This option will be most viable for students who do not require a wheelchair-accessible vehicle, since few co-workers will own one.

Getting into and Around a Business

A person who uses a special mobility device may face difficulties getting in and maneuvering around a business. It is true that government regulations require that companies that receive substantial federal support must be wheelchair accessible. However, it is likely that most individuals will be placed in private companies that are not required to be accessible (as stated earlier, many states do require private companies to make reasonable accommodations).

Many employers are willing to make accommodation and modifications to improve the accessibility of their companies. In addition, the Division of Vocational Rehabilitation will pay for or assist in paying for modifications to a business if it will result in the employment of a person with a disability.

In many cases, the difficulties that a person has getting into and around a business cannot be solved by a modification to the physical structure of the building. For example, a person may fall down due to lack of stability while walking, or run over co-workers' feet while driving his or her wheelchair around the work area. These problems are not accessibility issues, but rather issues related to the skills the individual has in maneuvering around the job site.

Getting into a Building   A student who walks or uses a cane, crutches, or a walker can get into a building that has one or more steps at its entrance. Training should be provided to ensure the student's optimal safety and independence moving up and down steps.

A person who uses a manual chair and who has good upper body strength and control may be able to maneuver his or her chair over a small step. If the person is light and the stairs are not too steep, another person may be able to pull them up and down the steps. Some individuals with disabilities can get out of their chair and walk a few steps with assistance. If this is true, another person could lift the chair up and down the steps.

Getting the door to a business open is another issue that must be considered with regard to getting in and out of a building. Opening doors can be quite difficult for individuals who have limited hand use. Even for persons with good use of their hands, maneuvering a wheelchair through a door while opening it can be challenging. However, many students, even those with limited hand use, can learn with systematic training to independently open doors. A strategy for getting different types of doors open and the wheelchair through them that is most effective and efficient for a particular student should be designed. Physical and occupational therapists are extremely useful in designing such strategies.

Getting Around a Business   There are two major critical issues related to how a student will move around a community-based business. The first is safety. Safety is typically of greatest relevance for students who will walk at the job site. A person who appears unsteady on his or her feet or falls frequently will understandably raise concerns in an employer's mind. If it is hoped that walking will be the primary means by which a student will maneuver around a job site, it is critically important that part of the training focuses on controlled and safe walking.

The second major issue related to getting around a business is how independently and accurately the student is able to do so. This issue is most relevant to persons who use wheelchairs or motorized carts. Of greatest importance is whether the student can maneuver the device without running into co-workers, walls, or equipment. A systematic intervention program should be implemented to ensure that the student drive accurately and independently.

Issues related to mobility are probably those that most frequently become barriers to the employment of persons with disabilities. As with many other areas, school programs often focus on the present when choosing the mode of mobility students will use and training mobility skills. To ensure that mobility does not decrease students' opportunities to access employment, schools must think about how they will get to work when there is no school van available and how they will get into and around employment sites.

DROOLING

Individuals whose neuromuscular disability has affected the nerves and muscles of the mouth or throat may drool (Brady, 1973; Koheil, Sochaniwskyj, Bablich, Kenny, & Milner, 1987). Unfortunately, a person who drools will face a particular challenge in being viewed as a competent employee as well as being accepted socially by his or her co-workers. Drooling can also interfere with one's task performance. For example, an individual may have difficulty keeping saliva off of the products, papers, and equipment with which he or she is working.

The traditional approaches utilized for controlling drooling have been drugs and surgery (Brady, 1973; Ekedahl, 1974; Illingworth, 1970; Wilkie, 1970). These interventions are aimed at reducing saliva production. Today there appears to be a consensus that drooling occurs because an individual does not swallow with sufficient frequency or completeness, rather than because of overproduction of saliva (Makhani, 1974; Van de Heyning, Marquet, & Cretin, 1980). Neurological treatment programs have been widely endorsed by therapists as a means to address swallowing difficulties (McCracken, 1978; Meuller, 1978). The goal of these programs is to increase jaw control and tactile awareness, which in theory improves control over drooling. However, no attempts have been made to experimentally evaluate the effectiveness of the approach.

A small number of studies have attempted to examine the effectiveness of behavioral approaches in the reduction of drooling (Drabman, Cruz, Russ, & Lynd, 1979; Garber, 1971; Koheil et al., 1987; Rapp, 1980). Rapp (1980) taught children with cerebral palsy and mental retardation to swallow more effectively using modeling, rehearsal, and feedback. They were then given a portable device that delivered an auditory cue (a beep) at programmed intervals and taught to swallow when the beep sounded. The children wore the device throughout their school day and teachers praised them when they swallowed at the beep. As a result of the intervention, the children's drooling was substantially reduced. However, no systematic attempts were made to remove the auditory cue that served to prompt the children to swallow. A similar procedure was used by Sowers, Gerdes, and Powers (1990) to assist an adult with cerebral palsy and mental retardation in a community work site to control his drooling. After the person was trained to swallow more effectively and to swallow at an auditory cue, the cue was then removed and he was praised for continuing to swallow without the cue and for keeping his mouth dry. The results demonstrated that the intervention was effective in increasing and maintaining the person's drool control across three work periods.

Program Description

The following provides a brief description of the drool control program utilized by Sowers, Gerdes, and Powers (1990). The program has been successfully implemented with approximately five individuals with physical and multiple disabilities.

1. The individual is first taught to suck the saliva present in the front of the mouth to the back of the mouth and then to swallow. This is extremely important because in most cases, drooling occurs when the individual has allowed so much saliva to accumulate in the front of the mouth cavity that it spills out of the mouth. The response is very similar to the one used to drink from a straw. Those individuals who can drink from a straw will have little difficulty learning to "suck and swallow" for the purpose of controlling drooling. Although the individual who participated in the Sowers et al. study had great difficulty learning the response (he had difficulty bringing his lips together), with instruction and practice he was able to learn to do so.

2. After the individual demonstrates the ability to "suck and swallow," the next phase of the program involves providing the individual with an auditory cue for executing the response. A bell or buzzer recorded on a tape can be used for this purpose. The tape recorder can be placed in a pouch on the person's wheelchair or on a table. The volume should be low enough to avoid calling undue attention to the person, but loud enough to insure that the student and trainer can both hear it. The individual is instructed to "suck and swallow" each time the cue is heard and when the student does so at the cue without a prompt, praise follows. The cue should be programmed to occur at intervals that will prevent drooling. This will vary depending on how much a person drools. An estimate of a person's drool rate should be obtained during baseline by simply noting each time the person drools. Typically, the cue should occur every 15 seconds to 2 minutes.

    A contingency for drooling should also be established during this phase. For example, the individual could receive a " + " on a card for every 5 minutes that he or she did not drool.

    This phase should be instituted long enough for the individual to become accustomed to "sucking and swallowing" regularly, but not so long that a dependence on the auditory cue is established. Generally, the phase should last between 1–3 weeks.

3. In the final stage of the program, the auditory cue is no longer provided. Although it may seem advisable to fade the cue by gradually reducing its volume, this technique actually results in making the person "more" dependent on it. In effect, the person struggles to try to hear the cue.

    When the cue is terminated, the person should be told that she or he is going to get the chance to swallow without the bell. The importance of doing it independently should be emphasized. The trainer should pre-prompt the person by saying, "Go ahead and get to work and begin sucking and swallowing." Each time the person "sucks and swallows" enthusiastic praise should be given. The contingency for not drooling (e.g., a " + " on a card) should also be continued. As time goes on, the praise should be faded (by gradually reducing the number of responses praised). For some individuals it may be possible to completely fade out the praise and feedback card. However, many individuals will require some ongoing feedback for sucking and swallowing and not drooling. The goal should be to reduce this feedback to as minimal a level as possible.

This program has been successfully implemented with a number of students and adults with disabilities. However, the program has not proven effective for individuals with very significant cognitive disabilities. It should also be noted that many students can learn to control their drooling without the need for the auditory cue phase of this program, by simply providing them with consistent feedback for swallowing and for maintaining a dry mouth. This less intrusive intervention is usually effective with students who do not drool a great deal and who function at higher cognitive levels.

This program does require a significant amount of time and effort commitment by staff. However, because drooling can serve as a significant barrier to a person's employment as well as general social acceptance, the time and effort are well worth it.

OTHER WORK-RELATED BEHAVIORS

To this point in the chapter, five work-related skills or behaviors that frequently must be addressed when placing an individual with physical and multiple disabilities into a job have been discussed. In this section, three additional work-related areas, which have been widely discussed elsewhere in the literature related to persons who experience mental retardation, are addressed (Sowers, Rusch, et al., 1979; Wehman, 1981). These behaviors and skills also contribute to the ease with which students with physical and multiple disabilities achieve successful employment.

Grooming

Employers expect employees to be well groomed: to have bathed and used deodorant recently enough to be free of body odor, to have clean and combed hair, brushed teeth, and clean and neat clothes that are appropriate to the business (Rusch, Schutz, & Agran, 1982; Sowers et al., 1979; Wehman et al., 1988). The grooming of many individuals with severe disabilities is often substantially controlled by their families or residential providers. This is particularly true for persons with physical and multiple disabilities, who may require considerable assistance with self-care activities. Because of the great effort that this assistance requires, the grooming of some students with physical and multiple disabilities is poor. Compared with community work sites, the standards for grooming in school are usually significantly lower, and are standards to which caregivers may become accustomed.

School programs should impress the importance of grooming upon the students and their parents or other caregivers. A natural starting point for this may occur when the student begins his or her first in-school work experience while in middle school. Students and their parents should be provided with an explanation of the importance of grooming for job success. This point should be emphasized to a greater extent when the student begins to participate in community work experiences. The student and parents should be provided with a clear description of the standards for acceptable grooming. For most parents and caregivers, it is helpful to receive a written description of the grooming standards. This document is particularly important for residential providers, where there are typically many different staff who may be involved in assisting the individual with basic care, and where there are frequent staff turnovers.

Some parents or other caregivers may balk at understanding why they need to worry about the student's grooming while she or he is still in school—after all, the student is not really employed; she or he is only participating in a work experience. Staff should emphasize the need to begin teaching the student the importance of good grooming and appearance before she or he is placed in a job. Parents, caregivers, and students should also be informed that even work experience site employers are concerned about how students look while they are there, and grooming problems may limit students' work experience options.

Attendance

School (special education) programs typically have very flexible attendance policies. Students, their families, and residential providers may become accustomed to frequent and lengthy vacations based on a school schedule or their own schedule's convenience. Students may also feel free to take a day off when they are a little under the weather (but not sick) and to schedule medical and other appointments during the school day.

Obviously, there is a much higher attendance standard in community-based employment situations. Employers expect employees to arrive on time each scheduled work day (Rusch et al., 1982). There typically is a specified and limited amount of vacation time allotted, and the use of it must be arranged at the convenience of the company. Employees will also be required or at least encouraged to schedule medical appointments during nonwork hours. The school program should at least begin to make students and parents aware of the attendance demands that will be present after graduation and to assist them to start adjusting their routines accordingly. In particular, the expectation for daily attendance at the student's work experience site should be established and reinforced.

If a student is being considered for placement into a permanent job, the school program should make sure that the student and his or her caregivers understand the vacation and sick-leave policy of a potential employer and that everyone makes a commitment to abide by it before the placement occurs.

It is certainly true that many individuals with multiple and physical disabilities experience a high number of illnesses and have medical needs that will require them to miss work. When this is the case, an employment situation must be found that can support this individual's need for additional time off.

Behaviors Deemed Inappropriate in an Employment Setting

Some individuals with disabilities have learned behaviors that may be viewed as "inappropriate" in a community work setting. In many cases the number and severity of "inappropriate" behaviors exhibited by an individual with disabilities will decrease as a simple effect of being in an environment where appropriate behaviors are being modeled by peers (i.e., co-workers), where there is an expectation for appropriate behavior, where the individual has an opportunity to show his or her competence, and where she or he is reinforced for other behaviors. In other words, many of the inappropriate behaviors displayed by a person in a special education class or a sheltered environment may well decrease in intensity and frequency when that person is placed into a community job (Romer & Heller, 1983).

The use of systematic behavioral instructional procedures to train tasks and work-related behaviors also contributes to appropriate behavior (Chadsey-Rusch, 1986, 1990; Chadsey-Rusch & Rusch, 1988). Behavior difficulties predictably arise when a person is frustrated by not being able to perform tasks, and thus experiences failure and a large amount of corrective feedback. The "art" of good training is to set up the training situation so that a person succeeds as much as possible and feels good about the situation, while learning new and possibly difficult tasks and skills (Carr & Durand, 1985).

It must be understood that there are different standards for behavior in different companies, and for different jobs within a company (Chadsey-Rusch & Rusch, 1988). In some companies and jobs, employees are expected to adhere to a standard norm, while the employees in other companies may be very accepting of behaviors that depart from the "norm." Many individuals have behaviors that may be long-standing and would require a great deal of intensive intervention to change. While students have a number of years left in school, the program should attempt to assist them to learn more appropriate alternative behaviors. However, when a student nears graduation, it would be better to find jobs for them in companies that would be accepting of these behaviors.

In a related point, "professionals" have a tendency to be far less accepting of certain behaviors than many others. For example, many years ago this author (Sowers) served as a trainer for an individual who had been placed into a dishwashing position in the cafeteria of a hospital. This man had learned his job quickly and was an excellent dishwasher. However, he had a stereotypic behavior of closing things twice: he would close a door, begin to walk away from it, then return and push it again to make sure it was closed. I was conducting a program to try to eliminate this behavior when his supervisor asked me why I was still at the site every day since David was doing so well. I explained that I was trying to stop him from doing this behavior. She indicated that she had not even noticed he was doing it and that she was not concerned about it as long as he got his job done. More often than not employers and co-workers are far more accepting of different behaviors than professionals are willing to give them credit for.

There will be many occasions when it will be necessary to develop and implement a specific behavior intervention program to decrease a behavior deemed "inappropriate" to a particular employment setting. The following guidelines can provide the basic components of social skill training (SST) packages, which have been demonstrated to be effective in teaching a wide variety of social behaviors (Chadsey-Rusch, 1990).

1. *Teach a more appropriate response that meets the same need.* Research has clearly demonstrated that the most effective way to decrease an unwanted behavior is not to punish the behavior or to even reinforce the person for not doing it, but rather to teach the individual an alternative behavior (Evans & Meyer, 1985). For example, on particularly busy days in the photocopy room where he worked, Jess would occasionally feel overwhelmed and would respond by screaming, beating his fists, and biting his hand. An alternative strategy was identified by his trainer, for Jess to point to the symbol on his communication card for a break when he began feeling upset. He would then go to the break room for 5 minutes and relax.

    Another example for identifying alternative behaviors is Max. Max was unable to speak, and the way that he had learned to express his happiness was to shriek, which was rather disruptive to the management and other clerical staff in the office where he performed computer data entry. He and his trainer discussed how he might be able to show that he was happy in another way, and they decided that he would shake his fist (a sign of victory), smile, and nod yes.

2. *Explain the rationale for stopping the behavior.* Trainers frequently tell a student to stop doing something or to do something without explaining why it is important to do so. However, few of us would be unwilling to comply with a request if we understood the reasons behind it. Students are also more willing to try to change their behavior if they understand the

reason why it is important. For example, "Jess, the reason I don't want you to scream at work is that it disturbs the other people who work here. When you scream, the other people who work here might think you are a kid and not very grown up. So we want to teach you a more grown-up way to act when you get upset."

3. *Explain how and when to perform the correct behaviors and have the student role play it.* The trainer should model the appropriate response and ask the student to demonstrate it. For example, before work, Max's vocational trainer conducted a brief training session to teach him what to do to express happiness at work, saying, "Max, when you are happy and excited about something, like when you are doing a really good job putting data in the computer, here is what you should do: make a fist and shake it like this. This is just like you see basketball players do when they are happy. Okay, let's practice. I am going to tell you how well you are doing putting data in and I want you to show me what you should do. Max, you put the whole form in without any mistakes. Good job!" (Max shakes his fist.) "Right." This practice and rehearsal of the correct way to respond to situations is particularly important for those that may occur in the job situation on a low frequency basis. For example, Jess typically became upset in the photocopy room only once or twice per month. Consequently, he would likely have difficulty remembering what he should do when the time comes, unless he has some regular practice and reminders.

4. *Provide assistance to perform the response and feedback.* The trainer of course should provide the student with feedback related to how well she or he performed the trained behavior. During initial phases of the program, the feedback should come directly after each opportunity to perform it. When Jess self-initiates taking a break, the trainer would provide him with praise. If he failed to do this and had a "temper tantrum," the trainer would remind him of the need to take breaks when he is beginning to feel frustrated, and possibly have him role play this situation again. It is also useful to provide the student with feedback at the end of the work period about his or her overall performance of the social behavior that day.

CONCLUSION

In this chapter, a number of work-related areas that are frequently challenges that students with physical and multiple disabilities will face in gaining employment have been addressed. The requirements that typically exist in employment settings, along with possible interventions and strategies that school programs can use to assist students to meet these challenges, have been described.

As suggested, work-related issues can frequently serve as major barriers to the community-based employment of persons with physical and multiple disabilities. A person who cannot use or gain access to a public bus, or who requires assistance using the bathroom or eating, will pose support challenges that most supported employment programs have not encountered and may find difficult to provide given their financial limitations. School programs can and should make every effort to teach students skills that will allow them to function as independently as possible. However, training and adaptive strategies will in many cases not be sufficient to permit a student to perform many behaviors independently. For example, if there are no wheelchair-accessible buses, no amount of training will permit John, a student who uses a wheelchair, to get to work using the public bus system. Consequently, it is imperative that the schools play a major role in working with students and their families and the adult service agencies to identify arrangements that will permit these potential barriers to be overcome in order to allow the student to work at a community work site. Certainly, one arrangement frequently proposed is to have the student work as part of a group such as an enclave. This arrangement would allow a van to pick up several persons to deliver them to and from work and the assignment of a program staff person at the site to provide personal support assistance. However, this is not a solution that provides the student with the optimal opportunity to work in a normal and integrated fashion. The school program should advocate for more creative arrangements that will allow the student to achieve this outcome. For example, arrangements may be made to have a local group home transport the student to and from work and for the student to pay for this service through an Impairment-Related Work Expense (IRWE) plan. Teachers and school staff need to be able to reconceptualize their roles, become knowledgeable of adult service issues, and become involved in local community employment related issues in order to contribute in a meaningful fashion to the successful transition of students with physical and multiple disabilities.

REFERENCES

Allaire, J. H., & Miller, J. M. (1983). Nonspeech communication. In M. E. Snell (Ed.), *Systematic instruction of the moderately and severely handicapped* (2nd ed.) (pp. 289–311). Columbus, OH: Charles E. Merrill.

Bigge, J. (1982). Self-care. In J. L. Bigge (Ed.), *Teaching individuals with physical and multiple disabilities* (2nd ed.) (pp. 290–313). Columbus, OH: Charles E. Merrill.

Bigge, J., & O'Donnell, J. (1976). *Teaching individuals with physical and multiple disabilities*. Columbus, OH: Bell & Howell Company.

Brady, G. S. (1973). Surgical control of drooling in cerebral palsy. *Developmental Medicine, 15,* 227–233.

Capozzi, M., & Mineo, B. (1984). Nonspeech language and communication systems. In A. L. Holland (Ed.), *Language disorders in children: Recent advances* (pp. 173–209). San Diego: College Hill Press.

Carr, E. G., & Durand, V. M. (1985). The social-communicative basis of severe behavior problems in children. In S. Reiss & R. Bootzin (Eds.), *Theoretical issues in behavior therapy* (pp. 219–254). New York: Academic Press.

Chadsey-Rusch, J. (1986). Identifying and teaching valued social behaviors in competitive employment settings. In F. R. Rusch (Ed.), *Competitive employment issues and strategies* (pp. 273–288). Baltimore: Paul H. Brookes Publishing Co.

Chadsey-Rusch, J. (1990). Teaching social skills on the job. In F. R. Rusch (Ed.) *Supported employment: Models, methods and issues* (pp. 161–180). Sycamore, IL: Sycamore Publishing Co.

Chadsey-Rusch, J., & Rusch, F. (1988). Ecology of the workplace. In R. Gaylord-Ross (Ed.), *Vocational education for persons with handicaps* (pp. 235–256). Baltimore: University Park Press.

Dailey, R. H. (1983). Acute upper airway obstruction. *Emergency Medicine Clinics of North America, 1,* 261–277.

Drabman, R. S., Cruz, G. C., Russ, J., & Lynd, S. (1979). Suppression of chronic drooling in mentally retarded children and adolescents: Effectiveness of a behavioural treatment package. *Behavior Therapy, 10,* 46–56.

Ekedahl, C. (1974). Surgical treatment of drooling. *Acta Oto-Laryngologica, 77,* 215–221.

Evans, I. M., & Meyer, L. H. (1985). *An educative approach to behavior problems: A practical decision model for interventions with severely handicapped learners.* Baltimore: Paul H. Brookes Publishing Co.

Foxx, R. M., & Azrin, N. H. (1973). *Toilet training the retarded: A rapid program for day and nighttime independent toileting.* Champaign, IL: Research Press.

Gallender, D. (1979). *Eating handicaps.* Springfield, IL: Charles C Thomas.

Garber, N. B. (1971). Operant procedures to eliminate drooling behaviour in cerebral palsied children. *Developmental Medicine and Child Neurology, 13,* 641–644.

Greenspan, S., & Shoultz, B. (1981). Why mentally retarded adults lose their jobs: Social incompetence as a factor in work adjustment. *Applied Research in Mental Retardation, 2*(1), 23–38.

Hanley-Maxwell, C., Rusch, F. R., Chadsey-Rusch, J., & Renzaglia, A. (1986). Factors contributing to job terminations. *Journal of The Association for Persons with Severe Handicaps, 11*(1), 45–52.

Harris, C. S., Baker, S. P., Smith, G. A., & Harris, R. M. (1984). Childhood asphyxiation by food: A national analysis and overview. *Journal of the American Medical Association, 251*(2), 2231–2235.

Illingworth, R. S. (1970). Control of excessive drooling. *Clinical Pediatrics, 9*(A), 13.

Jones, M. L. (1985). *Home care for the chronically ill or disabled child.* New York: Harper & Row.

Koheil, R., Sochaniwskyj, A. E., Bablich, K., Kenny, D. J., & Milner, M. (1987). Biofeedback techniques in the conservative remediation of drooling in children with cerebral palsy. *Developmental Medicine and Child Neurology, 29*(1), 19–26.

Lindemann, J. E. (1981). *Psychological and behavioral aspects of physical disability.* New York: Plenum Press.

Makhani, J. S. (1974). Dribbling of saliva in children with cerebral palsy and its management. *Indian Journal of Paediatrics, 41,* 272–277.

McCracken, A. (1978). Drool control and tongue thrust for the mentally retarded. *American Journal of Occupational Therapy, 32,* 79–85.

Meuller, H. A. (1978). Feeding. In N. R. Finnie (Ed.), *Handling the young cerebral palsied child at home* (pp. 113–132). London: Heineman.

Mirenda, P. (1985). Designing pictorial communication systems for physically able-bodied students with severe handicaps. *Augmentative and Alternative Communication, 1,* 58–64.

Moon, S. M., Inge, K. J., Wehman, P., Brooke, V., & Barcus, J. M. (1990). *Helping persons with severe mental retardation get and keep employment: Supported employment issues and strategies.* Baltimore: Paul H. Brookes Publishing Co.

Morris, S. E. (1978). *Program guidelines for children with feeding problems.* Edison, NJ: Childcraft.

Morris, S. E., & Weber, J. S. (1978). Problems of cerebral palsy and oral-motor functions. In J. M. Wilson (Ed.), *Oral-motor function and dysfunction in children* (pp. 163–166). Chapel Hill: University of North Carolina, Division of Physical Therapy.

Musselwhite, C. R., & St. Louis, K. W. (1982). *Communication programming for the severely handicapped*. San Diego: College Hill Press.

Orelove, F. P., & Sobsey, D. (1987). *Educating children with multiple disabilities: A transdisciplinary approach*. Baltimore: Paul H. Brookes Publishing Co.

Rapp, D. L. (1980). Drool control: Long-term follow-up. *Developmental Medicine and Child Neurology, 22,* 448–453.

Renzaglia, A., & Hutchins, M. (1988). A community-referenced approach to preparing persons with disabilities for employment. In P. Wehman & M. S. Moon (Eds.), *Vocational rehabilitation and supported employment* (pp. 91–110). Baltimore: Paul H. Brookes Publishing Co.

Romer, D., & Heller, T. (1983). Social adaptation of mentally retarded adults in community settings: A social-ecological approach. *Applied Research in Mental Retardation, 4,* 303–314.

Rusch, F. R., & Mithaug, D. E. (1980). *Vocational training for mentally retarded adults: A behavior analytic approach*. Champaign, IL: Research Press.

Rusch, F. R., Schutz, R. P., & Agran, M. (1982). Validating entry-level survival skills for service occupations: Implications for curriculum development. *Journal of The Association for the Severely Handicapped, 1,* 32–41.

Sailor, W., & Guess, D. (1983). *Severely handicapped students: An instructional design*. Boston: Houghton-Mifflin.

Sowers, J., Gerdes, J., & Powers, L. (1990). *Training a person with cerebral palsy and mental retardation drool control in a supported employment setting*. Eugene, OR: Oregon Research Institute.

Sowers, J., Jenkins, C., & Powers, L. (1988). Vocational education of persons with physical handicaps. In R. Gaylord-Ross (Ed.), *Vocational education for persons with handicaps* (pp. 387–416). Mountain View, CA: Mayfield.

Sowers, J., Rusch, F. R., & Hudson, C. (1979). Training a severely retarded young adult to ride the city bus to and from work. *AAESPH Review, 4*(1), 15–22.

Sowers, J., Thompson, L., & Connis, R. (1979). The food service vocational training program. In G. T. Bellamy, G. O. O'Connor, & O. C. Karan (Eds.), *Vocational rehabilitation of severely handicapped persons: Contemporary service strategies* (pp. 181–206). Baltimore: University Park Press.

Stauffer, D. T. (1983). A spina bifida student? You may have to catheterize! *DPH Journal, 7*(1), 14–21.

Van de Heyning, P. H., Marquet, J. F., & Cretin, W. L. (1980). Drooling in children with cerebral palsy. *Acta Oto-Rhino-Laryngalogica Belgica, 34,* 691–705.

Wehman, P. (1981). *Competitive employment: New horizons for severely disabled individuals*. Baltimore: Paul H. Brookes Publishing Co.

Wehman, P., Moon, M. S., Everson, J. M., Wood, W., & Barcus, J. M. (1988). *Transition from school to work: New challenges for youth with severe disabilities*. Baltimore: Paul H. Brookes Publishing Co.

Wehman, P., Wood, W., Everson, J. M., Goodwyn, R., & Conley, S. (1988). *Vocational education for multihandicapped youth with cerebral palsy*. Baltimore: Paul H. Brookes Publishing Co.

Wilkie, T. F. (1970). Surgical treatment of drooling: A follow-up report of five years' experience. *Plastic and Reconstructive Surgery, 45,* 549–558.

TRAVIS

Travis, who lives in a small rural community, is 12 years old and has some functional use of his hands. At present, his primary means of mobility is via a manual wheelchair pushed by others. He has recently received a power wheelchair and is beginning to communicate with a picture symbol board.

Travis's school district is committed to providing work experiences to all of its students with disabilities, beginning in the middle-school grades. Travis began receiving vocational training this year. His team decided that picking up milk and lunch orders for the cafeteria would be a particularly good work experience for him. The task involves going to classrooms, getting the order slip (which is hung from a clip outside the room), and taking them to the front office. In addition to actually gaining experience working and learning a task that is criterion-referenced (i.e., delivery is a task for which jobs can be found in his community), this task provides him opportunities to practice driving his wheelchair. It also requires him to lift his arm high enough to pull the slip from the clip which improves his range of motion. A teaching assistant accompanies Travis on his rounds each morning to provide him with instruction and assistance. The greatest amount of assistance required relates to wheelchair driving. Travis's major difficulty in driving is caused by his failure to attend to where he is going. A device was purchased and installed on

TRAVIS
(continued)

his chair that allows it to be turned on and off by remote control. The aide turns the wheelchair off if Travis is not attending to where he is going. This device allows Travis a greater sense of independence, for the aide can stay several yards behind him when he is working. The device is also a means to provide a consequence for inattention. The aide also provides verbal and physical assistance in grasping the slip and is gradually reducing the amount of assistance provided. A box for keeping the slips attaches to his lapboard with velcro. Travis particularly enjoys his job when he takes the slips to the front office and the office staff thank him for his help. Through his job, Travis is getting his first real sense of contributing to others and the accompanying feelings of accomplishment and competence that come with this.

4 Developing Work Training and Experience Sites

Traditionally, vocational programs offered by schools for students with severe disabilities involved training on simulated tasks in classroom settings. This was an appropriate approach when the only employment option available to these students as adults was in sheltered workshops or work activity centers (Wilcox, McDonnell, Bellamy, & Rose, 1988). Along with the adult service movement to provide these individuals with the opportunity to work in nonsheltered settings, most school vocational programs have shifted their focus to community-based work experiences (Wehman, Kregel, & Barcus, 1985; Wehman, Moon, Everson, Wood, & Barcus, 1988). Using this approach, employers are recruited who are willing to offer students the opportunity to receive training and gain work experience at their companies. Community work experience programs allow students to learn specific tasks as well as critical work-related skills (Gaylord-Ross, Forte, & Gaylord-Ross, 1986; Hutchins & Renzaglia, 1990).

Today most students with mild and moderate disabilities and even those with more severe mental retardation are actively involved in community-based work experience programs during their high school years. However, this is not typically true for students with severe physical and multiple disabilities (Sowers, Jenkins, & Powers, 1988; Wehman, Wood, Everson, Goodwyn & Conley, 1988). In many cases, these students may receive no vocational training at all. For those students who do receive training, the old in-class model is typically utilized. One reason for their lack of inclusion in community-based work experience programs is that staff may still doubt the feasibility of nonsheltered employment for these students. Another reason why these students are not included in work experience programs is the many logistical difficulties that staff face when attempting to do so. Primary among these difficulties are staff resources (Baumgart & Van Walleghem, 1986; Hutchins & Talarico, 1985). To date, the most common work experience approach has been to place a student at a site, provide short-term training, and then provide routine monitoring checks (Stainback, Stainback, Nietupski, & Hamre-Nietupski, 1986). Many students with severe physical and multiple disabilities need lengthy training before they can work independently, while independent work is not feasible for many others. Work experience programs also frequently utilize work experience crews and enclaves, in which a group of students work at a site or sites as a group (Wilcox et al., 1988). The crews and enclaves permit one staff person to supervise several students at one time. However, these work experience crews and enclaves are frequently structured in such a way as to make it difficult for them to accommodate a student who requires a significant amount of training to learn new skills. This point is particularly important to emphasize. Students with physical and multiple disabilities can learn new and relatively complex vocational tasks. However, to do so they will often require more intensive instruction than students who experience less severe disabilities. It may be possible to place a student with physical and multiple disabilities at a community site by identifying a simple task that he or she can learn to do with the same amount of instruction provided to other students in the program, but this is not enough. Students with physical and multiple disabilities should also have the opportunity to learn new tasks and skills and to achieve their optimal vocational functioning. If this requires, and it frequently does, more intensive training, then every attempt should be made to provide it.

Transportation is another logistical difficulty encountered when trying to provide students who have severe physical and multiple disabilities with community-based work experiences (Hutchins & Talarico, 1985; Wehman, Wood, et al., 1988). Schools typically get students to and from work experience sites by training them to use public buses or by providing a school van. If the public buses are not accessible in a community, the first option cannot be utilized for students who use wheelchairs. Many school districts also have only a limited number of wheelchair-accessible vehicles that can be allocated for transporting students to and from work experience sites. This chapter focuses on describing strategies that can be used to overcome the resource difficulties that many districts encounter when trying to provide students who have severe disabilities with the opportunity to participate in their work experience program.

COMMUNITY-BASED WORK EXPERIENCE SITES

The steps involved in establishing and managing work experience sites are very much the same as those that should be followed when developing and creating paid employment for individuals. A detailed description of job creation strategies is provided in Chapter 7. There are also several excellent descriptions available in the literature related to establishing and conducting work experience sites for students with disabilities (Pumpian, West, & Shepard, 1988; Stainback et al., 1986). The procedures are generally the same for all of the

students, regardless of the nature of their disabilities. The focus here is on issues that will assist districts to deal with resource difficulties that may impede
participation in the work experience program by students who need intensive
training and high amounts of supports, such as those with physical and multiple
disabilities.

Characteristics of Work Experience Sites

As has been emphasized, students with physical and multiple disabilities
should have the opportunity not only to participate in work experience, but also
to receive the type of training that they need to learn new skills. A commitment
to this belief will influence the type of sites that are recruited for community
work experiences, as well as how they are organized. The following are three
characteristics that should guide this recruitment and organization:

1. *Employers should understand that students will be there primarily to receive training and experience, not to produce work.* If an employer views
   students as a means to get a substantial amount of work performed (free of
   charge), there will be little time available to devote to training; instead the
   student and probably the trainer will be required to spend most or all of
   their energy simply getting work completed. When organizing a work experience, a balance needs to found between the amount of work that students complete and their training needs. On the one hand, having some
   production requirements is important for preparing students to learn to
   meet these requirements. On the other hand, the requirements need to be
   established in a way that permits training on new and challenging tasks.
   In most cases, the work that students produce should be viewed as
   supplementary.

2. *Sites should offer opportunities to perform a variety of tasks.* This characteristic also reflects the importance of using work experience sites to
   train students rather than for producing work for employers. If the emphasis were on production, it is likely that sites would be sought that allowed
   students to perform one simple task that could be learned with relatively
   little instruction (Bellamy, Rose, Sheehan, Horner, & Boles, 1980). When
   placed at a site with multiple tasks, a student can learn to perform two or
   three tasks simultaneously as part of a natural work schedule. For example,
   John does photocopying during the first half hour, then delivers the photocopying orders that he has completed to the offices of the employees, and
   then after a 15-minute break in the employee lounge he goes to the main
   office to enter data for about an hour. This is a more efficient method of
   service delivery than moving a student to a new site each time there is a
   desire for him or her to learn a different task. It also allows students to learn
   to use natural task completion and time cues to move from task to task in
   sequence, a skill that they probably will use when placed into a paid job
   (Berg, Wacker, & Flynn, 1990).

3. *Sites should provide the optimal opportunity for students to work and interact with nondisabled employees.* One of the most important advantages of community-based work experience sites is the chance for students to learn how to work alongside and interact with nondisabled co-workers (Chadsey-Rusch, 1990; Wehman, Moon, et al., 1988). Although there may be a number of co-workers at a particular site, there may be few real interaction opportunities. An attempt should be made to find sites not only where there are co-workers without disabilities present, but where it is likely that they and the student will interact. When analyzing a site, staff should note how much the employees interact with each other, assess the extent to which the assigned tasks will require them to actually work with the employees, and judge the receptiveness of the employees to the idea of having students with disabilities at the business.

Decreasing Staff Resource and Transportation Difficulties

Unfortunately, no strategy or group of strategies (except unlimited funds) will eliminate the difficulties that arise from district staff resource and transportation limitations. However, there are a number of things that staff can do to make better use of the limited resources available.

Develop a Work Experience Site Pool   In many cases, school vocational programs utilize an approach to community work experience site development whereby a new site is sought and set up each time a student is in need of a work experience. Finding and setting up sites requires a significant amount of staff time. A more efficient alternative is to establish a "pool" of sites, composed of a number of employers who have agreed to allow students from the program to rotate through their businesses on an ongoing basis (Bellamy et al., 1988; Stainback et al., 1986). When one student completes his or her work experience at the site, the employer will expect another one to be introduced. Students in the program move from site to site within the pool. Once a pool is established, staff no longer need to devote as much time to locating new sites, to analyzing or structuring new tasks, or to developing a rapport with new staff.

The number of sites in a work experience pool should be determined by the number of students in the program. In addition, the total "pool" of sites should offer students experience performing each task on the Task Pool List (Chapter 2). Figure 1 is an example of a format that could be used to assist staff in summarizing the tasks that are available at each site. The form could be enlarged and tags with the names of the student(s) who are currently at each site and performing each of the tasks could be placed in corresponding squares. Figure 2 provides an example of a form that could be employed to provide a description of each site and each task performed at the site.

The Work Experience Enclave

A strategy frequently used by school districts as a means to overcome resource difficulties is the work experience enclave, whereby a number of students work

	American Heart Association	Planned Parenthood	Good Samaritan Hospital	Baptist College
Photocopying	✓	✓		✓
Data entry	✓		✓	
Delivery		✓	✓	
Telephone answering	✓			✓
Light cleaning		✓	✓	✓
Packaging	✓	✓	✓	
Mail preparation	✓	✓		✓

(Row label: TASKS)

Figure 1. Work experience site pool.

Site: _____   Contact person: _____

Tasks available: _____
_____
_____

Accessibility of site:
  Entrance(s) _____
  Bathrooms _____
  Other areas _____
  _____
  _____

Transportation:
  Bus stop locales _____
  _____
  Buses _____

Preferred hours: _____

Other information about site: _____
_____
_____
_____
_____

Task: _____

General task description: _____
_____
_____
_____

Area(s) task performed: _____
_____

Production demands: _____
Quality demands: _____
Interaction opportunities: _____

Figure 2.   Work experience site description.

at the same business (Hutchins & Talarico, 1985). This arrangement allows one
staff person to supervise a group of students. As typically structured, the work
experience enclave has three major weaknesses. First, in many cases, students
work as a group in the same location in the company at the same time. For

example, a school district might establish an enclave at an electronics assembly company and structure it so that three or four students arrive as a group and work together in one area. Clearly, the opportunities for individual students to become integrated with the employees at the company and to learn social interaction skills that come with integration are seriously hampered by such an arrangement. Second, students with the most severe disabilities, such as those with physical and multiple disabilities, frequently are unable to receive the training needed to acquire new skills in such enclaves. The third disadvantage of this structure is that it usually does not allow students to perform more than one task or type of task in one location. Moving students as a group from one task to another, especially if they occur in different locations in a business, is extremely difficult and thus is usually not done.

With some restructuring, enclaves can offer students greater integration and training opportunities, while still retaining the staff resource advantages by having students work at one site at the same time, but in different locations in the company. For example, an enclave could be developed in an office building for three students from 9:00 A.M. to 12:00 P.M. During the first hour, one student might be assigned to work in the photocopy room, a second student assigned to deliver messages, and the third to enter data into the computer in the front office. During the second and third hours, each student could rotate to one of the other tasks and locations. In order for this arrangement to be possible, a company has to be fairly large. Another key to this alternative approach is that students with more severe disabilities are placed into enclaves with students who require less training and supervision. It may also be useful to have the student with more severe disabilities begin at the site 1–2 weeks after the other students. During this initial time, the two students would receive training and become fairly independent. When the third student arrives, the trainer would be able to focus attention on him or her, while maintaining some contact with the other two to monitor their performance. The specific arrangement described here is only one example of how an enclave can be organized to enhance integration and training qualities for students. Depending on the specific students in the program, scheduling and staffing factors, and the characteristics of the business where the enclave will operate, other variations can be devised.

It should be emphasized that, while these authors support the use of enclave arrangements for training and work experiences, we do not support this approach when placing students into paid employment.

Strategies to Reduce Transportation Difficulties

Although not always the case, many school buildings are located in close proximity to businesses. Work experiences that are established in these companies will have many of the same advantages as in-school work experiences with regard to staffing and transportation. When seeking work experience sites for the pool, staff may want to contact these employers first.

In many cases, a student is brought to school by a school bus or parent, goes to a community work experience later in the day, returns to school, and is taken home. One simple way to decrease the transportation demands is to schedule the work experience first thing in the morning or at the end of the day so that the parent or school bus could drop the student off or pick the student up.

If accessible buses or other public transport (e.g., subway, light rail) are available, the school program should take the time and effort to train the student to use it. The up-front cost, in terms of staff allocation, will likely be high. However, over time the program and student will benefit greatly. Once the student can use the system independently or with minimal support, the concerns related to transporting him or her to work experience sites decrease. Most importantly, one of the major barriers to future employment will be greatly alleviated.

IN-SCHOOL WORK EXPERIENCE SITES

Community-based work experience sites offer students the best opportunity to learn about the skills and requirements that will exist in the types of businesses where they may later seek employment. However, as previously stated, there are numerous resource and other logistical difficulties in providing these opportunities to students with physical and multiple disabilities. In the previous section, some strategies to alleviate these difficulties have been discussed. Another strategy to consider is that of using the offices and other areas in a student's school building as work experience sites. In-school work experiences are particularly useful for middle school students who have little or no previous exposure to vocational training and work. They provide students the opportunity to gain exposure to a variety of tasks and to begin to learn critical work-related skills and behaviors. If a program's resources limit the ability to get students into community sites, in-school work experiences also should be considered a viable option for older students. If there is a choice between putting a student into a community site with several other students, in which he or she will receive little intensive training, and an in-school site where a classroom aide is available to provide this training, the in-school option may well be the one that should be selected. Table 2 provides a list of some of the locations and types of tasks typically available in most schools that may be appropriate for training to students with physical and multiple disabilities.

Establishing and Conducting In-School Work Experiences

Convincing many personnel (e.g., librarian, office) in school buildings to provide work experience opportunities for students with disabilities (especially those with more severe disabilities) can be challenging. In fact, these staff may be less willing to cooperate with the program than community site employers. There are a number of things that may increase staff willingness to cooperate. In most cases, it proves most successful for the classroom teacher to recruit in-

Table 2. In-school work experience sites and tasks

POSSIBLE SITES
1. Main office
2. Attendance office
3. Library
4. Audio-visual room
5. Student newspaper/yearbook room
6. Athletic office
7. Teacher's work room
8. Nurse's office
9. Counselor's office
10. Cafeteria

POSSIBLE TASKS
1. Enter student attendance information on computer in attendance office or other office where this is done.
2. Enter student semester grades on computer in office where this is done.
3. Enter student test grades for teacher in teacher workroom.
4. Update student information files on computer in main, counselor, or athletic office.
5. Type memos for principal or other staff person.
6. Photocopy memos and other information for office.
7. Photocopy tests and hand-outs for teachers.
8. Enter new book catalogue numbers and check-out information in computer for librarian.
9. Put memos and other information in teacher mailboxes.
10. Deliver phone messages from front office to classrooms.
11. Pick up attendance slips from classrooms and deliver to attendance office.
12. File check-out cards in library.
13. Type information on check-out cards for new books.
14. Place protective covers on new books in library or repair old covers.
15. File correspondence and administrative information in main office.
16. File student record or attendance information in office where these are maintained.
17. Type articles for student newspaper.
18. Photocopy student newspaper.
19. Enter health status information for school nurse on computer.
20. Photocopy memos to be sent home by school nurse to students' parents.
21. Enter basic information about student athletes for athletic director and coaches on computer or assist in maintaining paper files of this information.
22. Help maintain records of equipment use in audio-visual room.
23. Answer phones in any of the offices.
24. Perform light cleaning duties in cafeteria.

school sites, rather than a person who does not routinely work in the building, such as a vocational trainer. School building staff usually are at least familiar with the teacher and may be likely to cooperate more with him or her than an outside person.

The proactive support of the school principal can also serve to encourage school building staff to cooperate in providing students with work experience opportunities. A meeting should be held with the principal to discuss the need for in-school work experience and to ask for his or her active support. It may be useful in this case for the teacher to be accompanied to the meeting by a special education administrator who is supportive of the work experience and vocational program for students. This individual will reinforce for the principal the importance of the request and reinforce that it is part of the district approved curriculum for students with disabilities. The principal should be asked to assist in gaining the cooperation of building staff by discussing the program at a staff meeting, sending out a memo asking staff to consider establishing a site, or speaking personally with one or two staff members who might be willing to establish a site.

If one staff person is willing to establish a site, this will go a long way in serving as an example to other building staff to cooperate. A teacher may know of one building staff member who has been responsive to and interested in students with disabilities. It may be a good strategy when first beginning an in-school work experience program to place a student at this person's site even before approaching other staff. After the student is functioning well at the site, the teacher will be able to point to it as an illustration of how the program works when attempting to recruit other sites.

In-school work experiences should be conducted in no less a systematic and professional manner than community sites. This will include conducting a detailed analysis of the tasks that will be performed, using systematic training strategies, and ensuring that all assigned duties are completed to high quality standards. In addition, students should be required to tell the site supervisor at least several days in advance when they will not be at work due to a planned absence, and to call the supervisor (with assistance from a parent if necessary) if unable to report to work because of illness. The teacher should also ensure that students consistently arrive at the site at the designated time and as neatly groomed as possible. All of these efforts help the supervisor to regard the work experience program positively and contribute to teaching the student important work skills.

CLASSROOM AND SIMULATED TRAINING: WHEN IS IT USEFUL?

This chapter has emphasized the value of providing work training and experience to students in real settings. Classroom-based, simulated training is a poor substitute for these settings when attempting to prepare students to work in community-based jobs. However, on a very limited basis classroom-based training can serve a useful purpose. The following provides a description of three ways in which classroom or simulated training may be appropriately used.

Brief Initial Training

Initial simulated training may be appropriate to use before placing a student into a work experience if the work experience site and the tasks that the student will perform have been identified so that training in the classroom can be provided on these specific tasks. This use of simulated training may be helpful if the student has never performed this type of task and may have difficulty learning the basics of the task at the site itself. For example, a goal for Sam is to learn to enter student attendance data on the computer in the attendance office. Sam has only used a computer before to play games. The attendance office is quite hectic, and the supervisor is particularly concerned about how the computer is operated and the accuracy of the data input. With all of these factors taken into account, it was decided that it would be helpful to provide Sam with training on the task for a few weeks in his classroom before moving him to the attendance office. His teacher got several old attendance forms, set up a program on the computer to match the one used in the office, and provided Sam with training on how to input data into the program. She did not wait to move him to the office until he mastered the program or was even close to achieving independence, but only until he had begun to learn the basics of the task.

Initial Design and Try-Out of Adaptations

If the analysis of the task that a student will perform at a work experience site reveals that an adaptation is required, the initial identification, design, and try-out of the adaptation may be more efficiently done in the classroom than at the site. For example, it was felt that Jim's stapling jig should be redesigned to assist him to work more productively. The teacher and vocational specialist had him try out several variations of a modified jig in the classroom, identified the best one, and then implemented it at his work site.

Extra Practice on Difficult Steps

One of the best uses of classroom-based training is as a supplement to the training the student receives in the real work setting. Specifically, students can be provided with additional practice on steps that they are having difficulty mastering at the work experience site. For example, John is working in the photocopying room of the school and is having trouble learning to correctly align copies before stapling them. In addition to working on aligning copies at his work experience site, John's teacher provides him with practice on this step before he goes to the photocopy room each day.

CONCLUSION

Students with severe physical and multiple disabilities should have the same opportunity as other students to participate fully in work experience programs. Because of the high training and support needs of many of these students, and the staffing and transportation constraints present in most districts, creative strategies must be utilized in order to realize this goal. This chapter has provided some suggestions that will at least serve as a starting point from which staff can begin to identify the strategies that will work for their district and students.

REFERENCES

Baumgart, D., & Van Walleghem, J. (1986). Staffing strategies for implementing community-based instruction. *Journal of The Association for Persons with Severe Handicaps, 11*(2), 92–102.

Bellamy, G. T., Sheehan, M. R., Horner, R. H., & Boles, S. M. (1980). Community programs for severely handicapped adults: An analysis of vocational opportunities. *Journal of The Association for Persons with Severe Handicaps, 5*(4), 307–324.

Berg, W., Wacker, D., & Flynn, T. (1990). Teaching generalization and maintenance of work behavior. In F. R. Rusch (Ed.), *Supported employment: Models, methods and issues* (pp. 145–160). Sycamore, IL: Sycamore Publishing Co.

Chadsey-Rusch, J. (1990). Teaching social skills on the job. In F. R. Rusch (Ed.), *Supported employment: Models, methods and issues* (pp. 161–180). Sycamore, IL: Sycamore Publishing Co.

Gaylord-Ross, C., Forte, J., & Gaylord-Ross, R. (1986). The community classroom: Technological vocational training for students with serious handicaps. *Career Development for Exceptional Children, 9*, 24–33.

Hutchins, M. P., & Renzaglia, A. (1990). Developing a longitudinal vocational training program. In F. R. Rusch (Ed.), *Supported employment: Models, methods and issues.* Sycamore, IL: Sycamore Publishing Co.

Hutchins, M., & Talarico, D. (1985). Administrative considerations in providing community integrated training programs. In P. McCarthy, J. Everson, S. Moon, & M. Barcus (Eds.), *School to work transitions for youth with severe disabilities* [Monograph], pp. 109–112. Richmond: Virginia Commonwealth University, Project Transition Into Employment.

Nietupski, J. A., Hamre-Nietupski, S., Welch, J., & Anderson, R. J. (1983). Establishing and maintaining vocational training sites for moderately and severely handicapped students: Strategies for community/vocational trainers. *Education and Training of the Mentally Retarded, 18*(3), 169–175.

Pumpian, I., West, E., & Shepard, H. (1988). Vocational education of persons with severe handicaps. In R. Gaylord-Ross (Ed.), *Vocational education for persons with handicaps* (pp. 355–386). Mountain View, CA: Mayfield Publishing Co.

Sowers, J., Jenkins, C., & Powers, L. (1988). Vocational education of persons with physical handicaps. In R. Gaylord-Ross (Ed.) *Vocational education for persons with handicaps* (pp. 387–416). Mountain View, CA: Mayfield Publishing Co.

Sowers, J., & Powers, L. (1989). Preparing students with cerebral palsy and mental retardation for the transition from school to community-based employment. *Career Development for Exceptional Individuals, 12*, 25–35.

Stainback, W., Stainback, S., Nietupski, J., & Hamre-Nietupski, S. (1986). Establishing effective community-based training stations. In F. R. Rusch (Ed.), *Competitive employment issues and strategies* (pp. 103–113). Baltimore: Paul H. Brookes Publishing Co.

Wacker, D. P., & Berg, W. (1987). Generalizing and maintaining work behavior. In F. R. Rusch (Ed.), *Competitive employment issues and strategies* (pp. 129–140). Baltimore: Paul H. Brookes Publishing Co.

Wehman, P., Kregel, J., & Barcus, J. M. (1985). From school to work: A vocational transition model for handicapped students. *Exceptional Children, 52*(1), 25–37.

Wehman, P., Moon, M. S., Everson, J. M., Wood, W., & Barcus, J. M. (1988). *Transition from school to work: New challenges for youth with severe disabilities* (pp. 1–27). Baltimore: Paul H. Brookes Publishing Co.

Wehman, P., Wood, W., Everson, J. M., Goodwyn, R., & Conley, S. (1988). *Vocational education for multihandicapped youth with cerebral palsy.* Baltimore: Paul H. Brookes Publishing Co.

Wilcox, B., McDonnell, J. J., Bellamy, G. T., & Rose, H. (1988). Preparing for supported employment: The role of secondary special education. In G. T. Bellamy, L. E. Rhodes, D. M. Mank, & J. M. Albin (Eds.), *Supported employment: A community implementation guide* (pp. 183–208). Baltimore: Paul H. Brookes Publishing Co.

MISSY

Missy is 21 years of age and is nearing school completion. She is able to stand and walk for very short distances. However, her primary mode of mobility is a scooter. Missy has functional use of one hand, and she uses a letter and word board to communicate.

Missy began receiving work experience when in middle school. Her first work experience was in the main office entering student attendance into a mainframe computer. The office administrator did not believe that she could learn to do this task accurately and was willing to give it a try only after encouragement from the school principal. The administrator also required that the information not be sent to the mainframe until she double-checked it. After several weeks, Missy was so accurate in entering the information that the administrator stopped checking her work.

Missy has had the opportunity to work at several community sites doing a wide range of clerical tasks. One site was a veterinarian's office, where she typed vaccine reminder cards and filed patient records. She also worked in the local university's computer center, where she handed out software program disks to students, refiled disks, and did some data entry. Work-related skills that were targeted included bus riding, work "attitude," social interactions, and eating. Missy is unable to swallow and, thus, there was a need to identify foods that she could "eat" independently and neatly at a job site.

5 Training the Movements and Discriminations Required by Vocational Tasks and Work-Related Skills

Jane and Sam have been placed in a work experience at an insurance office in the community. Jane works in the morning and Sam in the afternoon. One of the tasks assigned to both of these students is to staple papers in the photocopy area. There are four basic steps involved in stapling papers: 1) straightening the papers so that all of the edges are even, 2) inserting the papers in the stapler with the top left hand corner under the staple hole, 3) pushing down on the stapler arm until the staple is secured, and 4) removing the papers from the stapler.

Jane, who experiences severe mental retardation but has no physical disabilities, has several problems learning this task. She has difficulty recognizing when the papers are correctly straightened. Specifically, she lines up the top and bottom of the pages but forgets that the sides also must be even. Jane also does not consistently insert the papers in the stapler at the correct position. Sam has cerebral palsy with limited control of his arm, but does not experience mental retardation. Sam has difficulty performing many of the same steps as Jane. Sam's difficulties, however, are different in an important way. He understands what he is supposed to do, but he has difficulty executing the movements required to perform the steps correctly. For example, he recognizes when the papers are not even, but due to the poor control in his arms he has difficulty getting them straight. Sam also knows where the papers should be inserted, but again has difficulty physically getting it done.

The examples of the performance difficulties that Jane and Sam experience illustrate the difference between *discrimination* and *movement* requirements of task performance. Discrimination requirements include the following:

1. Knowing what steps to perform. For example, at the beginning of training, Jane did not know that stapling involved straightening papers.
2. Recognizing when the step should be performed. For example, the papers must be inserted into the stapler before it is pushed down.
3. Recognizing the criteria for the correct completion of steps. For example, the papers cannot simply be inserted into the stapler at any location. They must be inserted so that the very top, lefthand corner is placed under the stapling mechanism.

Motor response requirements are the movements a worker must execute to complete the steps of a task. For example, to insert papers at the correct position for stapling, the student must be able to grasp the papers and simultaneously maneuver them in a relatively precise manner. In most cases, persons who experience mental retardation and who have no physical disabilities have little difficulty leaning to execute the movements required by vocational tasks. Training for these individuals typically focuses on teaching the discrimination requirements of tasks (i.e., what steps constitute the task, when the steps should occur, and the criteria for step completion). A person with a neuromuscular disability may understand what step to perform, when to perform it, and to what criteria. However, the challenge is teaching the individual to execute the required movements. Individuals who experience both cognitive and physical disabilities are challenged to learn both the discrimination and motor response requirements of tasks.

During the past 2 decades, a powerful technology of vocational training has been developed for persons with mental retardation (Bellamy, Horner, & Inman, 1979; Gold, 1972; Moon, Inge, Wehman, Brooke, & Barcus, 1990; Wehman, 1981). This technology is based on and derived from the philosophy and methods of applied behavior analysis. The behavior analytic philosophy holds that the behaviors and skills of a person are determined by his or her environment and the number and nature of the opportunities afforded for learning. Such environmental factors contribute as much, if not more, to an individual's skills than do inborn characteristics. Applied behavior analysis focuses on the systematic manipulation of the environment in order to enhance the learning of behaviors and skills that contribute to a person's ability to function as fully and competently in life as possible.

Behavioral training techniques such as reinforcement, instructional cues, shaping, and fading have been successfully used to train an array of skills to persons with mental retardation (Alberto & Troutman, 1982; Horner, Meyer, & Fredericks, 1986). Researchers interested in employment issues have identified the specific manner in which these techniques can most effectively be used to train vocational skills (Bellamy et al., 1979; Connis, Sowers, & Thompson, 1978; Renzaglia & Hutchins, 1990; Rusch & Mithaug, 1980). This behaviorally based vocational technology is widely practiced by professionals in training tasks to persons with mental retardation.

Although the behavioral approach has been widely accepted for training discriminations to persons with mental retardation, there has been little attempt to use these techniques to train motor movements to persons with neuromuscular disabilities, such as cerebral palsy. Because cerebral palsy is caused by defects to the central nervous system, it is generally believed that to improve the motor control of these persons, the central nervous system must be improved. In fact, most physical therapy approaches and programs of intervention are based on this belief. Through therapy, it is hoped that the person's underlying system will be repaired, and the extent to which this occurs will directly influence his or her ability to perform movements required by functional skills and life tasks (Bobath & Karel, 1975; Gilette, 1969; Scrutton & Gilbertson, 1975).

There have been a number of studies that have investigated the extent to which biofeedback can affect the general level of muscle tension and spasticity experienced by persons with cerebral palsy (Cataldo, Bird, & Cunningham, 1978; Inman, 1979; Skrotsky, Gallenstein, & Osternig, 1978). There have also been a small number of studies that have used more direct behavioral techniques (i.e., prompts, reinforcement) to improve motor control or to teach movement responses to persons with physical disabilities (Horner, 1971; Rice, McDonald, & Denney, 1968; Thompson, Iwata, & Poynter, 1979). With the exception of these studies, there has been little other research focusing on the application of behavioral strategies to teaching motor skills to persons with movement disorders (Sowers & Powers, 1989). However, the small number of experimental studies that are available and the experience that these authors have gained clinically training students and adults with physical and multiple disabilities do strongly suggest that behavioral techniques are effective for teaching these individuals the movements required by tasks. In many cases, these techniques need to be applied in a slightly different fashion than when they are used for teaching discriminations. In addition, there are a number of strategies that can be effective for teaching movements that typically have not been employed when teaching discriminations to persons with mental retardation. Many of these techniques are ones that have been researched and reported in the literature pertaining to motor learning and training of persons who do not experience disabilities (Singer, 1980).

This chapter provides the reader with a detailed description of techniques that can be used to assist students with physical and multiple disabilities in acquiring the discriminations and movements required by vocational tasks and work-related skills. Issues that staff can use to encourage the generalization of the skills are also briefly addressed. Finally, a number of strategies that have been found to be effective in enhancing job maintenance are discussed.

TRAINING STRATEGIES

This section describes those strategies that have been shown to be effective for training discriminations to persons with cognitive disabilities, and delineates how to use these for training discriminations. In addition, the manner in which these techniques can be applied for teaching movements to students with neuro-muscular disabilities is discussed.

Task Analysis

A task analysis identifies each of the steps that constitute a task and that must be performed to complete it (Bellamy et al., 1979; Crosson, 1969; Gold, 1972; Mank & Horner, 1988). The critical role that task analysis plays in designing tasks is clear. The efficiency and effectiveness of training is also affected significantly by task analysis. In essence, a task analysis serves as a training guide. It helps to ensure that the trainer instructs the learner to perform the task in a consistent manner. Without a task analysis, the trainer may instruct the individual to perform the task one way on some occasions and in a different manner on other occasions. Consistency of training is extremely important when attempting to teach an individual who has difficulty learning the discriminations required by a task. Training consistency is also important when training a person with a neuromuscular disability to execute a motor movement required by a vocational task. Learning a movement involves programming and reprogramming the nerves and muscles of the body. Each slight variation in the movement that a person makes will cause this programming to become inconsistent. By requiring the person to perform the movement the same way each time, the body is more effectively programmed to execute the movement in the manner required to perform each step correctly.

One of the issues faced by trainers when constructing a task analysis is deciding how far steps should be broken down (Bellamy et al., 1979). The mailing task that John was assigned by his employer will illustrate this issue. The mailing task could be broken down into large or major steps, as shown in Figure 3. Each of the major steps (e.g., "staple pages together") could be broken down into smaller or ministeps. Each of the ministeps (e.g., "push down on the stapler") can be broken down even further into movement steps. The primary determinant of how small or large a step should be is the amount and nature of the difficulty that a person experiences in learning it. Large or major steps are sufficient if an individual experiences little difficulty learning to perform a task. However, if a trainer believes, based on his or her knowledge of a student, that he or she will experience difficulty learning a major step, then that step should be broken down into smaller or ministeps.

Ministeps identify the subbehaviors that constitute a major step and the sequence in which they must occur in order for the major step to be completed correctly. The ministep level will typically be adequate for teaching a new step or task to an individual who, due to his or her cognitive disability, has difficulty learning the discriminations (what steps to perform, when to perform each, and to what criteria) required by the task.

If an individual experiences difficulty in executing the movements re-

MAILING TASK ANALYSES:
DIFFERENT SIZE STEP ILLUSTRATION

Major steps	Mini steps		Movement steps	
1. Collate 3 pages of document (ordered correctly).				
2. Staple pages together. (Staple at top left-hand corner; pages even.)	2.1.	Straighten pages.		
	2.2.	Insert pages into stapler.		
	2.3.	Align top left-hand corner under staple hole.		
	2.4.	Push down on stapler.	2.4.1.	Move hand next to stapler.
			2.4.2.	Close hand into fist.
			2.4.3.	Lift fist and place on end of stapler arm.
			2.4.4.	Lean forward.
			2.4.5.	Push down on stapler arm.
3. Fold (3 folds, folds even).				
4. Insert in envelope.				
5. Seal envelope.				
6. Place label on envelope. (Label centered 2 inches from top, 3 inches from left side.)				
7. When 10 envelopes complete, bind with rubber band.				
8. If more materials needed, ask supervisor.				

Figure 3. Mailing task analyses to illustrate different sizes of steps.

quired by a ministep, the trainer will need to analyze the step further, to the movement-step level. Consequently, when training individuals with physical disabilities, trainers must be prepared to construct much more detailed task analyses. In most cases, it is best to first construct a major-step analysis of a task. If an individual experiences difficulty learning a major step, it should be broken down into ministeps. If the individual has difficulty executing the movements required by one or more ministeps, these should then be broken down into movement steps.

Whole-Task Versus Part-Task Training

When training a new task to a student, all of the steps can be trained simultaneously. This training format is commonly called *whole-task training* (Bellamy et al., 1979; Orelove & Sobsey, 1987; Wehman, Wood, Everson, Goodwyn, & Conley, 1988). An alternative to the whole-task approach is *part-task training* (Bellamy et al., 1979; Gold, 1968). In part-task training, the first step is trained until it is mastered, then the second step is trained until it is learned, and this process continues until the individual can perform the whole task. This approach is also referred to as forward chaining. Another part-training variation is backward chaining, in which the steps are successively trained beginning with the last one in the task analysis (Alberto & Troutman, 1982).

There have been numerous studies conducted to determine the relative effectiveness of whole-task or part-task training formats. The results of these studies have been mixed; some favor whole-task training, some favor one or both of the part-task formats, and other studies favor none of the approaches (Blake & Williams, 1969; Kayser, Billingsley, & Neel, 1986; Naylor & Briggs, 1963; Orelove & Sobsey, 1987). It appears that the whole-task method is as good as part-task formats unless the task being trained is particularly complex, in which case the part-task training procedures may be more effective (Walls, Zane, & Ellis, 1981). Interestingly, the same results have been shown in research comparing the use of whole- and part-task formats for training motor skills to individuals who do not experience a disability (Briggs & Brogden, 1954; Wickstrom, 1958). Based on available research, it might be concluded that part-task training should be the format of choice for training new motor movements to individuals with neuromuscular disabilities, or for teaching potentially difficult discriminations to persons with mental retardation. However, there are at least two factors that may recommend otherwise. First, part-task training is logistically cumbersome to execute, particularly in community-based employment situations. Second, in most cases, the entire task is not complex or difficult for an individual. Rather, some steps of the task are difficult while others are relatively easy to learn. The part-task format has been found to be particularly effective because it enables greater opportunity for practice of individual difficult steps than is accorded in using a whole-task method. It would appear that the effectiveness of the whole-task method could be enhanced if there was a way to use this method and still provide the opportunity to receive increased practice on those specific steps that are difficult for a particular student. In fact, Gaylord-Ross and Holvoet (1985) suggest such a format whereby an individual is trained on the whole task and additional practice is provided on those steps that he or she has particular difficulty learning.

Reinforcement

Reinforcement is probably the most important and powerful training tool available (Bellamy et al., 1979; Mank & Horner, 1988). Reinforcing a student after she or he has emitted a particular response will serve to increase the liklihood of that response occurring in the future (Kazdin, 1980). To be effective, reinforcers must be given contingently. A contingency is a rule that the trainer formulates to define what behavior or responses will be reinforced. The "art" of training involves continuously changing these reinforcement contingency rules in order to gradually move the learner toward greater levels of independence (i.e., with the least amount of assistance and reinforcement possible).

The only way to determine if an event or item is reinforcing for a particular student is to try to use it to consequate a response (Orelove & Sobsey, 1987; Wacker, Berg, Wiggins, Muldoon, & Cavanaugh, 1985). If the rate of response increases, then the event is a reinforcer for that person. In contrast, if the rate of response does not increase, then it may not be a reinforcer. Trainers must understand that what may be reinforcing for some or most persons may not be for others. For example, individuals have greatly varying preferences for food, drink, music, and free time.

During the initial stages of task acquisition, it is usually necessary to deliver a great deal of reinforcement to a person for task performance. Praise is the most useful reinforcer for this purpose. Praise, if used correctly, will not interrupt the individual or pull the person off-task (Bellamy et al., 1979).

The praise delivered during task performance can and in most cases should be supplemented with reinforcement following task completion. For some individuals, this additional reinforcement will be critical for adequate progress in learning a new task (Alberto & Troutman, 1982; Connis et al., 1978; Mank & Horner, 1988). However, the most important role of post-task completion reinforcers is to assist the individual to maintain performance when the trainer's assistance and praise during task performance is decreased (faded). In theory, anything that is a reinforcer for a particular person can be used for this purpose. However, if the reinforcer is going to be delivered at the job site, it is important that it is appropriate to the setting. Obviously, offering a person a beer or the opportunity to play with a toy truck are not acceptable in most employment settings. Breaks, looking at a magazine, or listening to a radio are reinforcing events that nondisabled employees typically have access to at work, and that could be used as reinforcers for a person with disabilities. It is important to recognize, however, that these reinforcers are not given to nondisabled employ-

ees contingently. Using them contingently for individuals with disabilities may
be illegal in some instances (e.g., breaks), and in most cases will serve to further identify them as different from their co-workers. A strategy that the authors have used with students at work experience sites is a job feedback form
like the one shown in Figure 4. The trainer targets several task performance and
work-related behaviors on the form and the criteria for each. The student and

Student _____Fred D._____   Site _____Library_____
Date _____5/10_____

My goal	How I did	Did I meet my goal?
FOLD 10 or more letters evenly	LHt LHt ||	+
Pick up letters without crumbling- 15 or more	LHt LHt ///	—
Complete mail delivery by 1:00p.m.	By 12:55	+
Go to break on own	yes	+
Say hi back to co-workers- all	/// - yes / - no	—

Figure 4.   Job performance evaluation form.

trainer review the behaviors at the beginning of the day and again before each task that is targeted. After the task has been completed, the trainer gives the student a plus (+) if he or she met the standard. The form indicating the student's performance on each of the targeted behaviors is then reviewed at the end of the day. This system is one that many students seem to like and respond well to. It provides the student and the trainer with clear goals to focus on each day and provides the student with tangible feedback. To increase the value of the system, students can take the form home to their parents, who are asked to review it with the student and to provide him or her with encouragement related to job performance. The form can also be used as the basis for providing other reinforcers away from the job site. For example, the trainer and Steve will go out for a soda after work on those days when he meets all of his goals. Parents have reported that the forms allow them an easy way to stay informed and involved with their child's vocational program.

Assistance Prompts

Under most circumstances, individuals with or without disabilities require assistance when learning new tasks and skills. Prompts are methods that can be used to provide this assistance (Bellamy et al., 1979). More specifically, assistance prompts are tools that a trainer can use to systematically communicate to a learner how to perform the steps of a task.

Prompt Types   There are four major types of assistance prompts: verbal, gesture, model, and physical. *Verbal prompting* is used when the trainer tells the student what major step, ministep, or movement step to perform. For example, the trainer might say "staple the papers," "insert the papers into the staple," or "move your hand next to the stapler." A trainer could also tell the student under what circumstances to perform a step (e.g., "after you insert the papers, straighten them"). In addition, verbal prompts can be used to indicate to what criterion a step should be done (e.g., "the papers must be even").

Gesture prompting involves pointing to or touching the task in such a way as to communicate to the student what step to perform and when to perform it. For example, a trainer could touch the stapler as a signal to the student that she or he should staple the papers after they are collated. Or, if a student does not get the papers straightened adequately, the trainer could point to the edges of the papers as a way to communicate that she or he should try to straighten them.

Model prompting is used when the trainer demonstrates a step or series of steps and then asks the student to imitate him or her. For example, a trainer might ask John to first watch her perform each of the ministeps involved in stapling and then attempt to do these himself. Modeling prompts are particularly useful when attempting to teach an individual how to execute a movement required by a step. For example, the trainer could model each of the movement steps that John is supposed to use when pushing down on the stapler.

Physical prompting involves the trainer moving or manipulating the student's body (usually arm or hand) through the movements required to complete a step. For example, the trainer could hold John's hand and move it to the top of the stapler. Physical assistance may be required for teaching what steps to perform and when to perform them if a person has difficulty understanding verbal instructions, gestures, or model prompts. However, physical assistance is often most useful for assisting an individual to learn *how* to execute the movements required by the step.

Prompt Strategies   There are two major approaches suggested for giving prompts (Orelove & Sobsey, 1987; Snell, 1983). The most popular and widely practiced approach is the least-to-most prompting strategy. This system is based on the amount of assistance that various prompts provide. A verbal prompt provides the least assistance, a gesture prompt slightly more, a model prompt even more, and physical assistance the greatest amount. When using a least-to-most approach, the learner is always provided with an opportunity to attempt to perform a step independently. If an error occurs, a verbal prompt is given, followed by a gesture prompt, model, and ultimately physical assistance, until the learner performs the step correctly.

An alternative approach to the one just described is sometimes called the most-to-least prompt strategy. Using this strategy, the trainer prompts the student before he or she attempts to perform the step. Typically this procedure is used with physical prompts, although another type of prompt can be used if the trainer finds it more appropriate. The prompt is then systematically faded. Fading involves slowly reducing the amount of assistance provided. For example, at the beginning of training, the trainer puts her hand on Steve's, moves it to the stapler, and pushes down to staple the papers. As time goes on she gradually gives him less physical help. Fading can also be done by moving to a different type of prompt that provides less assistance. As the trainer physically assists Steve, she also verbally prompts him to push down on the stapler. As she reduces her physical assistance, she continues to give him the verbal assistance until he can do the step with only the verbal prompt.

Although a number of studies have compared least-to-most and most-to-least prompting strategies, there is no clear evidence to indicate which is generally best or more effective for specific students and skills. Schoen (1986) provides an excellent review of the literature related to this issue. Each procedure has one major liability. The least-to-most procedure provides the greatest chance that learners will make errors during training. Errors may interfere with learning because by performing an error a student may actually learn the error. In addition, when an error occurs the student will need to be corrected. The motivation of a student to learn a task may suffer if he or she experiences a great deal of error correction feedback. Conversely, the most-to-least procedure has a greater potential of making the student dependent on assistance. Trainers must be extremely adept at fading to avoid this result.

In general, the least-to-most strategy is typically used by practitioners for training most skills to the majority of students, although the most-to-least procedure is commonly used when training students with the most significant disabilities. Based on clinical experience, these authors favor a combination of the two procedures (Bellamy et al., 1979). This variation involves identifying the prompt that a student requires to perform the step correctly by using the least-to-most procedure and then giving this prompt before the step is attempted (the most-to-least procedure) for several trials. The student is then permitted to attempt to perform the behavior without a prompt or with less assistance for several trials (again using the least-to-most procedure). If he or she does require a prompt of lesser assistance, this prompt is then used for several trials. For example, the trainer used a least-to-most prompting sequence to determine that Don needed a gesture prompt in order to figure out which side of the disk to hold when putting it into the drive slot. She pointed to the correct side for several trials before he attempted to pick it up and then went back to the least-to-most procedure for a couple of trials to see if he could do it without assistance or with less assistance. She found that he could do it without any assistance so she stopped giving it to him. This combination of the two strategies takes advantage of the strengths of both—it decreases the number of errors that a student makes and it helps to prevent giving the student too much assistance.

Are there any differences in using prompts to train discriminations versus movements, especially to students with neuromuscular disabilities? There has been no research related to this question. Based on the authors' experiences, the procedure described above is effective when training discriminations and movements to students with physical and multiple disabilities. However, trainers need to be cautioned to limit their use of physical assistance when training movements to these students. This recommendation appears strange to many practitioners, since it would appear that physical prompts would be especially needed for this purpose. Most of the students with physical disabilities who are served by districts will probably experience cerebral palsy, and many if not most of these students will experience spasticity or athetosis. The muscles in the arm of a student with spasticity are particularly resistive to attempts from others to manipulate or move them. By attempting to do so, the trainer may actually interfere with the student's attempts to perform the movement required by a step. Although the muscles in the limbs of the student with athetosis are not as resistive to manipulation, the writhing and flailing nature of these students' movements also do not lend themselves to physical assistance when trying to teach them a motor response. With these students it is best to use other prompts, especially modeling, when teaching them to perform a movement required by a step. The trainer should then reinforce the student for movements that more clearly approximate the one that is desired. For example, Don, who has spastic cerebral palsy, had difficulty picking up a computer disk. The trainer identified the easiest way for him to pick it up off the table by putting one finger on its edge and then sliding it off the table and bringing his thumb up to grasp it. She modeled this strategy for Don several times and then encouraged him to try to do it on his own. She did not attempt to take Don's hand and guide it through the grasp; however, she did put her hand on the disk to help hold it in place while Don attempted to grasp it, to decrease the chance that he would knock it off the table. When training began he struggled a great deal to get his arm and hand to make the required movements, and it usually took several attempts before he could grasp the disk. The trainer reinforced him for attempts that were slightly better, and as training proceeded he was able to perform the step with increasing ease and fewer attempts.

Performance Assessment

In this chapter, a number of different techniques that are effective in training tasks to individuals with disabilities are described. Some of the techniques will be very effective with some individuals while ineffective with others. In addition, different techniques are more or less effective for a particular individual, depending on the specific type of problem he or she experiences in learning a task. One of the most important responsibilities of a trainer is to determine which strategies to use with a particular person at the various phases of task acquisition. Data on a student's task and step performance will assist a trainer to make these critical decisions (Sowers, Thompson, & Connis, 1979; Wehman, 1981; Wehman et al., 1988).

There are many systems or formats that can be used for collecting performance data. One such format is shown in Figure 5. The task analysis (the major steps) for John's mailing task is entered on the form. A plus (+) was recorded each time a step was performed correctly and independently and a minus (−) was recorded each time John performed it incorrectly. By looking at the data (the + 's and − 's), the trainer can determine which steps John is learning successfully and which are difficult for him. Important aspects of this particular form are the areas labeled *Motor Problem* and *Discrimination Problem*. Here the trainer can note the specific difficulty that the student is having in attempting to perform a step. This information can serve as the basis for identifying training or design strategies that might alleviate the problem(s).

It is also useful for a trainer to be able to look at a student's overall progress in learning and performing a task. One method for summarizing task performance data is to compute the percentage of steps performed correctly (divide the number of steps for which a (+) was recorded during a day by the total number of steps performed during data collection that day). The percentage of correct and independent performance can then be graphed.

The amount of data that should be collected is frequently debated. Some professionals advocate for collecting data each and every time a trainee performs a task during the acquisition phase. Others believe that less data is needed. The purpose of collecting data is to obtain a good representation of the learner's

| Student _Jane C._   Site _City Records_ |||||
| Date _8/1_ |||||

Steps	+/−	Motor problem	Discrimination problem
1. Collate document	+ + + + + + + + + +		
2. Staple pages together	+ + + + + + + + + +	Stapling jig has eliminated problem getting pages aligned.	
3. Fold	− − − − − − − − − −	Can't do this with one hand – need a jig.	
4. Insert in envelope	+ − + + − + + + − +	Couldn't get letter in smoothly – tried to force, which caused crumbling.	
5. Seal envelope	+ + + + − + + − + +		Twice didn't wipe entire sticky surface with sponge.
6. Place label on envelope	− + − − − − − − − −	Label sticks to fingers – crumbles	Didn't put in correct location – without assistance

Total steps performed: __60__   Speed standard: _2 per min._
Correct/independent steps: __36__   # of work minutes: _10_
Percentage correct/independent: _36/60=60%_ $ completed: __3__
                                        Productivity: _.3 per min.= 15%_

Figure 5.   Task performance probe form.

performance in order to make training decisions. To be able to make such decisions, it is the authors' opinion that it is sufficient to collect data on a probe basis (e.g., once or twice a week), rather than every time the individual attempts to perform the task.

INCREASING TASK PERFORMANCE PRODUCTIVITY

The rate at which a worker completes his or her assigned tasks is important in most employment situations (Moon et al., 1990; Wehman et al., 1988). Behavioral strategies have been shown to be effective for increasing the vocational task productivity of persons with cognitive disabilities.

Many individuals with physical and multiple disabilities have particularly low task-completion rates. As with acquisition training, there has been little attention given by researchers to identifying those strategies that can help these individuals to perform at higher rates. In fact, a review of the literature reveals no study that has addressed this issue. This section reviews those training strategies that have been found to be effective for assisting persons with mental retardation to increase their rate of task performance, and includes suggestions for applying these strategies to an individual who experiences difficulty executing the movements required by a task.

The basic method for increasing a student's rate of task completion is simple: reinforce the person for working faster (Bellamy et al., 1979; Davis, Bates, & Cuvo, 1983; Wehman et al., 1988). However, there are a number of extremely important rules that should be followed in implementing a program to reinforce rate improvements in order to be optimally successful.

1. *The rate criteria for reinforcement should be gradually increased.*   One of the errors that trainers make when attempting to get a person to work faster is to set the rate criteria at levels too high during the initial stages of the program. Setting rate criteria that are significantly greater than current performance typically results in a negative outcome. As much as the person tries, he or she will have a great deal of difficulty achieving the goal. After several days or weeks of failing, the individual may understandably become discouraged and stop trying. Consequently, a student should first be asked to work slightly faster than his or her current rate of performance, and then should be reinforced for doing so.

2. *If a person's quality of task performance decreases after a rate criteria increase, maintain the criteria until the quality is reestablished.*   Performance quality often suffers when a person attempts to work at a rate to which he or she is unaccustomed. The movement responses of persons with neuromuscular disabilities, especially individuals with spasticity and athetosis, are particularly affected when they attempt to move more quickly. However, the quality usually returns to its previous level a few days after the rate increase (Sowers, Jenkins, & Powers, 1988). It appears that individuals require a few days to "learn" how to work more quickly, while concurrently maintaining control of their movements.

3. *Maintain a high criteria for quality of task performance during rate training.*   As described above, rate training often results in initial decrements in the execution of movements required by the task. In many cases, the

quality does return to previous levels. However, to help insure that this occurs, it is important to clearly communicate to the student that quality cannot be sacrificed to speed. Consequently, reinforcement contingencies should continue to remain in effect for the quality of task performance during rate training.

4. *After the student has achieved the rate criteria and his or her task performance quality has improved, the rate criteria should again be slightly increased.*   This pattern of gradual criteria increases should be repeated until either the student fails to achieve the criteria or achieves the rate criteria but his or her movement quality deteriorates and does not improve over time. If either of these situations occur, the rate criteria should be returned to the level at which the student can achieve and maintain task performance quality.

5. *Collect speed and productivity data.*   This data will serve as the basis for making rate criteria changes and determining the effectiveness of training and design strategies on students' productivity. This information will also be critical when identifying the tasks that should comprise a paid job for a student. Figure 5 provides a means to obtain this information.

Using the strategies described in this section, the task completion rate of persons with physical and multiple disabilities can be improved. However, it is likely that even with the use of these strategies as well as job design strategies, their rate will still be significantly lower than persons without disabilities. Other job creation and support strategies addressed elsewhere in this book will also need to be used so that these students' low production rates do not serve as a barrier to their employment.

Summary

Conventional behavior training strategies developed for training discriminations can be used to assist persons with motor disabilities to perform movements required by tasks and work-related skills. In some cases, these techniques need to be slightly modified for this purpose.

STRATEGIES SPECIFICALLY DESIGNED FOR TRAINING MOTOR RESPONSES TO PERSONS WITH NEUROMUSCULAR DISABILITIES

To this point an attempt has been made to describe the strategies that are key to training discriminations to persons with cognitive disabilities, as well as the manner in which these strategies can be applied to training movements to individuals with motor disabilities. In this section, a number of strategies are described that are uniquely useful for training movements.

Relaxation Training

Persons who exhibit a high level of muscle tension face a particular challenge when attempting to learn new movements. With the use of sophisticated bio-feedback equipment, it has been demonstrated that these individuals can learn to control muscle tension levels (Cataldo et al., 1978; Inman, 1979; Nielson & McCaughey, 1979; Skrotsky et al., 1978). Unfortunately most school districts and adult service programs do not have access to this equipment. Based on the authors' experience, however, it does appear that individuals can learn to decrease their muscle tension without the use of such equipment.

The specific strategy for teaching a person to relax (keep his or her muscle tension under control) varies depending on the student's cognitive abilities as well as the degree of muscle tension that is experienced. The following describes a simple relaxation promotion procedure that these authors have used with a number of students as part of their work experience training:

1. Before the student begins to perform a task, explain the importance of keeping the muscles "relaxed" while doing it. Attempt to determine if the student understands what it means to "relax." This can be done by asking the student to demonstrate what he or she looks like when relaxed and by providing him or her with appropriate feedback such as, "That's right, your muscles are soft and your arms are very still." If the individual has a difficult time achieving a relaxed state, the trainer should demonstrate how the student should look and feel when relaxed as compared to when tense. Comments like, "When you're relaxed, your muscles are real soft, and your arms are quiet and loose like spaghetti," paired with trainer demonstration of exaggerated looseness and relaxation, communicate this notion.
2. Prompt the student to get relaxed before starting the task. Do not allow the student to begin the task until he or she becomes relaxed and stays that way for at least a few seconds.
3. As the student performs the task, continue to verbally prompt him or her to remain relaxed. These prompts should be given in a quiet and controlled fashion. The trainer should also provide the student with feedback on how relaxed he or she is remaining: "You are really staying relaxed. Oops! You are starting to tighten up—try to get relaxed again."
4. If the student becomes so tense that he or she begins to lose control in executing the movements required by the task, the trainer should stop him or her, and require a return to a relaxed state before allowing the student to begin the task again.

One-Step Strategy

Most individuals do not perform each of the movements required by a step one-at-a-time. Rather, they "blend" movements. For example, when stapling papers, most individuals will do the following steps almost simultaneously: insert the papers in the stapler, place a hand on the stapler arm, and push down on it. Individuals who do not experience a neuromuscular disability can "blend" movement steps together and still maintain the quality of each of the movements. This is not the case with some students who have neuromuscular disabilities. When they attempt to begin one step before they complete another, the quality of both movements is often negatively affected. To maintain the quality of the movements, these students have to concentrate on doing one movement step at a time. Often these students will attempt to "blend" their movements, which results in quality deterioration. If this occurs, the trainer will need to encourage the student to concentrate on one step at a time.

Warm-Up Sessions

Athletes routinely warm up before beginning to perform: the baseball pitcher throws pitches in the bullpen, the basketball player shoots baskets before the game, and the golfer practices his stroke before teeing off. Research does in fact suggest that warming up, practicing a movement or a series of movements, can improve the performance of individuals without disabilities (Schmidt, 1976). Warming up has the greatest impact on skills that are particularly difficult for an individual to perform.

Applying this research to the training of tasks to individuals with neuromuscular disabilities, a trainer could establish a brief warm-up or practice session before an individual begins performing actual work tasks. During this session, those movements that are particularly difficult for the student would be practiced. For example, Steve had difficulty getting the disk into the disk drive without bending it. Consequently, before attempting to insert the "real" disk with important data on it, Steve practiced with an old disk.

Slowly Increase Work Period

Common sense suggests that it is difficult to learn and perform tasks when one is experiencing fatigue. In fact, research on individuals without disabilities reveals that fatigue does have deleterious effects on task learning and performance (Carron, 1972; Schmidt, 1969). Many persons with neuromuscular disabilities have been required to engage in very little physical effort of any kind. These individuals may find working for even short periods of time to be extremely tiring. This is especially true for individuals who are being trained to perform new motor movements.

The length of time that a student can work before fatigue occurs varies among individuals. During the first few days of training, the trainer should watch the student carefully for signs of fatigue. When fatigue begins to occur, the individual should be provided with a break. After several days, or possibly weeks, the student will probably begin to experience less fatigue at the end of work intervals. When this occurs, the work intervals should be increased slightly (i.e., by 5 or 10 minutes). When the student again appears to experience no fatigue, the work interval should again be slightly increased. This process of gradually increasing the work interval should be continued until it is clear that the longest interval that the student is capable of working without experiencing significant fatigue has been reached. With some students, this interval may remain relatively short, while others may be able to work several hours without needing a break. This information will be of particular utility when planning for a student's future employment.

Use of Videotape for Modeling and Feedback

The use of videotaped demonstrations to teach athletic skills such as a golf or tennis swing is quite common. Research has shown that, when used appropriately, videotape models can be equally as effective as live demonstrations for teaching athletic skills to persons who do not experience disabilities (Del Rey, 1971; Landers, 1978). Video modeling in conjunction with other techniques (e.g., prompting, reinforcement) has been shown to be successful for teaching social and self-help skills to individuals with mild mental retardation (Browning, White, Zembrosky-Barkin, & Nave, 1988; Nelson, Gibson, & Cutting, 1973).

The most frequent use of instructional videotapes is for the learner to view demonstrations of other individuals modeling desired behaviors. A variation of this approach is called self-modeling, whereby videotapes are produced of the learner performing the response to criterion. Dowrick and Dove (1980) edited videotapes to show children with spina bifida performing targeted water skills. Each child then viewed the tapes of him- or herself. The procedure seemed to have a positive effect on the children's swimming.

In the two uses of videotapes described above, the demonstration is shown to the learner before the response is attempted. Videotape can also be used for feedback purposes. Using this approach, the individual is videotaped attempting to perform the response. The individual is then shown the tape and typically, with the assistance of an instructor, the positive and negative aspects of the attempted response are pointed out to the learner (Singer, 1980). No attempts to utilize videotaping for training vocational skills have been published. However, it may be a technique worth exploring for teaching the movements required by vocational tasks to students with motor disabilities.

Imagery

A popular technique used by athletes is imagery or mental practice. Using this technique, the individual imagines and visualizes him- or herself performing the movements required to achieve the desired outcome. At least 100 studies have been conducted to determine the impact of imagery on motor performance (Wollman, 1986). Although the results to date are mixed, some studies have found that imagery can enhance motor performance (Corbin, 1972; Feltz & Landers, 1983; Richardson, 1967).

There has been no empirical validation of any attempt to use imagery to improve the motor performance of individuals with physical disabilities or to teach skills to individuals with any type of disability. It may well be a technique that trainers wish to try, in combination with more straightforward training. It is likely that imagery will have the greatest potential for success with individuals who do not experience significant levels of cognitive disability.

Summary

Strategies such as relaxation, focusing on one step at a time, introducing warm-ups, gradually increasing work intervals, providing instructional videotape, and imagery have unique application to training motor responses to individuals with neuromuscular disabilities. These techniques can be used in conjunction with traditional training methods to optimize the performance of such individuals.

STRATEGIES TO ENHANCE GENERALIZATION

It is hoped as a result of participating in a school vocational program students will be able to perform the tasks and skills required by future jobs. In essence, skill generalization is the major goal of these programs. Generalization occurs when a student can perform a skill or behavior in situations other than those in which he or she received training (Mank & Horner, 1988). Research and experience suggest that individuals with severe developmental disabilities frequently have great difficulty generalizing skills (Stokes & Baer, 1977; Wacker & Berg, 1986).

There are three major types of generalization. The first type of generalization is across *settings*—can the student perform a skill that was trained in one setting in a new and different setting? The second type is generalization across *persons*—can the student, after learning to work for a particular supervisor and around co-workers in a training setting, perform as well for a new supervisor and with different co-workers? The third type is *task* generalization—after the student has learned to perform one variation of a particular task or skill (e.g., working on one type of photocopy machine), can he or she perform other variations of this task or skill (e.g., photocopying using a different type of machine).

Enhancing Generalization Across Settings

The primary reason that community-based work experience training has been strongly advocated is that it enhances the extent to which a student is able to generalize the skills learned during training to future employment situations. This is based on the fact that the more similar the training environment is to the one in which a person will ultimately be expected to work, the greater the likelihood that generalization will occur.

It is important that school programs attempt to select training sites that have characteristics similar to those in which students are likely to work in the future. Those characteristics that are important to think about when recruiting sites include the number of persons around whom the student will work, the amount of communication and interaction that will occur among co-workers, the actual physical appearance of the setting (what the building and work area look like), the noise level of the setting, and the standards of conduct.

Clearly, there is great variation among employment sites in terms of their characteristics, and it will not be possible to predict the exact nature of the possible sites where a student may work in the future. Consequently, students should have the opportunity to work at sites that represent a range of characteristics.

Enhancing Generalization Across Persons

The second type of generalization of which school staff should be aware is generalization across persons. Students with disabilities frequently learn to perform well in the presence of staff with whom they have worked for a period of time. However, when new staff begin to work with the students, they may not perform at the same level. Consequently, effort should be made to have the student receive vocational training from a variety of different staff and to take direction from regular site supervisors.

Enhancing Task Generalization

The importance of training students to perform the tasks that they may perform in future jobs has been outlined in an earlier chapter. The greater the similarities between the tasks trained and those that will be performed in the future, the greater the generalization that the student can be expected to make—the student will be able to perform these tasks with the least amount of instruction. Again, there is a great amount of variation in the way the tasks are performed. In order to enhance generalization, students should be given the opportunity to learn and perform a number of different variations of tasks (Horner & McDonald, 1982; Wacker & Berg, 1984). For example, when training a student to perform computer data entry, the student should have the opportunity to perform different types of data entry tasks and to work on different computers and computer programs.

Summary

Generalization is the extent to which individuals can utilize the skills learned in training situations in future performance situations. Consequentley, the extent to which students generalize is a primary indicator of the effectiveness of school vocational preparation programs. In this section, a number of strategies that can be used to enhance generalization are described.

STRATEGIES TO ENHANCE MAINTENANCE

Issues of maintenance involve the extent to which a student continues to perform a learned skill or behavior when trainer supervision (i.e., prompting and feedback) and presence is decreased (Berg, Wacker, & Flynn, 1990). Although the supported employment approach decreases the *requirement* that students be able to work without assistance and support, the availability of support does not change the importance of making every effort to assist students to work as independently as possible. Job design strategies contribute to this outcome. Task acquisition and rate building strategies also help to insure that persons reach their highest levels of independence. In this section, additional techniques that can be utilized specifically to decrease the need for trainer supervision and presence are described.

Fading

In previous sections the importance of fading trainer prompts, reinforcers, and presence have been discussed. Fading is one of the most powerful maintenance-enhancing strategies (Mank & Horner, 1988).

Natural Support Systems

Wacker and Berg (1986) have suggested that trainers utilize consequences that are typically available in work settings. As suggested earlier, praise is the most commonly and widely used reinforcer in work settings. Another strategy suggested by Wacker and Berg (1986) is to teach students to solicit feedback from co-workers and supervisors. One strategy that students can use to get feedback is the *Job Feedback Form* (Figure 4) described earlier. The feedback review can be turned over from the trainer to the supervisor. Many students, of course, require substantially higher levels of ongoing assistance and support. Shafer (1986) and Nisbet and Hagner (1988) have described ways in which supervisors and co-workers can be recruited and trained to give assistance, feedback, and support to individuals with disabilities.

Self-Management Techniques

One set of strategies that have shown promise for the maintenance of behaviors by persons with developmental disabilities fall under the rubric of self-management techniques (Berg et al., 1990; Mahoney & Thoresen, 1974; Mank & Horner, 1988). Among the self-managment strategies most frequently and successfully utilized with persons who experience disabilities are self-monitoring (also called self-recording and self-assessment), self-instruction, self-delivered reinforcement, and antecedent cue regulation.

Self-Monitoring   Using this procedure, an individual is trained to take data on his or her own performance. The information collected by the student can then be used by the trainer to provide reinforcers or the student may reinforce himself or herself.

When establishing a self-monitoring system for an individual with a disability, an attempt should be made to develop one that is as easy to use as possible. This is particularly true for an individual with physical and multiple disabilities. For example, if John, a young man with cerebral palsy, had to make a mark on a piece of paper after he entered each form in the computer, his productivity would probably suffer because of the time spent recording. An alternative would be to have John use a mechanical counter mounted on the table so that he could simply push a button to record a number.

Self-Delivered Reinforcement   This strategy involves teaching a person to judge whether his or her performance or behavior has met an established standard for reinforcement and to deliver this reinforcement to himself or herself. A number of studies has demonstrated that this procedure can be effective or more effective than the delivery of reinforcers by another person (Horner & Brigman, 1979; Wehman, 1981). Typically, this procedure is used in conjunction with self-monitoring. For example, John could be taught to take a break after his counter reached 10.

Self-Instruction   Training persons to cue themselves has been shown to be effective in assisting individuals to manage their own behavior (Wacker & Berg, 1986). Crouch, Rusch, and Karlan (1984) trained individuals with mental retardation to cue themselves to work faster. Wacker and Greenebaum (1984) trained students with mental retardation to label the critical dimensions (e.g., big, little) of the objects that they were sorting. This technique could also be used for the training of motor skills to persons with physical disabilities. For example, an individual could be taught to prompt himself or herself to relax during the execution of a task.

Antecedent Cue Regulation   This is a strategy that can be used to assist students who have difficulty using the stimuli provided by the natural work setting to make discriminations (Berg et al., 1990). Sowers, Rusch, Connis, and Cummings (1980) provided persons with pictures of clock faces to assist them to independently go to and from breaks at their assigned times. Berg and Wacker (1989) taught a person who was hearing and visually impaired as well as cognitively disabled to use tactual cues to perform an envelope stuffing task involving different sized envelopes and fillers. Tactile cues were placed into each page of a cue book that was provided for her before beginning. The book she was given contained the cues corresponding to the size of the envelopes and materials to be stuffed. She then used the cues to identify the envelopes and materials on the table in front of her.

Summary

Maintenance of a student's behavior is potentially problematic. Fading and naturally maintaining contingencies can be used to enhance maintenance. Self-management strategies, such as self-monitoring, self-instruction, self-delivered reinforcement, and antecedent cue regulation can also contribute to maintenance.

CONCLUSION

Students with neuromuscular disabilities frequently experience difficulty executing the movements required by vocational tasks. Typically, job adaptations are used to assist students to overcome these problems. It is rare that attempts are made to teach students to make the movements. The experience of these authors suggests that the movements of individuals with neuromuscular disabilities can be greatly improved through direct instruction technologies. When students have several years remaining before graduation, school programs should take the time to train them to perform both the discriminations and movements required by tasks and work-related skills.

REFERENCES

Alberto, P. A., & Troutman, A. C. (1982). *Applied behavior analysis for teachers: Influencing student performance.* Columbus, OH: Charles E. Merrill.

Bellamy, G. T., Horner, R. H., & Inman, D. P. (1979). *Vocational habilitation of severely retarded adults: A direct service technology.* Baltimore: University Park Press.

Berg, W., & Wacker, D. (1989). Evaluation of tactile prompts with a student who is deaf, blind, and mentally retarded. *Journal of Applied Behavior Analysis, 22,* 93–99.

Berg, W., Wacker, D., & Flynn, T. (1990). Teaching generalization and maintenance of work behavior. In F. R. Rusch (Ed.), *Supported employment: Models, methods and issues* (pp. 145–160). Sycamore, IL: Sycamore Publishing Co.

Blake, K. A., & Williams, C. L. (1969). Retarded, normal, and superior subjects, learning of paired associates by whole and parts methods. *Psychological Reports, 25,* 819–824.

Bobath, B., & Karel, B. (1975). *Motor development in the different types of cerebral palsy.* London: William Heinemann.

Briggs, G. E., & Brogden, W. J. (1954). The effect of component practice on performance of a lever-positioning skill. *Journal of Experimental Psychology, 48,* 375–380.

Browning, P., White, W. A. T., Zembrosky-Barkin, P., & Nave, G. (1988). Interactive video in the special classroom: A pilot study. *The Computing Teacher.*

Carron, A. V. (1972). Motor performance and learning under physical fatigue. *Medicine and Science in Sports, 4,* 101–106.

Cataldo, M., Bird, B., & Cunningham, C. (1978). Experimental analysis of EMG feedback in treating cerebral palsy. *Journal of Behavior Medicine, 1,* 311–322.

Connis, T. T., Sowers, J., & Thompson, L. (Eds.). (1978). *Training the mentally handicapped for employment: A comprehensive manual.* New York: Human Sciences Press.

Corbin, C. B. (1972). Mental practice. In W. P. Morgan (Ed), *Ergogenic aids and muscular performance* (pp. 146–157). New York: Academic Press.

Crosson, J. E. (1969). A technique for programming sheltered workshop environments for training severely retarded workers. *American Journal of Mental Deficiency, 73,* 814–818.

Crouch, K. P., Rusch, F. R., & Karlan, G. P. (1984). Competitive employment: Utilizing the correspondence training paradigm to enhance productivity. *Education and Training of the Mentally Retarded, 19*(4), 268–275.

Davis, P., Bates, P., & Cuvo, A. (1983). Training a mentally retarded woman to work competitively: Effect of graphic feedback and a changing criterion design. *Education and Training of the Mentally Retarded, 18,* 158–163.

Del Rey, P. (1971). The effects of video-tape feedback on form, accuracy, and latency in an open and closed environment. *Journal of Motor Behavior, 3,* 281–287.

Dowrick, P., & Dove, C. (1980). The use of self-modeling to improve the swimming performance of spina bifida children. *Journal of Applied Behavior Analysis, 13*(1), 51–56.

Feltz, D. L., & Landers, D. M. (1983). The effects of mental practice on motor skill learning and performance: A meta-analysis. *Journal of Sport Psychology, 5,* 25–27.

Gaylord-Ross, R. J., & Holvoet, J. F. (1985). *Strategies for educating students with severe handicaps.* Boston: Little, Brown.

Gilette, H. E. (1969). *Systems of therapy in cerebral palsy.* Springfield, IL: Charles C Thomas.

Gold, M. (1972). Stimulus factors in skill training of the retarded on a complex assembly task: Acquisition, transfer, and retention. *American Journal of Mental Deficiency, 76,* 517–526.

Gold, M. W. (1968). Preworkshop skills for the trainable: A sequential technique. *Education and Training of the Mentally Retarded, 3,* 31–37.

Horner, R. H. (1971). Establishing uses of crutches by a mentally retarded spina bifida child. *Journal of Applied Behavior Analysis, 4,* 183–189.

Horner, R. H., & Brigman, T. A. (1979). Self management and on-task behavior in two retarded adults. *Education and Training of the Mentally Retarded, 14,* 18–24.

Horner, R., & McDonald, R. (1982). Comparison of single instance and general case instruction in teaching a generalized vocational skill. *Journal of The Association for the Severely Handicapped, 7,* 7–20.

Horner, R. H., Meyer, L. H., & Fredericks, H. D. B. (1986). *Education of learners with severe handicaps: Exemplary service strategies.* Baltimore: Paul H. Brookes Publishing Co.

Inman, D. P. (1979). Gaining control over tension in spastic muscles. In G. Hammerlynch (Ed.), *Behavioral systems for the developmentally disabled (Vol. II): Institutional, clinic, and community environments* (pp. 160–189). New York: Brunner-Mazel.

Kayser, J. E., Billingsley, F. F., & Neel, R. S. (1986). A comparison of in-context and traditional instructional approaches: Total task, single trial versus backward chaining, multiple trials. *Journal of The Association for Persons with Severe Handicaps, 11*(1), 28–38.

Kazdin, A. (1980). *Behavior modification in applied settings.* Homewood, IL: Dorsey Press.

Landers, D. M. (1978). How, when, and where to use demonstrations: Suggestions for practitioners. *Journal of Physical Education and Recreation, 49,* 65–67.

Mahoney, M. J., & Thoresen, C. E. (1974). *Self-control: Power to the person.* Monterey, CA: Brooks/Cole.

Mank, D. M., & Horner, R. H. (1988). Instructional programming in vocational education. In R. Gaylord-Ross (Ed.) *Vocational education for persons with handicaps* (pp. 142–173). Mountain View, CA: Mayfield Publishing Co.

Moon, S. M., Inge, K., Wehman, P., Brooke, V., & Barcus, J. M. (1990). *Helping persons with severe mental retardation get and keep employment.* Baltimore: Paul H. Brookes Publishing Co.

Naylor, J. C., & Briggs, G. E. (1963). Effects of task complexity and task organization on the relative efficiency of part and whole training methods. *Journal of Experimental Psychology, 65,* 217–224.

Nelson, R., Gibson, F., & Cutting D. S. (1973). Videotaped modeling: The development of three appropriate social responses in a mildly retarded child. *Mental Retardation, 11*(6), 24–28.

Nielson, P., & McCaughey, J. (1979). Self-regulation of spasm and spasticity in cerebral palsy. *Journal of Neurology, Neurosurgery and Psychiatry, 45*, 1123–1125.

Nisbet, J. & Hagner, D. (1988). Natural supports in the workplace: A reexamination of supported employment. *Journal of the Association for Persons with Severe Handicaps, 13*(4), 260–267.

Orelove, F. P., & Sobsey, D. (1987). Curriculum and instructional programming. In F. P. Orelove & D. Sobsey (Eds.), *Educating children with multiple disabilities: A transdisciplinary approach* (pp. 157–188). Baltimore: Paul H. Brookes Publishing Co.

Renzaglia, A., & Hutchins, M. (1990). A community-referenced approach to preparing persons with disabilities for employment. In P. Wehman & S. Moon (Eds.), *Vocational rehabilitation and supported employment* (pp. 91–110). Baltimore: Paul H. Brookes Publishing Co.

Rice, H., McDonald, B., & Denney, S. (1968). Operant conditioning techniques for use in the physical rehabilitation of the multiply handicapped retarded patient. *Physical Therapy, 48*, 342–346.

Richardson, A. (1967). Mental practice: A review and discussion: Part I. *Research Quarterly, 38*, 95–107.

Rusch, F. R., Connis, R. T., & Sowers, J. (1978). The modification and maintenance of time spent attending to task using social reinforcement, token reinforcement and response cost in an applied restaurant setting. *Journal of Special Education on Technology, 2*, 18–26.

Rusch, F. R., & Mithaug, D. E. (1980). *Vocational training for mentally retarded adults.* Champaign, IL: Research Press.

Schmidt, R. A. (1969). Performance and learning a gross motor skill under conditions of artificially induced fatigue. *Research Quarterly, 40*, 185–190.

Schmidt, R. A. (1976). Control processes in motor skills. In J. Keogh & R. S. Hutton (Eds.), *Exercise and sport sciences reviews (Vol. 4).* Santa Barbara, CA: Journal Publishing Affiliates.

Schoen, S. F. (1986). Assistance procedures to facilitate the transfer of stimulus control: Review and analysis. *Education and Training of the Mentally Retarded, 21*(1), 62–74.

Scrutton, D., & Gilbertson, M. (1975). The physiotherapist's role in the treatment of cerebral palsy. In R. L. Samilson, *Orthopaedic aspects of cerebral palsy.* London: William Heinemann.

Shafer, M. S. (1986). Utilizing co-workers as change agents. In F. R. Rusch (Eds.), *Competitive employment issues and strategies* (pp. 215–224). Baltimore: Paul H. Brookes Publishing Co.

Singer, R. (1980). *Motor learning and human performance: An application to motor skills and movement behaviors.* New York: Macmillan.

Singer, R. N., & Gaines, L. (1975). Effect of prompted and trial-and-error learning on transfer performance of a serial motor task. *American Educational Research Journal, 12*, 395–403.

Singer, R. N., & Pease, D. (1976). Effect of different instructional strategies on learning, retention, and transfer of a serial motor task. *Research Quarterly, 47*, 788–796.

Skrotsky, K., Gallenstein, J., & Osternig, L. (1978). Effects of electromyographic feedback training on motor control in spastic cerebral palsy. *Physical Therapy, 50*, 547–551.

Snell, M. E. (Ed.). (1983). *Systematic instruction of the moderately and severely handicapped* (2nd ed.). Columbus, OH: Charles E. Merrill.

Snell, M. E., & Gast, D. L. (1981). Applying delay procedure to the instruction of the severely handicapped. *Journal of The Association for the Severely Handicapped, 5*, 3–14.

Sowers, J., & Powers, L. (1989). Preparing students with cerebral palsy and mental retardation for the transition from school to community-based employment. *Career Development for Exceptional Individuals, 12*(1), 25–35.

Sowers, J., Jenkins, C., & Powers, L. (1988). Vocational education of persons with physical handicaps. In R. Gaylord-Ross (Ed.), *Vocational education for persons with handicaps*. Mountain View, CA: Mayfield Publishing Co.

Sowers, J., Rusch, F. R., Connis, R. T., & Cummings, L. E. (1980). Teaching mentally retarded adults to time manage in a vocational setting. *Journal of Applied Behavior Analysis, 13*(4).

Sowers, J., Thompson, L., & Connis, R. (1979). The food service vocational training program. In G. T. Bellamy, G. O'Connor, & O. Karan (Eds.), *Vocational rehabilitation of severely handicapped persons: Contemporary service strategies*. Baltimore: University Park Press.

Stokes, D. & Baer, D. (1977). An implicit technology of generalization. *Journal of Applied Behavior Analysis, 10*, 349–367.

Thompson, G., Iwata, B., & Poynter, H. (1979). Operant control of pathological tongue thrust in spastic cerebral palsy. *Journal of Applied Behavior Analysis, 12*, 325–333.

Wacker, D., & Berg, W. (1984). *Evaluation of response outcome and response topography on generalization of skills*. Unpublished manuscript, Division of Developmental Disabilities. Iowa City, IA: University of Iowa.

Wacker, D. & Greenebaum, F. (1984). Efficacy of a verbal training sequence on the sorting performance of moderately and severely retarded adolescents. *American Journal of Mental Retardation, 88*, 653–660.

Wacker, D. P., & Berg, W. K. (1986). Generalizing and maintaining work behavior. In F. R. Rusch (Ed.), *Competitive employment issues and strategies* (pp. 129–140). Baltimore: Paul H. Brookes Publishing Co.

Wacker, D. P., Berg, W. K., Wiggins, B., Muldoon, M., & Cavanaugh, J. (1985). Evaluation of reinforcer preferences for profoundly handicapped students. *Journal of Applied Behavior Analysis, 13*, 173–178.

Walls, R., Zane, T., & Ellis, W. (1981). Forward and backward chaining, and whole task methods. *Behavior Modification, 5*(1), 61–74.

Wehman, P. (1981). *Competitive employment: New horizons for severely disabled individuals*. Baltimore: Paul H. Brookes Publishing Co.

Wehman, P., Wood, W., Everson, J., Goodwyn, R., & Conley, S. (1988). *Vocational education for multihandicapped youth with cerebral palsy*. Baltimore: Paul H. Brookes Publishing Co.

Wickstrom, R. L.(1958). Comparative study of methodologies for teaching gymnastics and tumbling stunts. *Research Quarterly, 29*, 109–115.

Wilcox, B., & Bellamy, G. T. (1982). *Design of high school programs for severely handicapped students*. Baltimore: Paul H. Brookes Publishing Co.

Wollman, N. (1986). Research on imagery and motor performance: Three methodological suggestions. *Journal of Sports Psychology, 8*, 135–138.

Zeaman, D., & House, B. (1963). The role of attention in retardate discrimination learning. In N. Ellis (Ed.), *Handbook of mental deficiency*. New York: McGraw-Hill.

Zohn, J. G., & Bornstein, D. H. (1980). Self-management of work performance with mentally retarded adults: Effect upon work productivity, work quality and on-task behavior. *Mental Retardation, 18*, 19–24.

TIFFNEY

Tiffney is 25 years old and can walk, although unsteadily. She can speak, but is difficult to understand. She also wears hearing aids in both ears.

Tiffney learned a variety of tasks through her school's work experience program, including basic clerical and light cleaning tasks. A job was created for her during her last year of school at a hair salon where she has been employed for over 4 years. Her job title is Set-Up Assistant, which involves washing, drying, and folding towels, and supplying towels to the stylists. She also does a number of cleaning tasks, such as wiping off shampoo and styling stations, sweeping up hair, and taking garbage to the dumpster.

Tiffney was hired part-time, but due to bus schedule problems she now works about 3½ hours daily. She is paid based on her productivity, and is between 40% and 50% productive.

Only a few adaptations to the site or tasks were needed to enable Tiffney to perform her job. Containers that she needed to reach were put on lower shelves, and one large garbage can was exchanged for several smaller ones so that she would be able to lift the bags when full. A device that permitted her to turn the knobs on the washer and dryer was provided for her. Because Tiffney has difficulty holding and carrying more than one lotion bottle, she was given a colander to place the bottles into when

TIFFNEY
(continued)

carrying them from one room to another. This idea was borrowed from another hair salon that uses colanders for carrying curlers.

A job coach remained with Tiffney for about 5 months before beginning to fade. After several months of gradual fading, it became clear that Tiffney would continue to need daily support. The support was primarily around her need for monitoring and feedback in order to remain on-task and to maintain task performance standards. The adult service program contracted with the hair salon for them to provide this support to Tiffney. The receptionist was trained when to check on Tiffney's work and how to provide her with positive feedback. With this co-worker support, the adult service agency only checks in for a few minutes once a week.

6 Job Design Strategies and Adaptations

When a student who experiences physical and multiple disabilities is placed into a community job, a "gap" often exists between the requirements of the tasks and the ability of the person to meet these requirements. The goal is to close this gap in order that the person can work as independently and productively as possible. Figure 6 provides a graphic illustration of this concept.

There are two primary strategies that can be used to close the performance gap. First, the skills of the person can be increased through training. The second strategy is to decrease the requirements of the task by redesigning it and by using adaptations and modifications.

The importance of adaptations as a means to increase the participation, independence, and productivity of persons with disabilities, especially those students and adults who experience physical and multiple disabilities, has been widely recognized in the field of special education and rehabilitation (Barnes, Murphy, Waldo, & Sailor, 1979; Baumgart et al., 1982; Everson et al., 1990; Sowers & Powers, 1989; Wehman, Wood, Everson, Goodwyn, & Conley, 1988; York & Rainforth, 1987). The necessity of adaptations for providing these individuals with access to and full participation in community life including employment was reflected in the passage of the Technology Related Assistance for Individuals with Disabilities Act of 1988 as well as the Americans with Disabilities Act of 1990. As a result of both of these acts, the 1990s will be a time of growing attention to, exploration of, and utilization of adaptations as a means to increase and enhance the employment opportunities of persons with physical and multiple disabilities.

The purpose of this chapter is to describe job design strategies that can be used to enable persons with physical and multiple disabilities to use community job sites more independently and productively. The strategies are described, and a process for their design and selection is proposed.

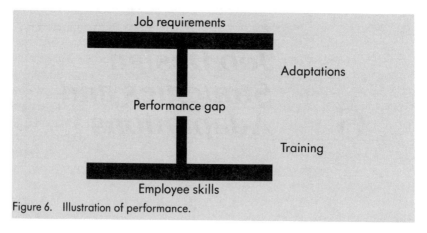

Figure 6.   Illustration of performance.

JOB DESIGN STRATEGIES

The purpose of task redesign, adaptation, and modification is to permit a worker to perform a task as independently and productively as possible. In some cases, there will be an adaptation technique (e.g., picture cues) or device (e.g., a keyguard) that has application across a number of students and tasks. Even in these cases, the adaptation will need to be designed to meet the specific needs of the student and the task being performed. However, in many other situations, an adaptation strategy will literally need to be invented in order for it to best match the individual difficulties that a person is having in performing a particular task (York & Rainforth, 1987). This requires that staff be familiar with the types of adaptation strategies and approaches that can be used and then to be creative in applying these to their students. A number of authors have identified categories or types of adaptation approaches that staff can use for this purpose (Orelove & Sobsey, 1987; York & Rainforth, 1987). In this section, six major types of task design and adaptation strategies are described, and examples for their vocational application are provided.

Strategy 1:   Redesign the Task
Sequence To Eliminate Difficult Steps

The first strategy that can be used to reduce the difficulty of a task involves redesigning it so that a step or aspect of the task that poses difficulty for the individual is no longer required for task completion (Orelove & Sobsey, 1987; York & Rainforth, 1987). In some cases, redesign may be done in such a way as to completely eliminate the difficult step, so that it is no longer performed by the worker with the disability, by any other worker at the site, or by the support trainer. In other cases, the redesign may result in the step being done by another person. This redesign strategy is at the basis of partial participation, which is a strategy that has been widely discussed in the special education literature

(Baumgart et al., 1982). This is a strategy aimed at students who may not be able to learn to perform an entire skill or task sequence independently but can perform part of the task. The remaining steps are then done by another person or adapted to eliminate the need for them to be done. This strategy has also been specifically addressed in the rehabilitation field under the rubric of job and task restructuring (McCray, 1987).

Eliminating Difficult Steps

Example A: Kelly's story provides an example of how a task can be made easier by designing it in such a way that the difficult step is completely eliminated. Kelly works at a deli, delivering and selling sandwiches to business persons who are unable to get away from their offices for lunch. He carries the sandwiches in a special box mounted on his wheelchair. While analyzing the job, the trainer found that the sandwiches were priced at $2.85, $2.95, $3.10, and $3.25; at these prices, Kelly would have to give his customers varying amounts of change, depending on how much money they gave him. Kelly did not know how to make change, and due to his physical disability handling coins was extremely difficult for him. These problems were explained to the owner of the deli, who agreed to price all of the sandwiches that Kelly sold at $3. Consequently, Kelly only has to determine how much change should be returned if a customer gives him a $5, $10, or $20 bill, and he does not have to handle coins.

Example B: John does photocopying for an insurance company. Before John was hired, the person who did the photocopying picked up the agents' photocopy orders from their desks. However, John was not able to maneuver his wheelchair through the small halls to reach their offices. Following discussion of this obstacle with the trainer, the agents agreed to bring their photocopy orders to a basket at the end of the hall where John could pick them up. This example demonstrates how a task can be redesigned so that a step that is difficult for a worker with a disability is now performed by other workers.

Strategy 2:   Alternative Response Strategies

If you ask several individuals who do not experience a disability to perform a simple task, one or two strategies for doing it typically emerge. For example, when asked to turn on a light in a room from a wall mounted switch, most individuals will use their index finger to flick the switch. Although there is usually a typical way that most people accomplish a simple task or movement, there are many variations that *can* be used to produce the same outcome. To illustrate this, the reader should try to think of as many different ways that she or he could turn on a wall light switch without using an index finger. Some alternative strategies include using the thumb, using the side of the hand, the elbow, the shoulder, or even the nose or chin. This exercise illustrates the old proverb that says there is more than one way to skin a cat. Students with disabilities may not be able to use the typical strategy that most people employ to accomplish a task or a step of a task. However, they may be able to do it via the use of alternative strategies (Wilcox & Bellamy, 1982).

Alternative Response Strategies

Example A: One of the steps involved in computer data entry is to put the disk into a disk sleeve after it has been removed from the disk drive. The typical strategy for accomplishing this step is to pick up the disk with one hand, the sleeve with the other, and insert the disk into the sleeve. Angela finds it difficult to get the disk inserted into the sleeve using the typical strategy, because she has very limited use of one hand. An alternative strategy was devised for her to use. First, she picks up the sleeve with her good hand and wedges it between her thighs. Next, she picks up the disk and inserts it into the sleeve. Finally, she removes the sleeve with the disk from between her legs and places it on the table.

Example B: Sue works at a company that has an employee cafeteria, where she likes to eat lunch. However, she has not learned money values. When the cashier tells her how much her lunch costs, she does not know how much money to give him. To get around this problem Sue's mother agreed to give her a $5 bill for her lunch each day (Sue never spends more than this on lunch). Sue simply gives the cashier the $5 bill. This strategy also eases her difficulty in getting money out of her wallet due to her limited hand use.

Environmental Rearrangement

Example A: The shelf on which the towels were stocked at the hair salon was too high for Tiffney to comfortably reach. There were several other shelves in the same area that were lower and were used to store items that Tiffney did not have to handle. The owner of the hair salon agreed to move the towels to one of the lower shelves and to move the materials on that shelf to the higher one. As a result, Tiffney was able to more easily and productively stock towels.

Example B: John, who uses a wheelchair, was being considered for employment by an insurance firm to perform a variety of clerical tasks, including updating client files on a microcomputer. Unfortunately, the microcomputer was located on the second floor of the office and there were no elevators. However, the owner of the company agreed to move the microcomputer to the first floor so that John could perform this task.

Strategy 3:   Environmental Rearrangement

The third strategy is to change the arrangement of equipment, furniture, walls, or other objects at the work site. In many cases, this strategy must be utilized to permit an individual to gain access to a business area. In other cases, rearranging the environment may be done to increase a student's task performance independence and productivity.

Strategy 4:   Equipment Positioning

One factor that can have a tremendous impact on the ease with which a person performs a movement is the position of the individual in relation to the equipment being used or the materials being manipulated (Inge & Snell, 1985; Rainforth & York, 1987; Trefler, Nickey, & Hobson, 1983). For example, slight

---

Equipment Positioning

Example A: Jeb works at a small parts manufacturing business. His task assignment is to package a particular part. After the worker next to him completes his work on a part, he places it in front of Jeb, who picks it up and places it in a box. During the first few days on the job, Jeb's trainer observed that Jeb usually had a very difficult time picking the part up. Occasionally, however, he could perform the step more easily. After carefully analyzing the situation, it became clear that the location of the part placed by the other worker appeared to affect how easily Jeb could pick it up. If the part was placed approximately 6 inches from the table edge, he could pick it up with some ease. On the one hand, if the part was placed closer than 6 inches, Jeb had to bend his elbow to get his hand down to it, which caused his hand to close into a fist before he could grasp the part. On the other hand, if the part was placed further than 6 inches from the table edge he had to extend his arm to reach it. When this occurred, Jeb's arm reflexively went into full extension, which caused him to reach beyond the part. Consequently, the trainer placed a mark on the table 6 inches from the edge, and Jeb's co-worker was instructed to place the part on the mark.

Example B: Tom was learning computer data entry. The copyholder was positioned on the table to the left of the computer. During the first few days of training, it became apparent that when Tom turned his head to look at the copyholder (to see what he was to enter into the computer), his left arm, which he uses to type, went into extension. As a result, it became extremely difficult for him to strike the keys on the keyboard. A physical therapist explained that this was caused by what is called Asymmetrical Tonic Neck Reflex—when he turns his head to the left, his left arm reflexively straightens, making it difficult to hit the keys on the keyboard. To eliminate this reflex and make it easier for him to enter the data, the copyholder was positioned on his right side, where he could turn his head without experiencing this reflex.

changes in the height at which a task is performed (in relationship to a person's body) can have a significant impact on how well a person with a motor disability is able to execute the movements required by that task. Some individuals may have better control if a task is located at mid-body, while a lower or higher work surface may enhance the motor response for other individuals. The degree to which the work surface should be lowered or raised varies greatly, depending on the student and the nature of the movement required. For example, it may be easier for a student to fold papers if the work surface is at chest level, whereas that same person may perform stapling most proficiently if the table surface is positioned at waist height.

The angle at which a person must move his or her arm can also affect the ease of movement execution. Many individuals with motor disabilities find it difficult to execute movements that require cross-body reaching. Consequently, task materials should be positioned in order to limit cross-body reaching. Furthermore, simply moving task materials a few inches to the left or right can greatly change the ease with which individuals can accomplish required movements.

The distance that task materials are positioned from a person's body can also affect motor performance. Reaching beyond a certain point can cause reflexive extension and decreased motor control in many individuals. Limitation in range of motion will also restrict how far some individuals can reach to perform a task.

The optimal position of task materials depends on the specific person and the particular movements that the person will perform. Determining the best positioning for a person involves having the individual perform the task at one position for several trials, assessing his or her performance, changing one aspect of the position (angle, height, distance), and reassessing the individual's performance. After trying numerous position variations, the optimal one can be selected.

Strategy 5: Environmental Cues

This strategy focuses on discrimination problems that an individual might encounter in performing a task. Specifically, if a student is unable to use the naturally existing cues provided by the work environment or task, additional cues can be added (Berg, Wacker, & Flynn, 1990). A picture prompt is one of the most common example of this strategy (Connis, 1979; Johnson & Cuvo, 1981; Sowers, Rusch, Connis, & Cummings, 1980; Sowers, Verdi, Bourbeau, & Sheehan, 1985; Wacker & Berg, 1984; Wacker, Berg, Berrie, & Swatta, 1985). Sowers et al. (1985) gave students with mental retardation photographs of task assignments, which they were trained to use to independently move from one task to another. Written, tactile (Berg & Wacker, 1989), and tape-recorded (Alberto, Sharpton, Briggs, & Stright, 1986) cues have also been used.

Environmental Cues

Example A: Linda was unable to discriminate which button on the photocopy machine should be pushed to start it. The trainer simply put a piece of colored tape on this button as a means to highlight for Linda that it was the button that started the machine.

Example B: David was learning to do a computer data entry task. To start up the computer, he had to perform 10 steps that involved inserting and removing multiple disks as well as inputting different codes. After several weeks of training, he still had a difficult time remembering to do each step in the order it should be done. Because David was able to read, the trainer provided him with a written step-by-step description of the start-up procedure. After completing each step, he would place a mark next to it in order to not lose his place.

Strategy 6:   Assistive Devices

The use of assistive devices is one of the most important strategies for increasing the ease of task performance for students (Barnes et al., 1979; Campbell, Green, & Carlson, 1977; York & Rainforth, 1987). There has been a tremendous growth in the number of commercially available assistive devices that have been designed to alleviate the difficulties that individuals with physical disabilities frequently encounter in performing tasks. In fact, new technology innovations come on the market with each passing day. Staff must attempt to become knowledgeable of and stay updated about these innovations. However, staff should be aware of the utility of other types of devices. Common office, hardware, and household supplies and equipment can often be used as adaptive devices for students with disabilities. In addition, staff frequently will need to design and construct devices to meet the unique needs of a particular student.

Commercially Available Assistive Devices   Persons with multiple and physical disabilities vary a tremendous amount in terms of the nature and degree of their disabilities. A device or adaptation that may be extremely useful for one person may not be usable by another person with a slightly different type or degree of disability. The amount of leg, arm, hand, and head control a person has as well as how proficiently she or he can see, hear, speak, and make discriminations can all affect the type of adaptive device that is most useful.

Unfortunately, commercial producers cannot tailor their devices for each and every person who possibly could benefit from them. In most cases, a device is designed to meet the needs of persons with a particular set of disability characteristics. For example, many computer assistive devices on the market are most appropriate for persons who use a wheelchair but have excellent use of their hands, no vision impairments, and extremely good cognitive abilities.

Commercial manufacturers also do not always make clear the types of skills that are needed to use a device effectively. For this reason, it is wise to avoid purchasing an assistive device until the user has an opportunity to try it out. Most companies will permit a short trial period before a device is purchased or will offer a short-term lease agreement. They typically require a refundable deposit before they send the device for trial use. If a company does not permit a trial period, every attempt should be made to borrow the device from someone who currently uses it, or at least to observe someone else using the

---

Commercially Available Assistive Devices

Example A: David is a 16-year-old student with mild mental retardation who also experiences very severe cerebral palsy. He has no use of his hands and arms and is pushed in a wheelchair. David is unable to speak, but he communicates by directing his eyes to letters on an alphabet board to spell words. The most viable job area for David, given the nature of his disabilities, appeared to be computer-related work. After talking with a number of persons with knowledge of computer applications for persons with disabilities, the staff at David's school discovered that there were two devices that would allow him to use a computer. These devices are the Adaptive Firmware Card and the PC-AID, which work with the Apple 2E and IBM compatible computers respectively. Briefly, both of these products allow computer access by activating one switch. When the devices are used, an alphabet or number array appears at the bottom of the computer screen. A cursor scans the letters or numbers. When the cursor appears on the letter or number that the operator wishes to enter, the switch is activated. There are a large variety of switches, including those that are activated by pushing, squeezing, blowing into, and licking. The type of switch purchased and where it is positioned is determined by the characteristics of the person who will be using it. In David's case, he can control his head better than any other part of his body. Consequently, a special head switch was purchased for him. By using an Adaptive Firmware Card and PC-AID, David has learned to perform computer data entry and word processing.

Example B: John was trained to answer telephones in the main office at his middle school and at a downtown business where he participated in a work experience. Because John has little functional use of his arms or hands, he was unable to lift up and hold the receiver. Two devices were purchased to assist him with these difficult steps. A gooseneck receiver-holder was positioned next to his head so that he could speak to and hear the caller. A second device, a spring-loaded bar, was positioned over the telephone receiver cradle. When the telephone rings, the bar is pushed up to engage the phone; to disengage or hang up the phone, the bar is pushed down. Both of these devices were purchased from Extensions for Independent Living. Similar devices are available from other companies, including Zygo Industries and TASH, Inc. See the Appendix to this chapter for addresses of some companies.

device. Some companies will provide names and telephone numbers of individuals who have purchased their device living in the vicinity of the interested party.

Commercially Available Assistive Devices that Are Generic in Design
Generic assistive devices, or those that are not specially made for persons with disabilities, can also be of great assistance in making tasks easier to perform for these individuals. A tour of an office supply store will illustrate the vast array of devices that have been designed to make clerically related tasks easier to perform. Hardware and restaurant-supply stores are also excellent sources of devices that may be useful for easing the difficulty of a task for individuals with and without disabilities.

Generic Assistive Devices

Example A: Even with eyeglasses, Phil had to strain to see the figures both on the hard copy and on the monitor when he did his computer data entry task. A visit to an office supply store revealed a product that many people with a problem similar to his use. This device is a magnifier in the form of a plastic strip, which attaches to a copyholder on a roller. The strip can be positioned directly over the lines that are being entered and then easily moved to the next lines as the person progresses down the page.

Example B: One of Tiffney's tasks at the hair salon is to refill hair solution containers. Tiffney was unable to unscrew the container lids due to the lack of movement and strength in her hands. There are several different types of devices available to assist individuals to open container lids. These devices are available at most hardware and kitchen supply stores. The one that seemed most useful for Tiffney was purchased, and the task became much easier for her to accomplish.

Constructed Assistive Devices   Although there are many specially designed or generic assistive devices that can be purchased, it is also possible to make them or have them made. Making a device that is similar to a commercially available one can frequently result in significant cost savings. In many cases, it is necessary to build a device because the one that is needed is not commercially available.

The amount of money and time required to design and build a device will of course depend on what is being constructed. In many cases, the cost and time involved can be significant. As York and Rainforth (1987) point out, most devices will need to be modified many times before they meet the needs of the student. It should be standard practice to create inexpensive prototypes of a device that can be field-tested and modified until the specifications that are desired are targeted. The final version of the device can then be built professionally using more expensive materials.

Constructed Devices

Example A: Due to Cindy's poor hand control, she was unable to insert or remove the disk from the disk drive. There are commercially available devices, called disk insertion guides, which can be purchased. This device is really no more than a platform with edges to "guide" the disk. The disk is placed on the platform and then pushed into the drive opening. Commercially available disk guides typically cost at least $50. Cindy's teacher showed a picture of the device to the school's shop teacher, who asked his students to build one. It took the students less than 2 hours in time and less than $5 in materials to make it.

Example B: In order for Kelly (mentioned in a previous example) to be able to deliver and sell sandwiches, he needed some way to carry the sandwiches on his electric wheelchair. The sandwich container needed to meet several important criteria, including that Kelly could easily get to the sandwiches, that it not interfere with his driving, and that it keep the sandwiches fresh and dry. There was obviously no such piece of equipment available commercially. However, Kelly's grandfather has a home workshop and likes to build devices for Kelly. He found an old metal ammunition box and fabricated a top that was easy for Kelly to open and that sealed the box from moisture when closed. He also placed metal prongs on each side of the box, which allows it to easily attach to Kelly's wheelchair in front of his legs. This position allows him to reach the sandwiches, but does not interfere with his driving.

TASK DESIGN: A PROCESS

The previous section illustrates that there are many task design adaptation and modification strategies that can be used to assist a student to perform a task more independently and productively. The challenge is to determine the strategy that is most effective for a particular student who is attempting to perform a specific task at a work site. In this section, a process that can be used for this purpose is described. This process is similar to ones that have been described by York and Rainforth (1987), Baumgart et al. (1982), and Nisbet et al. (1983). The phases and activities that are included in the process are illustrated in Figure 7.

Design Phases

There are three major phases involved in designing a task: Initial Design, Intensive Design, and Design Refinement. The Initial Design Phase occurs *before* an individual begins work at a job site, as part of the Job Creation process. The purpose of this phase is to attempt to make the tasks as "do-able" as possible for the individual when she or he first begins work.

The ability to make design changes will be limited until the individual

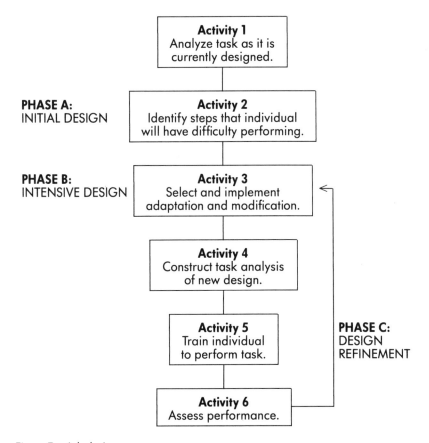

Figure 7.   Job design process.

actually has the opportunity to perform the tasks at the site. The Intensive Design Phase begins when this occurs. During this phase, the trainer will be able to observe and assess the individual's ability to perform the task as it is designed, and to identify the specific difficulties that she or he experiences.

As Figure 7 reflects, the design process is dynamic and ongoing. Design changes are made, training is provided, and assessment of these changes is conducted. The assessment then provides the basis for additional design changes and the process begins again. This feedback loop continues until it appears that the person can function as independently and productively as possible. Although most of the design changes typically occur during the Intensive Design Phase, ongoing refinements of the task design will often be required as the individual becomes progressively more familiar with and adept at the tasks, and as changes in the task and job site occur. This period, which may go on indefinitely, is called the Design Refinement Phase.

Design Activities

There are six activities that if utilized will result in task designs that optimally increase the participation, independence, and productivity of individuals with physical and multiple disabilities. The reader is again referred to Figure 7 for a picture of how these activities interrelate. A case study example illustrates how these activities can be applied in designing a task for a student. Beth experiences limited use of her hands and uses a wheelchair. A job has been created for her at the Acme Insurance Company, doing computer data entry. There are three main components to this task: 1) preparing to enter data, 2) entering data, and 3) computer close down. The first component, preparing to enter data is focused on for illustration purposes.

Activity 1:   Analyze how the task is performed as it is currently designed. The first activity in designing a task is to analyze how it is currently done by employees at a job site. As indicated earlier, this activity should occur during the job creation process and the initial design phase. The support trainer should observe one or more employees performing the task and list each of the steps performed in the order that they occur. The task of preparing to enter data will be used for illustration purposes. The four steps that make up this task are: 1) obtaining the disk from the disk holder, 2) removing the disk from its sleeve, 3) inserting the disk into the drive, and 4) pushing the switch to turn on the computer.

Activity 2:   Identify the steps of the task that the student may have difficulty performing.   When an employee is being observed performing the task as it is currently designed and each of its steps are listed, an attempt should also be made to identify those steps that the student may have difficulty performing. The Job Design Analysis Form (Figure 8), provides space to describe the specific physical and discrimination difficulties that a student may have in performing the steps of a task.

The ability of staff to accurately identify the types of difficulties that a particular student will encounter in learning and performing a task is greatly influenced by the amount and nature of their prior experience with the individual. If staff have previously trained an individual to perform a task very similar to the one under consideration, they will be able to identify most of the difficulties that the person is likely to encounter when performing the task at the new site. However, if staff have little prior experience in training the student, it will be possible for them to identify only the very most obvious difficulties that the person may have in performing the task. For example, even if the staff have no experience training Beth, it is obvious that she will have difficulty performing Step 1 for two reasons. The first difficulty is a physical one. The disk box is kept on a tall file cabinet and because she uses a wheelchair she will not be able to reach the box. The second difficulty is discriminative in nature. There are 20 different disks stored in the holder and they are coded in such a manner that Beth will have difficulty identifying the one that she is supposed to use. Staff would also know that Step 4, pushing the switch to turn on the computer, would

JOB DESIGN ANALYSIS FORM

Task <u>Preparing to enter data</u>   Staff   <u>Steve</u>

Site <u>Acme Insurance</u>   New Employee <u>Beth</u>

Step	Physical difficulties	Discrimination difficulties
Obtain disk from disk holder.	Holder located on high shelf. Beth cannot reach.	20 disks in holder. Coding of disks complicated. Beth will have difficulty identifying the one to use.
Remove disk from sleeve.		
Insert disk into drive.		
Push switch in back of computer to turn on.	Switch is located in back of machine. Beth will not be able to reach it.	

Figure 8.   Job design analysis form.

be difficult because the switch is located in the back and requires the worker to stand up and lean over the computer to reach it. Beth will not be able to do this from her wheelchair.

Activity 3:   Select the design modifications and adaptations that decrease the difficulty of each step.   Activity 3 involves the selection of the design strategy that will be used to decrease the difficulty of a step and thus will permit the individual to perform the task as independently and productively as possible. There are many factors that should be considered when selecting a design strategy. The following identifies and describes three of the most important factors:

1. *Effectiveness*   Obviously, the most important factor in selecting a strategy is the extent to which each possible strategy will be effective in decreasing the difficulty of the step for the student. During the Initial Design Phase, the amount of prior experience that staff have in working with an individual will affect their ability to predict how effective different strategies will be. Once the Intensive Design Phase begins, the effectiveness of a strategy can be determined by collecting data on the actual degree to which it increases the independence and productivity of the individual.

2. *Impact on Site*   When considering a job design alternative, the degree to which each possible strategy will impact the manner in which other employees perform their tasks, will affect the general operations of the site, or will change the physical structure of the work environment should be considered. The greater the potential impact on a site, the more likely that employer and co-worker resistance will be encountered. Obviously, if an employer is unwilling to permit a certain modification or adaptation to be made to the task or job site, it must be eliminated from consideration. The cooperation and goodwill of co-workers can be critical to the job success of an individual with a disability (Shafer, 1986; Sowers, Thompson, & Connis, 1979). A design change that requires the person's co-workers to perform their jobs in a very different way, or in their minds unduly inconveniences them, may serve to decrease the amount of cooperation that they will accord the individual. Acceptance and support of design changes will vary from co-worker to co-worker. Co-workers' acceptance of such changes can be greatly enhanced by discussing with them the problem and need for a solution prior to a final selection of a design strategy. In this way, the co-workers are provided with an opportunity to voice their concerns, make suggestions, and feel a part of the process. In addition, the greater the impact of a design change, the more attention it will call to the "special needs" of the person and thus potentially contribute to co-workers viewing him or her as "different." For all these reasons, an attempt should be made to use modifications and adaptations that have a minimum impact on the site.

3. *Cost*   Later in this chapter sources for funding modifications or adaptations are identified. However, the amount of financial support available from these sources is typically quite limited. Consequently, it is usually necessary to select the strategy that is the least expensive.

When selecting a design strategy, an attempt should be made to identify as many different strategies as possible that have a potential for decreasing the difficulty of a step. Staff should review the six major strategy categories and then try to think of specific strategies in each category that may decrease the difficulty of a step. They can then discuss their ideas with the three considerations in mind and identify the "best" one for the student, problem, and job site. Some design strategy ideas that might be generated to eliminate or decrease the difficulty that Beth would have in pushing the switch to turn on the computer are shown in Figure 9. Following discussion, the staff decided that the power cord strategy was the best. The strip could be placed on the floor where Beth could push the on/off switch with her foot. This strategy was effective, inexpensive, and acceptable to the employer and to Beth's co-workers.

Activity 4: Construct and revise the task analysis to reflect the new task design. During the first activity, a task analysis was constructed that identified the steps required to complete the task as it was originally designed. The implementation of design changes for the student with disabilities resulted in the modification of those steps. Consequently, it is important to revise the task analysis so that it reflects the new design. In fact, each time the task design is changed, the task analysis should also be revised to reflect the new design. The task analysis will serve as the basis for training and for assessing the effectiveness of the design and training strategies that are used. For the simple task design change used for making turning on the computer easier for Beth, Step 4 was rewritten: "Push switch on floor with foot."

Activity 5: Train the individual to perform the task. The implementation of a design strategy will usually not be sufficient to permit an individual to perform a task independently and productively. In most cases, the individual will still require task performance training (Maloney & Kurtz, 1982; Walmsey, Crichton, & Droog, 1981; York & Rainforth, 1987). If an assistive device is in use, the individual will also typically need instruction in how to operate it. For example, Beth never had used her foot to turn on a switch. She had to be taught to touch the switch with her toe gently and then to pull her foot away, so as not to inadvertently turn the computer off.

Activity 6. Assess the extent to which the implemented strategies are effective. The sixth activity is crucial in the job design process. This activity involves collecting task performance information to determine the extent to which a design modification or adaptation, in conjunction with training, is effective in increasing the individual's independence and productivity.

This information will provide the basis for further refining the adaptation being used or to determine the need to try another one. For example, after Beth attempted to use the powerstrip on the floor for several days, it was clear that she had a great deal of difficulty activating it. In part, this was because other staff using the computer would frequently push the power cord out of her reach, but she also had less strength and control of her foot than originally anticipated. Consequently, the decision was made to tape the switch to the leg of the table, so that she could reach it with her hand.

DESIGN STRATEGY IDEAS

Task _Preparing to enter data_   Worker _Beth_

Difficult step _Push switch to_   Site   _Acme Insurance_
turn on computer

Strategy type	Specific design strategy ideas
Eliminate step	Have someone else turn on computer for her.
Alternative response strategy	
Rearranging environment	Have table on which computer is placed pulled away from wall so Beth could move her chair behind it and turn it on.
Repositioning equipment	
Environmental cues	
Assistive devices— special	Buy & install switch that fits on side of computer—available at all computer stores.
Assistive devices— generic	Buy a power cord—plug into computer & place on the floor.
Assistive devices— constructed	

Figure 9.   Design strategy ideas.

CONSIDERATIONS WHEN USING ADAPTATIONS

Adaptations can be an invaluable tool for increasing the vocational competence of students with physical and multiple disabilities. However, several authors have pointed out that assistive devices can be overused (Baumgart et al., 1982; Davis, 1981; York & Rainforth, 1987). Providing a student with an assistive device may decrease his or her opportunity to learn the discriminations or movements that are required to perform the step without the adaptation. As Chapter 5 stressed, students can frequently learn difficult discriminations and movements if provided with systematic instruction. In general, students should always be given the chance to learn to perform a task without an adaptation before one is introduced. Of course, there will be situations when it is clear that the student will not be able to perform the task, regardless of how much instruction is provided, unless an adaptation is used. For example, a student who has no functional hand use should not be expected to learn to input information into a computer without some type of adaptation, such as a switch system.

INFORMATION SOURCES FOR
ADAPTATIONS AND MODIFICATIONS

In the previous sections, design strategies have been described and a process for designing tasks has been proposed. The extent to which staff can apply this information will depend on their knowledge of specific design options or at least their awareness of resources for gaining such knowledge. A description of the major types of resources that can be used to identify design options will be presented in this section. In addition, a list of specific resources is provided in the Appendix.

Commercial Catalogues

Large companies that specialize in the sale of equipment for persons with disabilities distribute product catalogues that describe each of their products. These catalogues can be obtained by calling the companies. Information regarding the availability and cost of commercial products, as well as ideas for constructing similar ones by hand, can be obtained through a review of these catalogues.

In most cases, several companies will offer similar devices. The products, however, may differ in their specific characteristics and prices. As when buying any product, it is important to compare prices and features of similar devices offered by different companies, in order to obtain the one that best suits the needs of the person who will be using it.

Directories

A number of organizations and projects have compiled lists and descriptions of adaptation products and ideas. Some of these are generic adaptation guides, while others focus specifically on those that have vocational applications. In most cases, these directories emphasize assistive devices as opposed to other types of design strategies.

Local Medical Supply Store

Most medium-size communities have several stores that specialize in selling medical equipment and supplies for persons with disabilities. The range of products that are carried varies greatly from store to store. Many stores only carry mobility equipment (wheelchairs, walkers) and such things as beds, lifts, and toilet seats. Others offer a wider array of equipment and devices. The equipment on display in a local store is only a small portion of what these companies can supply. The device being sought should be described to a salesperson, who can order it from a manufacturer. Sales persons should also be able to describe any variations in devices, design, and price across manufacturers.

Organizational Information Services

A number of organizations involved with persons with disabilities assist in the identification of adaptations. One of the most useful services is called ABLE-DATA, which is conducted under the auspices of the National Rehabilitation Information Center. The address of this organization as well as other information services can be found in the Appendix.

Therapists (Physical and Occupational) and Specialists (Speech, Vision, and Hearing)

School programs typically have physical and occupational therapists as well as speech, vision, and hearing specialists on staff and available for assistance. Without doubt, they can be a great source of information and assistance in identifying, selecting, designing, and constructing adaptations. However, most therapists have little understanding of vocational training and employment issues. To benefit from their expertise, it is important that these therapists and specialists receive training related to these issues, and are actively involved in the vocational preparation of students.

Rehabilitation Engineers

Rehabilitation engineers are trained to design and build adaptations for persons with disabilities. Obviously, these professionals have a great deal of expertise in this area and can be of tremendous assistance. However, most school and adult service programs cannot afford to have a rehabilitation engineer on staff. Nonetheless, programs should identify a person or persons who could be consulted when necessary. Again, hospitals are good resources.

Carpenters, Electricians, and Handypersons

Individuals who have building and electronic experience can be of great assistance in getting ideas for, designing, and constructing devices. Friends or relatives of the person with the disability as well as those of staff who have such skills should be recruited for their help. In addition, a brief presentation to a fraternal or service organization may create a pool of persons willing to assist in constructing devices.

LAWS AND REGULATIONS

In order to be able to utilize job and task adaptations for a student to gain access to employment and increase his or her independence and productivity, employers must be willing to permit adaptations to be made. There are three major laws that relate to job site adaptations. The Architectural Barrier Act of 1968 was passed to increase access to publicly funded facilities. The Architectural and Transportation Barrier Compliance Board (ATBCB) sets standards and oversees their compliance. The standards adopted are those published by the American National Standards Institute (ANSI, 1986).

The focus of the Architectural Barrier Act is not on employment, but rather on general public access. Accessibility requirements as they relate specifically to employment are covered under the reasonable accommodation regulations that are contained in Sections 503 and 504 of the Rehabilitation Act of 1973. These two sections require that employers who receive federal assistance or those who have contracts with the federal government make "reasonable accommodations" that will enable persons with disabilities to be employed at their companies. Reasonable accommodation includes job restructuring, making the site accessible, and task adaptations including equipment and devices (McCray, 1987).

Sections 503 and new 504 of the Rehabilitation Act of 1973 did not cover private employers. The Americans with Disabilities Act of 1990 extends the reasonable accommodation protections to private businesses that have more than 15 employees.

CONCLUSION

The successful use of design strategies requires practice, ingenuity, and above all adherence to a belief that physical and cognitive challenges do not inherently limit vocational success. Utilizing such an approach does not emphasize deciding whether a student with a disability can or cannot perform a task. Rather, the focus shifts to systematically identifying strategies that can be used to enable him or her to do so as independently and productively as possible.

REFERENCES

American National Standards Institute specifications for making buildings accessible to, and usable by, physically handicapped people. (1986). New York: American National Standards Institute.

Alberto, P. A., Sharpton, W. R., Briggs, A., & Stright, M. H. (1986). Facilitating task acquisition through the use of a self-operated auditory prompt system. *Journal of The Association for Persons with Severe Handicaps, 11,* 85–91.

Barnes, K., Murphy, M., Waldo, L., & Sailor, W. (1979). Adaptive equipment for the severely, multiply handicapped child. In R. York & E. Edgar (Eds.), *Teaching the severely handicapped* (Vol. IV) (pp. 108–152). Seattle: American Association for the Education of the Severely/Profoundly Handicapped.

Baumgart, D., Brown, L., Pumpian, I., Nisbet, J., Ford, A., Sweet, M., Messina, R., & Schoeder, J. (1982). Principle of partial participation and individualized adaptations in educational programs for severely handicapped students. *Journal of The Association for the Severely Handicapped, 7*(2), 17–27.

Berg, W., & Wacker, D. (1989). Evaluation of tactile prompts with a student who is deaf, blind, and mentally retarded. *Journal of Applied Behavior Analysis, 22,* 93–99.

Berg, W., Wacker, D. P., & Flynn, T. H. (1990). Teaching generalization and maintenance of work behavior. In F. R. Rusch (Ed.), *Supported employment: Models, methods and issues* (pp. 145–160). Sycamore, IL: Sycamore Publishing Co.

Campbell, P., Green, C., & Carlson, L. (1977). Approximating the norm through environmental child-centered prosthetics and adaptive equipment. In E. Sontag, J. Smith, & N. Certo (Eds.), *Educational programming for the severely/profoundly handicapped* (pp. 300–319). Reston, VA: Council for Exceptional Children, Division on Mental Retardation.

Connis, R. (1979). The effects of sequential pictorial cues, self-recording, and praise on the job task sequencing of retarded adults. *Journal of Applied Behavior Analysis, 12,* 355–361.

Davis, W. M. (1981). *Aids to make you able: Self-help devices for the disabled.* New York: Beaufort Books.

Everson, J., Callahan, M., Hollahan, J., Gradel, C., Cohen, R., Button, C., Franklin, K., & Brady, F. (1990). *Getting the job done: Supported employment for persons with severe physical disabilities.* Washington, DC: United Cerebral Palsy Association.

Inge, K. J., & Snell, M. E. (1985). Teaching positioning and handling techniques to public school personnel through in-service training. *Journal of The Association for Persons with Severe Handicaps, 10*(2), 105–110.

Johnson, B., & Cuvo, A. (1981). Teaching mentally retarded adults to cook. *Behavior Modification, 5,* 187–202.

Maloney, F., & Kurtz, P. (1982). The use of a mercury switch head control device in profoundly retarded, multiply handicapped children. *Physical and Occupational Therapy in Pediatrics, 2*(4), 11–17.

McCray, P. M. (1987). *The job accommodation handbook.* Verndale, MN: RPM Press, Inc.

Nisbet, J., Sweet, M., Ford, A., Shiraga, B., Udvari, A., York, J., Messina, R., & Schroeder, J. (1983). Utilizing adaptive devices with severely handicapped students. In L. Brown, A. Ford, J. Nisbet, M. Sweet, B. Shiraga, J. York, R. Loomis, & P. VanDeventer (Eds.), *Educational programs for severely handicapped students* (Vol. 13, pp. 101–146). Madison, WI: Madison Metropolitan School District.

Orelove, F. P., & Sobsey, D. (1987). Curriculum and instructional programming. In F. P. Orelove & D. Sobsey, *Educating children with multiple disabilities: A transdisciplinary approach.* Baltimore: Paul H. Brookes Publishing Co.

Rainforth, B., & York, J. (1987). Handling and positioning. In F. P. Orelove & D. Sobsey, *Educating children with multiple disabilities: A transdisciplinary approach.* Baltimore: Paul H. Brookes Publishing Co.

Shafer, M. S. (1986). Utilizing co-workers as change agents. In F. R. Rusch (Ed.), *Competitive employment issues and strategies* (pp. 215–224). Baltimore: Paul H. Brookes Publishing Co.

Sowers, J., & Powers, L. (1989). Preparing students with cerebral palsy and mental retardation for the transition from school to community-based employment. *Career Development for Exceptional Individuals, 12*(1), 25–35.

Sowers, J., Rusch, F. R., Connis, R. T., & Cummings, L. E. (1980). Teaching mentally retarded adults to time-manage in a vocational setting. *Journal of Applied Behavior Analysis, 13*(4), 119–128.

Sowers, J., Thompson, L., & Connis, R. (1979). The food service vocational training program. In G. T. Bellamy, G. O. O'Connor, & O. C. Karan (Eds.), *Vocational rehabilitation of severely handicapped persons: Contemporary service strategies* (pp. 181–206). Baltimore: University Park Press.

Sowers, J., Verdi, M., Bourbeau, P., & Sheenan, M. (1985). Teaching job independence and flexibility to mentally retarded students through the use of a self-control package. *Journal of Applied Behavior Analysis, 18*(1), 81–85.

Trefler, E., Nickey, J., & Hobson, D. (1983). Technology in the education of multiply handicapped children. *American Journal of Occupational Therapy, 37*(6), 381–387.

Wacker, D., & Berg, W. (1984). Training adolescents with severe handicaps to set up job tasks independently using picture prompts. *Analysis and Intervention in Developmental Disabilities, 4,* 353–365.

Wacker, D., Berg, W., Berrie, P., & Swatta, P. (1985). Generalization and maintenance of complex skills by severely handicapped adolescents following picture prompt training. *Journal of Applied Behavior Analysis, 18,* 329–336.

Walmsey, R., Crichton, T., & Droog, D. (1981). Music as feedback for teaching head control to severely handicapped children: A pilot study. *Developmental Medicine and Child Neurology, 23,* 739–746.

Wehman, P., Wood, W., Everson, J., Goodwyn, R., & Conley, S. (1988). *Vocational education for multihandicapped youth with cerebral palsy.* Baltimore: Paul H. Brookes Publishing Co.

Wilcox, B., & Bellamy, G. T. (1982). *Design of high school programs for severely handicapped students.* Baltimore: Paul H. Brookes Publishing Co.

York, J., & Rainforth, B. (1987). Developing instructional adaptations. In F. P. Orelove & D. Sobsey, *Educating children with multiple disabilities: A transdisciplinary approach* (pp. 183–217). Baltimore: Paul H. Brookes Publishing Co.

Appendix

The following are specific names and addresses of resources for design adaptations, modifications, and devices.

ABLEDATA
National Rehabilitation Information
  Center
4407 Eighth Street, NE
Washington, DC 20017
Voice (202) 635-6090
TDD (202) 635-5884
(*Computerized databank of over 8,000
  commercially available devices.*)

Accent on Living
P.O. Box 700
Bloomington, IL 61702
(*Publication focuses on adaptations for
  persons with disabilities*)

**American National Standard
  Specifications for Making Buildings
  and Facilities Accessible and Usable
  by The Physically Handicapped
  (1980)**
American National Standards Institute
1430 Broadway
New York, NY 10018
(*Accessibility standards described in
  Section 50 of Rehabilitation Act and
  basis for most local and state
  accessibility codes.*)

Closing the Gap
P.O. Box 68
Henderson, MN 56044
(*A newsletter specializing in computer-
  related devices for persons with
  disabilities.*)

Computer-Disability News
c/o The National Easter Seal Society
2023 West Ogden Avenue
Chicago, IL 60612
(*A newsletter specializing in computer-
  related devices for persons with
  disabilities*)

Job Accommodations Network
Box 468
Morgantown, WV 26505
(*Provides assistance to employers in
  developing accommodations*)

Modified Equipment Catalog (1980)
Wisconsin Vocational Studies Center
University of Wisconsin-Madison
Madison, WI 53706
(*A catalogue that describes commercial
  and constructed devices for use in
  employment*)

RESNA
Suite 700
1101 Connecticut Avenue, NW
Washington, DC 20236
(*This is an organization that specializes
  in rehabilitation technology issues*)

**United Cerebral Palsy Associations
  (UCPA)**
Community Service Division
1522 "K" Street, NW
Suite 1112
Washington, DC
(*UCPA has several publications related
  to technology and employment issues*)

KELLY

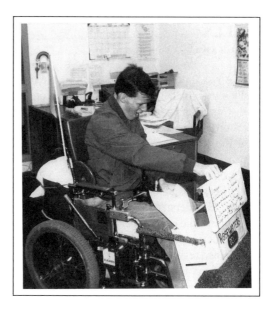

Kelly is 21 years of age and has just completed school. He uses a power wheelchair for mobility, has limited functional use of his hands, some visual deficits, and speaks but is difficult to understand.

Through his work experience program, Kelly had the opportunity to learn a variety of tasks, including stapling, postage metering, and photocopying at community sites. An attempt was made to train Kelly computer data entry. However, his poor motor control combined with visual deficits made this a difficult task for him to perform. He also learned to deliver telephone messages to employees' offices for receptionists. He liked this task a great deal because he enjoyed moving around and because it gave him the maximum opportunity to interact with people. His work-related skills included staying on task and wheelchair driving (not bumping into walls and people), as well as several bathroom-use skills.

A paid job was created for Kelly as a sandwich delivery person for a deli. The deli did not have a delivery service, but when approached with the idea of creating a job for Kelly, the owners indicated that they had talked about having such a service but had not had the time to get it together. This delivery job was created for Kelly when he still had several years of school left. He worked the job 2–3 hours each school day for almost 2 years, and then had to leave for a period to have surgery. He returned to the job during his last year of school and remains on it today. He now works about 4 hours daily and earns 50% of the minimum wage.

KELLY
(continued)

A box for carrying sandwiches on the front of his chair was built by Kelly's grandfather. The box was fabricated from an old ammunition box. Customers complete an order form, which they hand to Kelly. He takes orders to the deli, which makes and places the sandwiches in the box. Kelly then returns to the businesses with the sandwiches. Kelly cannot make change and has particular difficulty handling coins. To avoid this problem, the deli agreed to charge $3.00 for all sandwiches, rather than prices like $2.85 and $3.15. The customers on his route gradually learned to understand his speech with the help of the job coach.

One of the hardest parts of Kelly's job is getting into the doors of all the businesses to which he delivers. Over a period of several months he was trained regarding the best way to approach and position his chair next to each door as well as the movements required to open each door. He cannot open some doors so he uses different strategies to enter them. At some he has been taught to knock, at others to wave through the window to get an employee's attention, and at others to wait for someone else to go in or out of the door.

A trainer remained with Kelly for 6 months before he was able to perform the job independently. Follow-up checks are still made on a daily basis. The primary focus of these checks is to ensure his use of safe street-crossing procedures.

Placing
Students into
7 Paying Jobs

This book has focused on strategies that can be utilized by school programs to prepare students with physical and multiple disabilities for community-based employment. The most valid measure of the success of this preparation is whether students are employed when they depart from school. Traditionally, when a student reaches the point of transition, school programs have viewed their role as simply one of referral to an adult program. Using this approach, students have too often experienced a gap in services, remaining at home for several months while a job is being sought. In the worst of cases, the student receives no services or is placed in a sheltered program (McDonnell, Wilcox, & Boles, 1988; Wehman, Moon, Everson, Wood, & Barcus, 1988; Will, 1986). This remains the status quo for students with the most significant disabilities, including those who experience physical and multiple disabilities. To ensure that these students make the successful transition from school to community-based employment, schools must take an active, and possibly the lead, role in placing them into paid jobs and arranging for the supports that they will need to remain employed.

As indicated in Chapter 1, there are four major supported employment approaches that are used to provide persons who experience disabilities with the opportunity to work in community settings: individual placement (job coach), crews, enclaves, and small businesses (Bellamy, Rhodes, Mank, & Albin, 1988; Rusch & Hughes, 1990). The individual placement model, which offers the greatest opportunity for normalized and integrated employment has been used to a greater extent than any of the other models (Wehman, Kregel, & Shafer, 1990). However, the vast majority of those who have been individually placed and coached experience mild and moderate mental retardation. The components of the job coach model include: 1) An existing position that is opened in a company is identified, its performance requirements analyzed, and a person whose skills and abilities "match" these requirements is selected for placement. 2) The person is hired at the same wage, and thus is expected to be as productive as any worker filling the same position. 3) The person is expected to achieve independence after a few weeks of training by a job coach, and then to continue to work independently with routine but only periodic follow-up visits. It is not surprising that persons with physical and multiple disabilities have not been deemed capable of individual placement, when the current approach is viewed as "the model" to achieve this outcome. The skills and abilities of many persons with physical and multiple disabilities do not match existing jobs as they are currently structured. They also may not be able to approximate the productivity rates of employees without disabilities, and they may require longer periods of training and more intensive support than is provided through the existing job coach approach. However, the failure of these persons to achieve individual job placements should not be attributed to them, but rather to the inadequacy of the current approaches. In this chapter, alternative approaches and strategies that can be used to place these students into nongroup employment situations are described.

Many of the strategies discussed in previous chapters related to preparation are also ones that will be critical when placing students into paid jobs. These include job design and training strategies as well as strategies to overcome work-related challenges and to involve parents. The discussion in this chapter focuses on strategies that can be used to create employment situations for students with physical and multiple disabilities. Specifically, alternative job development, wage, and support strategies will be addressed. In addition, a description of the activities involved in the process of establishing individual employment situations for students who are nearing departure from school is provided. This process emphasizes the need for careful planning and collaboration between the schools, adult service agencies, and family.

JOB DEVELOPMENT STRATEGIES

Most job positions as structured by companies include a variety of different tasks. For example, a typical clerical position duty list might include typing, word processing, answering the telephone, photocopying, and filing. A particular student with physical and multiple disabilities may be able to perform some but not all of these tasks. Using the existing placement approach, this student could be not be considered for this position. In fact, it may be difficult to find any position as it is currently structured that a student with physical and multiple disabilities could perform. In this section, four alternative job development strategies are described that can be used for these students.

Restructuring an Existing Position

Job restructuring involves working with an employer to restructure and reassign job duties in such a way that a person with a disability could fill an opening at a company (McCray, 1987). Job restructuring would be utilized if an employee with a disability could perform most, but not all, of the tasks which comprise a job. The tasks the person could not perform would be assigned to other employees, while the employee with the disability would be responsible for performing a greater quantity of the work that he or she could do. For example, a moderate sized law firm employs several clerical staff and has a position opening. Each staff person is assigned primary responsibility for one or two of the attorneys, but they assist other lawyers as time permits and with general office assignments. As currently structured, all of the staff do word processing, photocopy, run errands (mostly delivering and retrieving documents at other law firms and the courthouse), and file and answer telephones. Jane can perform all of these tasks except telephone answering (she cannot speak) or errand running (she uses crutches and cannot travel long distances). It was clear that she would not be able to fill the position as it was structured. However, the school asked the firm to consider restructuring task assignment duties to enable Jane to fill the position. The restructuring involved assigning Jane major responsibility for all of the photocopying. In addition, she would also do word processing and filing as time permitted. The other staff used their time freed from photocopying to take responsiblity for running errands and answering telephones. They also continued to do word processing and filing.

Employers are willing to restructure positions if doing so does not negatively affect the efficiency of the business and other employees. In many cases, job restructuring that is implemented for a person with a disability can result in the increased efficiency of a company's operations in general. It is critical when considering job restructuring that the other employees are involved in planning task reassignment and are supportive of the changes that are proposed. An employer or supervisor may mandate that an employee no longer perform a preferred task or that the employee takes on less preferred job duties; however, this will not enhance the extent to which the new employee is accepted by his or her colleagues.

Creating a New Job from Existing Tasks

Job restructuring is primarily used to permit a person to fill an existing position at a company. Another placement strategy that can be used involves working with a company to actually create a new position that a student can fill. For example, the law firm described above may not have a position opening. However, they may realize that their existing staff have a difficult time getting all of the firm's work done. In particular, the clerical staff may find that the photocopying often does not get done because they must devote the majority of their time to word processing. They also often have to use an outside delivery service to take documents to the courthouse and other law firms because the staff cannot get away from the office. Given this scenario, the law firm may be very receptive to creating and adding a position in the company that is devoted to photocopying and running errands, for a student who is adept at these tasks.

Companies are particularly eager to create new positions for persons who will assist staff to complete routine tasks that may not require a high level of expertise but are essential to the function of the company. Until approached to create a special position from these tasks, companies often think that their only option is to hire another person into an existing job position. However, they may not be able to afford to do so. For example, the law firm pays their secretaries $9 per hour. This wage is paid primarily for the typing and word processing skills that these persons possess, although they also do other auxiliary tasks (e.g., photocopying, errand running). However, if a person was hired to perform these less skilled clerical tasks such as photocopying and errand running, the company appropriately could offer a lower wage (e.g., $5 per hour), which it may be able to afford.

In some cases, the amount of work available at one company is not sufficient to create a job with the number of hours that a student would like to be employed. Rather than turning these opportunities down, the possibility of arranging for the student to work at more than one site should be considered. For example, a student might work in the morning for a couple of hours at one company, and then in the afternoon at another company for a couple of hours. Although there are some obvious difficulties that may be encountered with this arrangement, there are also some benefits. In particular, working at two companies provides the student with the opportunity to get to know and interact with the employees at both companies. Also, if one job is lost, the student will still have the other while another is being sought.

Creating a New Job from New Tasks

Most employers want to offer their customers or clients new or improved service. However, they may not have the time or expertise to do what is needed to offer this service. In addition, if equipment is needed for the service, the company may not have the capital to purchase it.   For example, a dentist would like to computerize the office's patient record and billing system. However, neither the dentist nor the receptionist has any experience with computers and they do not have the time to learn about them. Also, because she has only been practicing for a few years, the dentist needs to spend what money is available on dentistry equipment rather than a computer. A program could use this situation to create a job for a student by offering staff time and expertise to set up the computer system if the dentist agrees to hire a student to operate or assist in operating it. The vocational rehabilitation agency may also be willing to purchase a computer for the student to use at the job site.

ALTERNATIVE WAGE STRATEGIES

Persons with disabilities, like all persons, should have the opportunity to work at jobs that will allow them to earn as high a wage as possible. One primary impetus for the supported employment movement was the poor wages earned by individuals in work activity centers and sheltered workshops. Data from supported employment programs substantiates that they have been able to assist individuals to earn higher wages compared to sheltered programs (Ellis, Rusch, Tu, & McCaughrin, 1990; Vogelsburg, 1990).

Programs should make every effort to find and create jobs for students with physical and multiple disabilities that will permit them to earn the same wage that other employees performing the same tasks at a company receive. However, many of these students will not be able to work at competitive rates, and most employers are not willing to hire and pay a competitive wage to a person who cannot approximate the amount of work produced by their other employees.

The Fair Labor Standards Act (FLSA) permits employers to pay less than the statutory minimum wage to a person who experiences a disability, if the disability contributes to the individual being less productive than a nondisabled employee performing the same job. To pay a person with a disability less than the minimum wage, a company must apply for and receive a special worker's certificate from the Department of Labor. With this certificate, the person's wage is based on his or her productivity in comparison to other employees at the same company performing the same tasks. For example, if the wage for a job is $5 per hour and the student produces 50 percent of the amount of work completed by other employees, the student's hourly wage would be $2.50. The clear intent of the FLSA is to decrease the economic disincentive to employers in hiring persons with disabilities. Until recently, the subminimum wage regulations pertaining to persons with disabilities were typically used only by sheltered workshops and work activity centers, because the FLSA provisions were fairly restrictive and cumbersome for use by regular businesses. Changes in the FLSA have eliminated may of these obstacles.

Using the alternative job development and job creation strategies discussed in the previous section can create some challenging wage determination issues. The example used earlier was the company that created a job for a student to assist with photocopying and errand running. These were tasks that the secretaries who are paid $9 per hour did before the new job was created. Should the student's base wage be $9 an hour (since the secretaries got paid this amount when they were doing these tasks) or should it be lower since she or he will not do the higher skilled tasks done by the secretaries? And if the wage should be lower, how do you go about determining what it is? There are no clearly established regulations for answering these questions. In general, it is the primary task responsibilities and assignments that should serve as the basis for determining the wage of a person. Although the secretaries photocopied, they spent the majority of their time performing other tasks (e.g., word processing), and thus their wage should be based primarily on these tasks and the skill level required by them.

The program that places the student, whether it is an adult service or school program, should assist the employer to obtain a subminimum wage certificate and to comply with the requirements of the regulations pertaining to the receipt and maintenance of the certificate. Specifically, the program should 1) determine the productivity standards for all tasks performed, 2) determine the employee's productivity, 3) reassess the employee's productivity on a routine basis, and 4) maintain records of all productivity assessment information collected.

SUPPORT STRATEGIES

The current models of supported employment reflect a belief that is still prevalent in human services, that the primary source of assistance and support for persons with disabilities must come from programs and specialized service providers. However, there has begun to be the realization in the field of disability services of the need to look to more natural providers of support (McKnight, 1987; O'Connell, 1988). This approach shifts the focus of support from disability agencies and staff to families, friends, and "regular" community people. Strategies and models that take advantage of nonspecialized sources of employment assistance and support have also begun to be explored (Moon, Inge, Wehman, Brooke, & Barcus, 1990; Nisbet & Hagner, 1988; Shafer, 1986). Nisbet and Hagner (1988) have written the seminal article advocating for the use of natural job support strategies. They identified four examples of alternative models of job support: mentoring, training consultant, job sharing, and attendant. Using the mentor option, a program job coach provides the initial job training. After the employee has learned the tasks and work-related behaviors required at the site, a co-worker would provide any ongoing support and assistance that the employee might need. Nisbet and Hagner (1988) suggest that the mentoring approach is most feasible for employees who do not require intensive, daily support. Another approach that works well for a person with minimal support needs is the training consultant option. Using this approach, an existing co-worker at a company provides the initial training as well as the ongoing support of the person. The program role in this approach is to provide initial instruction to the co-worker about how to assist and support the employee, and to consult with the co-worker related to any issues or difficulties that may arise. In both the mentor and training consultant approaches the provider agency might pay the company a service fee (stipend) for the time and effort that the co-worker devoted to the employee with the disability.

An approach that may be needed for a person with high support needs is the job sharing option. With this approach, an employer would agree to hire two individuals for one position, one with a disability and one without a disability. The co-worker would then provide ongoing assistance to the employee with the disability. Nisbet and Hagner suggest that the worker with the disability could be paid based on his or her productivity, while the co-worker is paid the remaining amount of the wage as well as additional monies from the program for the assistance provided. This approach is similiar to the support co-worker model described in Chapter 1, which has been used by these authors, with one major difference (Sowers, 1989). In our current implementation of this approach, a contract for services is made between the company and the program, and the two co-workers are employees of and paid by the program. The person with the disability is paid based on his or her productivity or half of the site-contract dollars (whichever is more). The worker without the disability is paid from the remaining contract dollars, as well as from program fee-for-service monies. In large part, this approach has been utilized because the concept of having two persons (one with very significant disabilities) to perform a job is extremely novel to employers, and they appear to be more willing to try it using a contract arrangement rather than to actually hire the two co-workers. However, a practical consideration has also forced this approach. If the base wage for a job is $5 per hour, then the co-worker with the disability who is 25% productive would earn $1.25 per hour, leaving only $3.75 for the company to pay the person without the disability. However, a person who does have a disability cannot be paid less than the minimum wage. This problem could be overcome if the program gave a portion of the fee-for-service dollars to the employer, who would use it to pay the person without a disability a higher wage. An alternative strategy that could be used to get around this problem is to use a Plan for Achieving Self Support (PASS), or an Impairment-Related Work Experience (IRWE). Using this strategy, the company could hire only the person with the disability, who would receive the entire wage although she or he might be 20% productive.The person with the disability would then hire a person without a disability to assist in completing the work (as well as assisting with personal needs). The person could then deduct this expense when calculating his or her monthly Social Security Income (SSI).The fourth support strategy, the attendant option, is primarily used by a person who requires assistance for personal care purposes, but not for actual job performance support. Again, the person could hire and pay the attendant using a PASS or IRWE.

PLANNING FOR AND
DEVELOPING EMPLOYMENT SITUATIONS

As suggested, the school program should take the responsibility for placing students into paid employment before they graduate or before their eligibility for school services is complete. Careful planning and collaboration is critical regardless of the student and the employment approach utilized. However, for a student who can be placed using the existing job coach model, this planning can be done in a relatively straightforward fashion. The school would place the student into a job and train the student until independent. When the student nears school departure, an adult service program would be identified that could provide the minimal amount of ongoing follow-up required. For students who may require high levels of support and for whom alternative job development, wage, and support strategies will need to be utilized, this planning process can be particularly complex. It requires analyzing the amounts and types of support that will be needed, determining the supports that are available now and in the future through the school and adult service agencies, identifying and determining the feasibility of other support options, and finally putting all of this information together to map out a plan for the employment support that will guide job development for the student. In this section, a description of the activities that can be used to guide the process for planning for and placing a student who may have high support needs into individual jobs will be provided.

Activity 1:   Obtain and Summarize Information About the Student

The first activity in creating a job is to gain a detailed and comprehensive description of the skills, support needs, and work preferences of the student for whom the job is being created. Using this information, an attempt should be made to identify strategies that can be used to decrease the amount of ongoing support that the student will require from the program. These strategies will include identifying the following: 1) types of tasks from which a job will be created (those the student can do most independently and productively), 2) the number of hours that the student will work and the optimal scheduling of those hours (which may determine whether a parent can assist with transportation), 3) work sites that meet the accessibility needs of the student, 4) the optimal location of the site (to insure that there is an accessible bus close to the site and that the student can get to work with the least amount of help), 5) strategies to avoid the need for a student to perform a high-support behavior (e.g., if the student needs help eating, he or she might be able to bring a high-protein drink to work and, thus, not have to eat there), 6) supports that the student's family might be able to provide (e.g., with the student's grooming and dress), and 7) supports that it might be feasible for a co-worker to provide (e.g., opening the door to the entrance). The Student Job Creation and Support Assessment Package (Appendix A) provides a format for collecting and summarizing this information. The assessment should be coordinated by one staff person, who obtains information from other staff members (teachers, vocational trainers) who have been involved with the student during his or her school career. A meeting should be held with the family to discuss and identify ways in which they can provide specific assistance to the student when he or she is placed on a job and indicate their preferences related to the job that is created. Of course, the preferences of the student should also be obtained.

As suggested, the purpose of the assessment is to attempt to identify the supports that a student may need on a job and to identify the strategies that may decrease the supports that a program would have to provide. The results of the assessment can also be used as a guide by the staff person, who will attempt to create a job for the student. Finally, the results of the assessment should permit staff to determine the overall amount of employment support that a program will need to provide to a student, and thus plan for how this support will be provided given the available funding levels and resources.

The forms shown in Appendix I have been completed for a student (Steve A.) as an illustration of the information that can be yielded from the assessment process. The general information page of the assessment (Part I) allows the recording of general information about the student. Part II of the package provides detailed task information about each of the student's work experiences. The work experience description form in Part II should be completed for each work experience in which a student participated during his or her school career. Steve participated in five work experiences, so five description forms would appear in Part II for him. In the interest of saving space, only one of the five work experience descriptions appears in Appendix A. A brief description of the tasks performed at the site should be provided on the form, with a complete task analysis of each attached to the form. In addition, the percentage of independence and productivity achieved by the student in performing each task should be recorded. Finally, any adaptations that were used to allow the student to perform the task and any supports that the student required should be indicated. It is recommended that the work experience description form be completed by staff at the conclusion of each work experience, and that it be filed in his or her records. This will make the process of obtaining this information for the job creation assessment much easier. All of the work experiences in which a student participated are then summarized on the work experience task summary form (Part III). In addition, based on the information about the student's task performance, as well as his or her task preferences, those tasks that should be targeted for job creation should be indicated at the end of Part III.

Part IV of the assessment package focuses on work-related issues and support needs. Using this form, the student's performance or functioning and support needs in each of twelve identified areas (bathroom, endurance, eating/drinking, communication, grooming, hand use, vision/hearing, medical needs, mobility, getting to and from work, behaviors, and academics) should be described, along with strategies that could be used to reduce the amount of support that the program will need to provide.

The job creation preferences form (Part V) of the package summarizes the students' and parents' preferences about the job that is to be created. The student's preferences can be obtained by asking him or her directly about each of the job creation issues (i.e., tasks, hours, schedule, wages/benefits, and location). Some students may not be able to answer these questions directly. In this case, staff can attempt to infer their preferences based on behavior indicators and knowledge of the student (e.g., he seems to perform best in the morning). Parent preferences can be obtained by directly asking the parent.

Activity 2: Analyze Support Resources and Determine Support Delivery Plan

Many students with physical and multiple disabilities will require periods of initial job coach training that are longer than those for other persons who have typically been placed into individual jobs in order to achieve optimal independence. Even with systematic job creation planning, many of these students will also require high levels of ongoing support. In some cases, the amount of training and support needed may be difficult to provide given the resources available. However, by carefully analyzing the resources that are available from the various funding and provider agencies (school, employment program, MRDD, DVR, PASS, and IRWE) a plan can be devised that will permit the services and supports that are needed to be provided.

This planning can most effectively occur at a meeting with all of the persons and agency representatives identified above. The meeting should include a discussion of each of the following topics: 1) a description of various support options; 2) the amount of money that the adult service funding agencies can make available for the provision of training and ongoing support to the student; 3) the student's support needs, which will have been summarized during Activity 1; and 4) a description of PASS and IRWE including how these programs can be used to supplement fee-for-service dollars and how they operate. Using all of this information, along with the information from Activity 1, the group should attempt to map out an initial plan for the type of employment situation and support arrangement, and how this support will be provided to best meet the needs of the student. Figure 10 provides a format for summarizing this information.

Activity 3: Approach Employers

After Activity 1 and 2 are complete, staff should have a good sense of the type of job, job site, and employment arrangement that should be sought for a student. The next activity is to approach employers about creating a job for the student. The first step in this process is to simply decide what companies to approach. There is no formula that can be used to develop "the" list of companies that should be contacted. In fact, probably the most valid indicator of success in developing and creating jobs is the number of companies contacted—the more contacts made, the more likely a job will be found. However, there are a few hints that may be helpful in increasing the likelihood of contacting those companies that may have job creation opportunities:

1. Check the help wanted ads. Even though a student may not be able to fill the position that is being advertised, a help wanted ad indicates that the

Student: Steve A.

Date: 3/5/90

Persons Present at Meeting: Steve, parents, David Long (school) Betty Hoder (Employment Service), John Davis (MRDD), Shirley All (DVR)

INITIAL TRAINING

How much program funded assistance is available?

DVR can allocate up to 10 hours per week of training fees for 3 months. School can support another 10 hours of training per week for 2 to 3 months. MRDD will pay up to $400 per month after DVR dollars are expended, but not prior to 3 months before graduation.

Will the amount of assistance available be sufficient for the student's needs?

If Steve is placed on part-time job, it should be sufficient. The amount of initial training that he will need will depend on the job, but it is likely that he will not require more than 4 months.

Is it feasible for this student to receive initial training by company's staff?

Probably not.

Could a PASS be utilized?

Steve and family are willing to use this if necessary.

Who will take responsibility for job development (initial training) and who will fund?

School program will do job development and initial training. DVR and school will fund. MRDD will begin in April. To insure that training will be available, job should be timed to begin in January; DVR and school will pay for the first 3 months, and then MRDD dollars will be available.

ONGOING SUPPORT

What type and how much support will student require?

He may need a small amount of daily support related to task performance —specific type/amount will depend on job. He will also need daily assistance to use the bathroom. Try to schedule work so that his mother can take him to the bus and pick him up. Also, have him take high-protein drink to work to avoid need for eating assistance.

How much (if any) program-funded ongoing support is available?

MRDD will provide up to $400 per month beginning 3 months prior to his graduation.

Figure 10.   Initial employment/support plan.

Figure 10. *(continued)*

Is the amount of program funded support sufficient to meet the student's support needs?	This is questionable. If the job offers the right schedule and co-worker supports can be established, then program supports will be needed approximately 1 hour a day—$400 will barely cover this. No additional hours can be provided by the Employment Service Program.
Is it feasible for a co-worker at a company to provide support?	It probably will be feasible for a company employee to provide the type and amount of support Steve will need, except for bathroom assistance.
Will an IRWE need to be considered?	Yes, it may be necessary to use IRWE to supplement MRDD dollars for a program staff or an attendant to help Steve to use the bathroom each day as well as other support needs—especially if a co-worker cannot be recruited to provide this support.

GENERAL SUPPORT PLAN

1. Will try to have his job begin in January.
2. School will seek job for student.
3. School will provide initial training. DVR will help pay for 10 hours per week for 2 months.
4. School will attempt to recruit company staff to provide task-related support. Whether the company/staff should be paid for this assistance will be determined by amount that is actually needed.
5. Steve's mother will provide transportation assistance if hours fit in her schedule.
6. The Employment Service Program will be responsible for managing Steve's employment and support after graduation. MRDD will allocate up to $400 in service fees to them.
7. The Employment Service Program will provide daily bathroom assistance or subcontract with an attendant to provide this.
8. The need for a PASS or IRWE will be determined later.

company is in need of staff and thus may be amenable to restructuring or creating a position.

2. Find out where the student's friends and relatives (as well as those of staff) work, and ask them to provide the name of a person who can be contacted within the company. Based on their inside knowledge of the company and how it operates, friends and relatives might even be able to suggest possible job creation opportunities there.

3. Approach companies that are similar to those where a job has been created for other students, since the types of tasks and organizational structures of these companies are also often similar. For example, if a job was successfully created at a bank for a student, other banks should be contacted.

The initial meeting with an employer is critical. The goals of the meeting are to "sell" the idea of hiring a student and to obtain some preliminary information about the potential employment of the student. It has been suggested that a job developer has 15 minutes to convince an employer to consider hiring a person. Consequently, it is critical that a well organized and practiced presentation is made. This is particularly true when attempting to explain to employers the idea of actually creating a new position for a student. An example of what a job creator might say during the initial meeting is provided in Figure 11. After this presentation, the employer would be asked to describe any jobs that are currently available or that may be opened in the near future, any tasks that the current staff have difficulty getting done, or new tasks that the company would like to have done.

It may have been determined that a particular student will need full-time support and that the adult service agency will attempt to utilize the support co-worker approach, including contracting with the employer, described in this chapter. If this is true, it is suggested that the adult service agency, rather than the school program, take the major responsibility for creating the job for the student. Most school districts will not permit such a service contract to be arranged with them or to act in the role of an employer for students. It would also be cumbersome to shift the contract from the school to the adult service agency when the student departs school.

It should be noted that up to this time specific students need not be discussed. In general, it is best to indicate during the initial contact that jobs are being sought for a number of different students with different skills and interests, and that the student best suited to a particular site and job is determined after a thorough job and site analysis.

When considering creating a support co-worker arrangement for a student, it is best to not describe this as an option during the initial contacts with the employer, since it is likely that direct-hire jobs are being sought for other students. Mentioning the contract option may decrease employers' interest in hiring (directly) these other students. Generally, it is best to wait until after the job analysis has revealed that the site is best suited for the student for whom the support co-workers arrangement is being sought, and then to propose this arrangement to the employer.

Activity 4: Conduct an Analysis of the Site and Each of the Tasks

If there appears to be a job opening that a student could possibly fill, or if there is the potential for restructuring or creating a job for a student at the company, a

The following is an example of an initial job creation presentation:

As I indicated to you when we first spoke, I am the Vocational Coordinator for the Jefferson Special Needs Program. The program works with students who experience disabilities. One of the most important goals of the program is to prepare our students for employment. Beginning in the middle school we start providing students with work experience training that teaches them critical work skills. Students in high school go to businesses in the community to gain experience working in actual employment settings. When students are in their last year of school we assist them to obtain paying jobs. We have been placing students into jobs for several years, and here is a list of the businesses where students are employed, as well as the names and telephone numbers of their employers, in case you would like to contact them.

I am now looking for paying jobs for several of our students who will graduate at the end of this school year. I would like to tell you a little bit about how we assist employers to hire students and to see if there might be a possibility now or in the future for a student to be hired by your company. We take two major approaches in working with employers. First, if an employer has a position opening, we analyze the requirements of the job and determine if one of our students could fill it. We are then available to provide initial training to the student or to work with the company to provide this training. After the initial training our staff are available to provide ongoing assistance to the student and company as needed. After the student graduates from school, this ongoing assistance will also be available from an agency that works with adults with disabilities.

We have also worked with companies who don't have any position openings, but whose current staff have a difficult time completing all of their task duties and would be interested in hiring a student to assist in performing these duties. For example, the United States Bank created a new job for a student to help out its tellers with microfilming checks. The tellers had a hard time keeping up with the microfilming given their other duties, so the bank hired this student for 4 hours a day to take over the microfilming.

You may be interested to know that companies can deduct the wages paid to an employee with a disability from their taxes (describe the current Target Job Tax Credits program in effect). Some companies are concerned about the impact of hiring a person with a disability on their liability insurance. Statistics show that the jobsite accident rates of persons with disabilities are equal to or lower than those of nondisabled persons. Do you have any job openings coming up? Are there any tasks that your current employees have a difficult time getting done?

Figure 11. Initial meeting script.

job site and task analysis should be arranged. This process involves actually looking at the site's physical design and observing the jobs and tasks identified by the employer. The analysis should yield information about the physical accessibility of the site, bus routes in proximity to it, social integration and interaction available, work-related requirements such as dress, and a detailed description of the requirements of the identified jobs and tasks. A format for collecting the information during the job analysis is provided in Appendix B. The basic information about the site (name, contact, and address), the date of the analysis, and the staff person completing the analysis is recorded at the top of the form. Information related to six site and job issues (hours/schedule, wages/benefits, accessibility, public bus, social environment/behavior requirements, and grooming/dress) are recorded in Part I. A task analysis (the major steps) of each of the identified tasks is written on Part II of the form. Each step should be briefly described. At the bottom of the form, the amount of work that is available (i.e., how much time employees spend or could spend doing the task) and the productivity demands for the task (i.e., how much of the task the employer expects to be completed in a specified amount of time) should be estimated. One form should be completed for each of the tasks analyzed. For illustration purposes in this book, only one of the five analyzed tasks (photocopying) is shown here.

Activity 5: Determine the Feasibility of Placing a Student at the Site

Using the information from the job analysis as well as the information summarized about the student, staff should determine the feasibility of placing a student at the site and plan how this will occur. Each of the issues in Part I of the job analysis/match form should be considered with the particular student in mind. In Part II of the form, staff can use a code system to indicate the likelihood that the student will be able to perform the steps of each task analyzed, as well as the difficulty the student may encounter in performing the steps and the possible ways in which each could be adapted to decrease the difficulty.

Activity 6: Develop a Job Creation Proposal

At the conclusion of the job analysis and match process, staff should be able to determine whether it is possible for a job to be created for a student at a particular site. To make a final decision about the feasibility of creating a job, staff should attempt to actually take the information gathered and develop a plan for how the job would be created, including how many hours the student would be at the site, what the student's work schedule would be (inclusive of transportation and breaks), what tasks would be done, and what supports and adaptations would be required to allow the plan to be implemented. Figure 12 provides an example of how this job creation summary/schedule proposal can be constructed.

It seems feasible for a job to be created for Steve at Acme. Based on the

Student: Steve A.

Number of hours on site: 5

Number of hours of work: 4

Projected productivity: 50%
(he will get 2 hrs. of work done)

Site: ACME

Number of hours of program support: 1

Base wage: $5.00/hr.

Actual pay: $2.50/hr.

Tasks analyzed: photocopying, filing, shredding, mail pick-up, postage metering

Created job tasks: photocopying, shredding, mail pick-up, postage metering

Schedule	Activity	Support/adaptation needed
7:15 A.M.	Get on #10 at Hwy. 99.	Mother will walk with him and help him on bus.
7:30 A.M.	Get off at mall.	
7:45 A.M.	Get on #15.	Program staff meets—help on bus, we will try to find someone who takes same bus to help with this.
7:55 A.M.	Get off bus/cross street/ enter site.	Receptionist can open door.
8:05 A.M.	Remove jacket/put drink and snack bag in refrigerator.	Ask co-worker to help with this.
8:15 A.M.	Shred paper.	Co-worker will be asked to remove full bags, put on new bags.
8:45 A.M.	Photocopy.	Lower tables, electric stapler, order form, in/out basket. Ask co-worker to remove staples.
10:15 A.M.	Take break.	Program staff will help with bathroom use.
11:30 A.M.	Collect mail/postage meter.	Lower mail holders.
12:00 P.M.	Return to photocopying.	*Same as above.*
1:15 P.M.	Prepare to leave—put on jacket.	Co-worker helps.
1:30 P.M.	Mother picks up.	

Figure 12. Job creation summary/schedule proposal.

analysis of the five tasks, it appears that Steve could perform all of them with adaptations and some minor co-worker assistance, except for the filing task. It also appears that Steve could complete the four identified tasks in 4 hours (he will be about 50% productive across the tasks). This will meet the employer's desire to create a 2 hour position (i.e., to pay someone for 2 hours of work) and Steve's desire to work part-time (and meet the criteria for supported employment). The plan, however, has Steve at the site for 5 hours. This schedule was devised to permit Steve to take an unpaid hour break, during which time he will be assisted to use the bathroom, to rest, and to have the opportunity to socialize with co-workers. The extra hour will also permit him to leave for work at 7:15 A.M., when his mother can help him get on the bus to work and to remain at the site until 1:30 P.M., when his mother will be available to pick him up. The plan identifies a number of ways in which co-workers will need to be utilized to provide support. Because the type and amount of co-worker support is fairly minimal, it is likely that the employer will be agreeable to allowing staff to give it and it is likely that co-workers will be found who are willing to do so. The adaptations that the employer will need to be willing to make or have made also seem feasible to implement. The amount of program support needed in this plan is about 1 hour per day. This will include meeting Steve at the mall and helping him to transfer to the bus going to the site. It is hoped that after a few weeks a person who takes the same bus as Steve can be identified and recruited to assist in getting him on the bus. A program support person will also come to the site daily to assist Steve in using the bathroom. As indicated in the original plan, this amount of support is realistic for the adult service program to provide on an ongoing basis.

The proposed job creation plan should be described in detail to the student and family, and their approval should be gained before proceeding to discuss it with the employer. Steve and his mother are very supportive of the planned job creation for him and have given their permission to pursue it with the employer.

Activity 7: Present a Proposal to the Employer

The employer can now be presented with a proposal for how a job could be created for the student at the company. The staff person should first indicate to the employer that it appears that there is a student for whom a job could be created at the company and give the employer the name of the student. The description should be accurate and complete, but done in a positive and respectful fashion. Personal information about the student that the employer does not need to know should not be revealed. For example, in describing Steve the following might be said:

> Steve is 20 years old and will be completing high school this year. He has had extensive vocational training and work experience. He has had work experiences in several businesses in the community including the County Records office, the

Heart Association office, and Good Samaritan Hospital. He performed many of the tasks that you identified as ones you would like to have done here, including photocopying, postage metering, mail pick-up, and shredding. Steve has cerebral palsy and uses a power wheelchair to get around. Because of his disability, he cannot use his left hand, but is able to get his work done with his right hand. Steve's speech has also been affected by his disability. At first it can be difficult to understand what Steve is saying, but after being around him for a period of time most people can understand him. Steve also experiences learning disabilities. It takes him longer to learn new things and he does not know how to read or write. Steve experiences epilepsy, but he is on medication and has not had any seizures for almost a year. He is highly motivated to work. He takes a lot of pride in doing a job, and the supervisors at his work experiences have always been very pleased with his work and attitude.

The proposed job creation plan should then be presented to the employer. The written proposal that was devised will serve as the basis for this description and it can actually be given to the employer to review during the discussion. (However, the employer does need to know information about how the student will get to and from work.) Each of the tasks that will constitute the created job should be identified as well as those which were analyzed but not included in the job. This issue can be one of the concerns of an employer when deciding to accept the plan and to hire a student. For example, the ACME may not be willing to hire a student unless she or he can perform all of the identified tasks. It may seem appropriate to ask this question of the employer initially, before the job analysis and job creation proposal is conducted. However, these authors have found this to not be advisable. Most employers will indicate that they would like to think a person could perform all of the identified tasks, which in effect limits the students for whom a job could be created. If we do not ask this question initially, but simply provide the employer with a proposal of those tasks that a student is able to do, most are open to accepting it. If at the point of presenting the proposal the employer is concerned that all of the identified tasks cannot be done by the student, the staff person may suggest that the base wage be decreased to reflect the reduced job duties. For example, if the employer had indicated a willingness to pay $5.00 per hour for the five identified tasks, the staff person might suggest that the wage be decreased to $4.75 because the student will not perform the filing task. The actual wage will have to be negotiated and, of course, must be in accordance with wage and hour regulations.

Particular emphasis should be placed on describing for the employer the issues surrounding work hours and productivity. In Steve's case, the employer would be told that he will work 4 hours, during which he will probably complete 2 hours of work (which is about how long it will take him to complete the work assignments and the amount of hours the employer desires). Consequently, the employer will pay Steve half of the base wage or the equivalent of two hours of work. A description of how the employer would obtain (with the assistance of the program) a subminimum wage certificate to permit him to pay the student based on his productivity would be provided. It should be emphasized that the productivity *estimates* provided are only that, and if the student is more productive, his or her wage would need to reflect this. The types of adaptations that will need to be made and the reason that they are needed should be described to the employer, and his or her willingness to make these or to allow them to be made determined. A description of the types of co-worker assistance and support that would be needed to allow the student to work at the company with the least amount of program support should be described to the employer. The extent to which the employer feels that this assistance could be provided and his or her willingness to allow this to occur should be determined. The types of ongoing program supports that the student will need should also be provided, and the plans for providing this should be discussed. For example, the ACME employer would be told that a program staff person will come by on a daily basis to assist Steve to use the bathroom. This point will raise the issue of Steve taking an unpaid, 1-hour break to rest and use the bathroom.

If the employer makes the decision to hire a student, it is useful to develop a written document that clearly specifies the issues that were discussed and agreed on related to the student's employment at the company and the roles and responsibilities of the company, school, and adult program. Figure 13 provides an example of such an agreement.

Activity 8:   Prepare Site and Co-workers

The final activity in the process is to actually prepare the work site for the student to begin working. This includes determining exactly how a task should be designed to enable a student to perform it as independently as possible, and writing a task analysis that reflects this design. In addition, any job site modifications should be made, and equipment should be put in place.

One of the most important reasons for placing individuals into community settings is the social integration and interaction opportunities available there. The hope is that the supported employee will be accepted by the other employees as a co-worker and that other employees will interact with him or her in the same fashion and to the same degree that they do with other employees at the site. In fact, some of the research related to the interactions and relationships between employees with mental retardation and their co-workers at community sites suggest that this hope is not always realized (Chadsey-Rusch, Gonzalez, & Tines, 1988; Shafer, Rice, Metzler, & Haring, 1989). The results of these studies generally found that there were relatively low levels of social interactions between supported work employees and their co-workers. In addition, there is evidence that severity of disability negatively affects employer and co-worker attitudes towards persons with disabilities (Bowman, 1976; Hartlage & Roland, 1971). This suggests that the amount of social interaction that will occur between students with physical and multiple disabilities and their nondisabled co-workers should be of particular concern. Few attempts have been

I. ACME Insurance agrees to employ Steve Anderson. Mr. Anderson is a student in the Jefferson Special Needs Program (JSPN). JSPN will provide initial training. Beginning in April, Mr. Anderson will be provided employment services through the Employment Services Program.

II. **Responsibilities:**
Jefferson Special Needs Program will:
   1. Provide the initial training to the employee.
   2. Train identified co-worker(s) to provide assistance to the student related to those issues identified in the job creation proposal.
   3. Provide bathroom assistance to Steve.
   4. Assist the employer to gain a special wage certificate from the Department of Labor and to collect productivity information on a monthly basis.

Employment Services Program (ESP) will:
   1. Assume responsibility from school program for representing Mr. Anderson on April 1, 1991.
   2. Coordinate developing contract with employer related to any assistance provided by a co-worker to Mr. Anderson.
   3. Arrange for the provision of additional support, assistance, and training needs that cannot be provided by the company.

ACME Insurance will:
   1. Assist to identify co-worker(s) who will provide ongoing support and assistance to Mr. Anderson.
   2. Inform the school program and ESP of any schedule or task assignment changes before they occur.

III. **Task assignments:**
   1. Mr. Anderson will photocopy, pick up mail/meter, and shred paper.
   2. The task schedule is attached.

IV. **Adaptations:**
   1. ACME agrees to allow photocopier to be moved to lower table, to lower mail boxes, and to have work table raised or replaced with a higher one.
   2. DVR will purchase tables for photocopier and workspace.
   3. Additional design and adaptations will be presented to ACME before they are made.

V. **Schedule:**
   1. The employee will work 20 hours per week.
   2. The employee's schedule will be 8:15 to 1:15, Monday through Friday. He will take a 1-hour and 15-minute break. He will be paid for 15 minutes of break time.

VI. **Wages and benefits:**
   1. The base wage is $5 per hour.
   2. Mr. Anderson will be paid based on his productivity. This productivity will be determined in accordance with Section 14 (c) of the Fair Labor Standard Act.

Figure 13.   Employment agreement.   (continued)

Figure 13. *(continued)*

> 3. Productivity information will be collected at least twice per month during the first 6 months of employment. The wage will be based on an average of these twice-monthly productivity checks.
> 4. The base wage will be increased in accordance with the regular company pay-raise policy.
>
> SIGNATURES OF AGREEMENT   Date
>
> ACME Insurance _____
>
> Steven Anderson _____
>
> Jefferson Special Needs Program _____
>
> Employment Services Program _____

made to identify strategies that can be utilized to increase the social acceptance and integration of supported employees. The focus to date has been on teaching the supported employee social skills and behaviors (Chadsey-Rusch, 1986; Chadsey-Rusch, 1990; Gaylord-Ross, Haring, Breen, & Pitts-Conway, 1984). This research has shown that even when these persons learn appropriate social interaction behaviors, the amount of interactions between them and their co-workers does not increase significantly. There is a clear need to identify and investigate other strategies, those that are aimed directly at influencing the willingness of nondisabled co-workers to interact with supported employees. The following provides a number of practical strategies that these authors have found useful and effective for enhancing the social acceptance and integration of employees with physical and multiple disabilities at community work sites:

1. *Provide information to the co-workers about disability issues, supported employment, the employee, and how to interact with him or her.* Most co-workers will have had little exposure to or opportunity to interact with persons with significant disabilities. Consequently, co-workers may feel uncomfortable or even fearful of a co-worker with a disability. They may also question the rationale for employing the person, especially if he or she has very severe disabilities and requires intensive work supports. In most cases, the rationale for supported employment and information about disability issues and the student being placed is provided to the employer during the job development and negotiation activities. However, it is not uncommon for little of this information to be conveyed to the co-workers in a straightforward fashion. Co-workers, who will be working with the supported employee on a daily basis, want and need this information as much if not more than the employer.

If a company has routine meetings that are attended by all or most of the employees, this is an excellent forum to provide this information. The presentation should include a rationale for placing individuals into community work settings. A description of the person should be provided in a positive fashion that conveys to the employees that the person should not be pitied or feared. Because many people are not sure when to provide or offer assistance to a person with a disability, this topic should be discussed in reference to the new employee. The topic of the employees' work productivity should also be addressed. If it is not, the co-workers may assume that the expectation is that the student will work as fast as other employees and then be disgruntled when this does not occur. In addition, they may feel that the employer is hiring the student for charity reasons, if they believe that the student is being paid a full wage although she or he is not fully productive. Particular emphasis should be placed on explaining to the co-workers how important it is that the supported employee is accepted by them and that they interact with him or her in the same way and as often as they do with other co-workers. Finally, the role that the school and employment staff will play in training and supporting the student and the site should be delineated. Figure 14 provides an example of a presentation that might be made to the co-workers of a new supported employee. During and after the presentation, the co-workers should be encouraged to ask any questions that they have about any of the information presented or any related issues. They should also be encouraged to express any concerns, fears, or reservations that they may have, and the presentor should address these in a positive and respectful fashion.

If it is not possible to have a meeting with a group of employees, staff should make the attempt to present the same information to as many individual employees as possible. If there are a large number of employees this may become a formidable task. In this case, those employees who will work most closely with the student should be approached.

2.   *The job coach or support worker should model how to socialize with the student.*   Chadsey-Rusch et al. (1988) documented that a substantial amount of the social interactions that occur among co-workers involves "kidding" each other (e.g., "John, I've noticed you putting some weight on, you better give me some of your cookies."). Co-workers might fear that the feelings of the supported employee would be hurt by such kidding. During the initial presentation, they should be told that this is not the case. It will be particularly important for the job coach to "kid around" with the student in front of the co-workers, to actually attempt to draw the co-workers into joking with the student, and to assist the student to kid with the co-workers. Individuals who do not speak can still be kidded with and can joke with others. For example, one of John's co-workers was often a few minutes late getting to work on Monday mornings. The other employees always kidded him when he came in about his wild weekends. John would laugh along with everyone and would point to the clock as his way of kidding the person.

3.   *Assist the supported employee to provide information about his or her interests and life to co-workers.*   In addition to kidding, employees also

The following is an example of one possible way to address co-workers regarding student placement:

PRESENTATION TO CO-WORKERS

My name is _____ and I am a vocational trainer with Jefferson Special Needs Program. Our program works with students who have disabilities. We teach them work skills while they are in school and then help them to get a job when they are close to graduation.

Your company has agreed to hire Steve Anderson, a student in our program. Mr. Davis is hiring Steve to help the secretaries with photocopying. Steve will also enter new policy information and shred old policy information as time permits. He will work from 9:15 to 1:15 each day.

Some of you may have never worked with a person with a disability or, for that matter, had any experience being around a person with a disability. I wanted to have the chance today to talk with you and give some information that may help you to feel comfortable when Steve begins work next week. Steve experiences cerebral palsy. Cerebral palsy affects a person's ability to control and use his or her muscles. However, the exact affect of cerebral palsy is different for different people. Steve cannot walk, so he uses an electric wheelchair to get around. He also cannot use one of his hands. Steve also has difficulty speaking because of his disability. At first, it will be very difficult for you to understand what he is saying. However, as you are around him you will find it increasingly easier to understand him. If you don't understand him, don't be embarrassed—just tell him you don't understand and he will repeat what he said. I will be here during the first few weeks to help train Steve, and I will help interpret for him until you can begin to understand him. Steve also has a communication book that he uses. Here is the communication book. It has pictures with associated words. He points to the picture of the word that he wishes to say. He usually will first try to tell you what he wants to say. If he has trouble getting you to understand, he will then pull out the book and use it.

Often people are not sure when they should help a person with a disability who seems to have trouble doing something like opening a door. The best rule of thumb is to ask the person. If you ask, Steve will tell you if he needs your help.

Steve also experiences what is often called mental retardation. All that means is that he has more trouble learning things than you and I might have. However, the term mental retardation is very negative. Today, we simply say that Steve has a learning disability. It is important that all of us understand that Steve is first and most importantly a person, a person who has the same emotions, desires, and dreams as the rest of us. He is not a physically disabled or mentally retarded person—he is a person who happens to have a physical and learning disability. He is also a person who likes to watch television, especially football, and go camping.

Figure 14.   Presentation to co-workers.   (continued)

Figure 14. (continued)

As I said, I will be here with Steve for several weeks training him to do his job. You should be aware that it will take Steve longer to get work done than it would take you. There is a special program that the Department of Labor has that allows an employer to pay a person with a disability based on how much work she or he can do compared to other employees at the company. So if Steve can do about half as much photocopying during his work period as you would get done, he would be paid half of his hourly wage. I am telling you this information so that you understand that Mr. Davis is not hiring Steve for charity purposes, and is paying him even though he is really not getting as much work done as other employees—Steve will get paid for what he contributes. We do believe that during Steve's shift he will be able to get all or most of the photocopying done and to help out with data entry and shredding.

Some people may wonder why we should go to the trouble of helping a person like Steve to work. They may even feel that it would be better if he stayed home or went to a special program for people like him. Until recently, people with disabilities did stay home or go to a special work program. Although Steve may not get rich working here, he will make a lot more than he could ever make in the sheltered workshop. However, the money is not the most important thing. Steve, and other people with disabilities, want more than anything to be a part of regular society, to do what other people do, to have the same experiences and opportunities as all of us. He does not want to be protected, he does not want to go to a special program—he wants to work in a real business, next to people like you, to earn money, to do work that he likes, and to know that he is making a contribution.

One of the most important things that I want to communicate to you today is how important it is for Steve to feel accepted by you, his co-workers. Simply going to work and getting our job done is not enough for any of us to feel good about where we work. The social aspects of the job are also very, very important—we enjoy chatting with our co-workers, joking and kidding around with them, taking breaks together, and developing friendships. These things are also very important for Steve. Steve has a great sense of humor and is a very social person. I would like to encourage you to get to know him and to show him that he is a part of the company.

socialize by talking about themselves, their lives, and their interests. This sharing of information serves as the basis upon which co-workers really begin to know each other and for the development of more in-depth bonding and friendships. Students who have problems speaking, who have limited vocabularies, or who are shy may find it difficult to share this information. The trainer can assist by asking the student questions in such a way that this information is conveyed. For example, at break time while Shirley and her trainer sit with a couple of employees, the trainer says, "Shirley, did you go camping this week-end as you had planned?" Shirley nods yes. The trainer says, "Boy, I bet the coast was nice. Did you go to Newport?" Shirley, nods yes again. The trainer says to the co-workers, "Shirley's family has an RV and they go camping a lot." Through this interaction, the co-workers now know something about Shirley's life at home, and they have something to talk with her about in the future.

4. *Assist the student to go to company parties and activities.* Most companies organize parties and other social activities for employees. This may be just an office party at Christmas and a Fourth-of-July picnic. Other companies are much more active in sponsoring social gatherings for their employees, including such things as softball and bowling teams. These events are typically advertised on a bulletin board or through informal word of mouth. Although a supervisor and co-worker may not mean to exclude a supported employee from these activities, they may not think to make him or her aware of them or to encourage the person to participate. Even if the supported employee is aware of the activity, he or she may not be able to attend without some special arrangements and assistance. The school or adult program should assist the student to participate in these activities. This may involve the trainer or co-worker going with the student, arranging for an attendant who will do so, or talking with a co-worker about helping out.

CONCLUSION

Students who experience physical and multiple disabilities should have the opportunity to work in regular employment situations and in nongroup situations. To achieve this outcome, alternatives to the existing individual placement supported employment approach must be identified and utilized. This chapter has described a number of these strategies and the major activities involved in developing individual placements for these students. The information presented here represents only the beginnings of the work that must be done to open greater employment opportunities for those individuals whom supported employment is intended to assist.

REFERENCES

Bellamy, G. T., Rhodes, L. E., Mank, D. M., & Albin, J. M. (1988). *Supported employment: A community implementation guide.* Baltimore: Paul H. Brookes Publishing Co.

Bowman, J. T. (1976). Attitudes toward disabled persons: Social distance and work competence. *Journal of Rehabilitation, 53,* 71–74.

Chadsey-Rusch, J. (1986). Identifying and teaching valued social behaviors. In F. R. Rusch (Ed.), *Competitive employment issues and strategies* (pp. 273–287). Baltimore: Paul H. Brookes Publishing Co.

Chadsey-Rusch, J. (1990). Teaching social skills on the job. In F. R. Rusch (Ed.), *Supported employment: Models, methods and issues* (pp. 161–180). Sycamore, IL: Sycamore Publishing Co.

Chadsey-Rusch, J., Gonzalez, P., & Tines, J. (1988). Social ecology of the workplace: A study of interactions among employees with and without mental retardation. In J. Chadsey-Rusch (Ed.), *Social ecology of the workplace* (pp. 27–54). Champaign: University of Illinois.

Ellis, W., Rusch, F. R., Tu, J., & McCaughrin, W. (1990). Supported employment in Illinois. In F. R. Rusch (Ed.), *Supported employment: Models, methods and issues* (pp. 31–44). Sycamore, IL: Sycamore Publishing Co.

Gaylord-Ross, R. J., Haring, T. G., Breen, C., & Pitts-Conway, V. (1984). The training and generalization of social interaction skills with autistic youth. *Journal of Applied Behavior Analysis, 17,* 229–247.

Hartlage, L. C., & Roland, P. E. (1971). Attitudes of employers toward different types of handicapped workers. *Journal of Applied Rehabilitation Counseling, 2,* 115–120.

McCray, R. (1987). *The job accommodation handbook.* Verndale, MN: RPM Press, Inc.

McDonnell, J., Wilcox, B., & Boles, S. (1988) Do we know enough about transition? A national survey of state agencies responsible for services to persons with severe handicaps. *Journal of The Association for Persons with Severe Handicaps, 11*(1), 53–60.

McKnight, J. L. (1987, Winter). Regenerating community. *Social Policy,* pp. 54–58.

Moon, S. M., Inge, K. J., Wehman, P., Brooke, V., & Barcus, J. M. (1990). *Helping persons with severe mental retardation get and keep employment: Supported employment issues and strategies.* Baltimore: Paul H. Brookes Publishing Co.

Nisbet, J., & Hagner, D. (1988). Natural supports in the workplace: A reexamination of supported employment. *Journal of The Association for Persons with Severe Handicaps, 13*(4), 260–267.

O'Connell, M. (1988, February). *The gift of hospitality: Opening the doors of community life to people with disabilities.* Chicago: Center for Urban Affairs and Policy Research, Northwestern University.

Rusch, F. R., & Hughes, C. (1990). Historical overview of supported employment. In F. R. Rusch (Ed.), *Supported employment: Models, methods and issues* (pp. 5–14). Sycamore, IL: Sycamore Publishing Co.

Shafer, M. (1986) Utilizing co-workers as change agents. In F. R. Rusch (Ed.), *Competitive employment issues and strategies* (pp. 215–224). Baltimore: Paul H. Brookes Publishing Co.

Shafer, M. S., Rice, M. L., Metzler, H. M., & Haring, M. (1989). A survey of nondisabled employees' attitudes toward supported employees with mental retardation. *Journal of The Association for Persons with Severe Handicaps, 14*(2), 137–146.

Sowers, J. (1989). Supported employment for persons with physical and multiple disabilities. *The Advance: The Association for Persons in Supported Employment Newsletter,* February.

Vogelsberg, R. T. (1990). Supported employment in Pennsylvania. In F. R. Rusch (Ed.), *Supported employment: Models, methods and issues* (pp. 45–64). Sycamore, IL: Sycamore Publishing Co.

Wehman, P., Kregel, J., & Shafer, M. (1990). *Emerging trends in the national supported employment initiative: A preliminary analysis of twenty-seven states.* Richmond, VA: Virginia Commonwealth University, Rehabilitation and Research Training Center.

Wehman, P., Moon, M. S., Everson, J. M., Wood, W., & Barcus, J. M. (1988). *Transition from school to work: New challenges for youth with severe disabilities.* Baltimore: Paul H. Brookes Publishing Co.

Will, M. (1986). OSERS programming for the transition of youth with disabilities: Bridges from school to working life. In J. Chadsey-Rusch & C. Hanley-Maxwell (Eds.), *Enhancing transition from school to the work place for handicapped youth: Issues in personnel preparation* (pp. 9–25). Urbana: University of Illinois, College of Education, Office of Career Development for Special Populations.

Appendix A

Student Job Creation and Support Assessment Package
General Information (Part I)

1. Name: <u>Steve Anderson</u>

2. Date of birth: <u>6/5/71</u>

3. Address: <u>212 Barger</u>

4. Telephone: <u>236-2636</u>

5. Social Security #: <u>267-81-6163</u>

6. Disabilities experienced: <u>cerebral palsy, moderate mental</u>
   <u>retardation</u>

7. Time remaining until graduation: <u>12 months</u>

8. High school: <u>Jefferson</u>

9. Teacher: <u>Dave Smiley</u>

10. Living with whom: <u>Mother</u>

11. Home support/involvement: <u>Mother is interested and involved.</u>
    <u>She has other small children—finds it hard to keep up</u>
    <u>with everything.</u>

Student Job Creation and Support Package

Work Experience Description (Part II)

Student: <u>Steve A.</u>

Site: <u>Hospital</u>

Start/stop dates: <u>9/15/89 to 12/10/89</u>

Number of other students at site: <u>2 — in different areas</u>

Hours/days worked: <u>3.5, M-F</u>

Task	Description (task analysis)	Independence Achieved	Productivity	Adaptations	Support needed
Photocopying	Copied patient front sheets—2 or 3 pages, and stapled.	90%–100%	40%–60%—varied	Had to take work to machine on low table. Stapling jig, electric stapler needed.	If machine jammed, or paper ran out. Some quality control on stapling. Secretaries removed staples for him.
Delivery	Picked up pharmacy order from 3 floors and took to pharmacy. Plastic bag held orders—kept behind desk. Nurse gave to him.	100%	60%–75%	None.	None.

Data Entry	Updated drug information for pharmacy. Simple copying, for the most part—pulled up record on machine, entered date of last drug order and drug code.	75%—90%	20%—30%	Key-guard, magnifier strip for copy holder.	Some help if printing not clear. Usually made 2 or 3 entry errors daily—out of about 10 forms and a total of about 50 letters/numbers (characters) entered.

Student Job Creation and Support Package
Work Experience/Tasks Summary (Part III)

Student: <u>Steve A.</u>

Site	Dates	Tasks performed
School Library	9/12/87—12/10/87	photocopying, shelving books, checking books in
School Office	1/15/88—6/1/88	delivery, putting videos away, photocopying
Heart Association	9/10/88—12/10/88	shredding, postage metering, photocopying
County Records	1/6/89—6/1/89	data entry, filing, delivery
Hospital	9/15/89—12/10/89	photocopying, delivery (pharmacy orders), data entry

Tasks to target in job creation (those student performed most independently and productively and those preferred):
photocopying, delivery, data entry, shredding

Student Job Creation and Support Package
Work-Related Issues and Support (Part IV)

Performance Area	Information/support needed	Job creation/ support reduction strategy
Bathroom: Is student continent (bladder/bowel)? Assistance needed? How long does it take? How often does he need to go? Is accessible bathroom needed?	He is continent. We have him on a schedule (between 11:00 and 11:30 A.M.) and once in afternoon (2:00 to 2:30 P.M.) He is able to stick with this schedule. He can do it all, except lifting and emptying urinal when it is full. Takes about 10 minutes.	Program support will need to be provided. Try to arrange bathroom time when other support will also be needed.
Endurance: How long can student work before becoming fatigued? Any limits on sitting? Do short breaks alleviate fatigue?	The longest he has worked is 4 hours—he did begin to tire at the end of that period. Mom reports coming home tired after work. Breaks do seem to help. He should be able to stay in chair up to 8 hrs, unless recovering from skin breakdown.	Keep work time to about 4 hours. Intersperse with long break—when he goes to the bathroom.
Eating/drinking: Type/amount of assistance? Any food restrictions? How long does it take student to eat?	He needs to have drink placed on table with a straw. He can eat finger foods by himself, including crackers, granola bars, fruit slices (things that are firm), which are easiest for him to pick up. Will choke on occasion—apple skins, hard candy.	Possibly have him not eat at work. Best strategy is to have Mom give him a high protein drink (breakfast type) to take to work. Co-worker could set up for him. Mom and Steve said they would support this approach.

(continued)

Performance Area	Information/support needed	Job creation/ support reduction strategy
Communication: Mode? How well does student use this mode? Can others understand? How quickly can it be used? How is his or her ability to understand others?	Steve is able to speak. Is somewhat difficult to understand initially—then most people can begin to interpret. His receptive abilities are fairly good—can understand simple requests, instructions, and questions.	Job coach will help co-workers to learn how to understand him and will show them how to use simple requests, instructions, questions.
Grooming: How well is s/he usually groomed? Type of clothes usually worn?	Steve has grooming problems, soiled clothes, dirty hair. He usually wears casual/older/worn clothes. We have worked with Mom and him on this—improved, but still an issue.	D.V.R. will buy new clothes, Mom has made renewed commitments to helping him with grooming. We have set up hair washing schedule and grooming checklist.
Hand use: Ability to grasp, manipulate or lift weight, reach forward/up, amount of control?	No functional use of left hand (can use as weight, can lift from lap to table). Right hand can grasp, pick up objects, lift no more than a couple of pounds, cannot do fine motor manipulation. Starts to go into extension when extends arm (loses control). Can reach length of arm—but poor control.	No tasks with very fine/precise manipulations, no heavy lifting. Will need to design/arrange to decrease reaching as much as possible.
Vision/hearing: How good is near/far vision? Is vision corrected? Any hearing loss/aides/adaptations?	Distance vision is fine. Some difficulty reading regular size print—uses magnifying device for data entry. He has glasses, but still has trouble. Has hearing aides in both ears. Environment with lots of noise (machine noise) can bother him.	Use magnifying glass device—attaches to copyholder or table if he has to read small print. Find low-noise site.

Medical needs: Any medications taken—when/how/how? Any medical conditions that may affect work?	Has seizures, but has had none in last 9 months. Takes seizure medications—at home. Missed total of 20 days due to upper respiratory infections/skin breakdown.	Mom has agreed to have nurse come in and give suggestions about diet and hygiene, to decrease health problems. Will need to find site where absences will not disrupt work—someone else can pick up.
Mobility: Mode? How safe, independent is student? How far can he or she go?	Uses power wheelchair—safe, independent, in close quarters, does not back chair up well. Chair battery will last for several miles—Mother and Steve need to make sure they plug in batteries *every night!*	Work areas should be fairly roomy—not a lot of furniture, equipment in close quarters. We will provide Steve/Mom with two checklists of things to do related to work—telephone to prompt/reinforce.
Getting to/from work: Can student use public bus? Does he or she need accessible bus? Is there a bus available? How much assistance is needed? Type? What assistance is needed to cross streets?	Has been trained to ride bus, which is accessible. Needs help backing chair on lift; drivers won't help. Accessible bus on stop at Hwy 99, which is two blocks from home and requires him to cross busy/uncontrolled street. He can cross safely at controlled streets, but not at very busy, uncontrolled streets.	Mom has agreed to take him to the bus in the morning, if he leaves before 8:00 A.M. She will also pick him up from work if he gets off between 1:15 P.M. and 2:00 P.M. This fits her work schedule and will help reduce program support. Find site where he doesn't have to cross uncontrolled streets. If possible, find site where he doesn't have to transfer buses.
Behaviors: Describe any behavior challenges and strategies to deal with them.	If Steve feels high pressure/frustrated, may cry or lose temper (yell, curse).	Make sure that task demands are not too high and provide quality instruction so that he learns how to do tasks effectively.
Academics: Reading/writing/math/number skills.	Steve does not read, except a few functional words (men, stop). He can match letters and numbers. He does not write at all. He can count to 20, and can identify numbers to 29.	Job should not require academics greater than his current skill level.

(continued)

Appendix A. *(continued)*

Issue	Student	Family
Tasks, types of tasks	Photocopying, data entry, delivery. He likes jobs that give him a variety of things to do.	"Whatever Steve likes."
Hours	He indicated part-time or less—"not all day."	Mother thought that part-time work would be best, because "he gets tired."
Schedule	He doesn't seem to have a preference.	Mother prefers morning hours, because that's when she works.
Wages/benefits	"A lot of money." (Steve does not understand money values.)	"Money is not really important . . . not so much that he loses his benefits."
Location	"Downtown"	"As close to home as possible." "Not in Springfield."

Student Job Creation and Support Package
Job Creation Preferences (Part V)
Student: <u>Steve A.</u>   Family member(s): <u>Mother</u>

Appendix B

Job Analysis/Match

Site ___Acme Insurance___   Date ___9/25/90___

Contact ___John Davis, Owner___   Staff ___Liza B.___

Address ___205 S.E. 5th___

Tasks analyzed: photocopying
                   filing
                   mail pick up
                   postage metering
                   paper shredding

Comments:

Appendix B. *(continued)*

Site: Acme		Student: Steve A.
Issue	**Information**	**Student match**
Number of hours/ schedule	John indicated that he would be willing to create a 2-hour job for someone. He indicated that mornings were preferred.	Steve wants 4 hours. Given his projected productivity, we can create a 4 hour job from these tasks—will take him 4 hours to get 2 hours of work done.
Wages/ benefits	Will pay $5 base wage. No benefits for employers who work less than 25 hours.	At 50% productivity, he will make $2.50 per hour—this is acceptable to Steve and Mom. They indicated that benefits were not critical. Will need to negotiate vacation/sick leave.
Accessibility Entrance	There are no steps at entrance. The door is heavy and hard to open.	Receptionist is at front—she can let Steve in and out.
Bathroom	Men and women's bathroom—large—plenty of room for chair. No hand rail for transfer. Regular seat height—may need to be raised.	Steve uses urinal—won't need hand rail or raised toilet seat.
Other areas	Lunch area accessible, but sink is not. Water fountains are not. Work areas all on ground level.	If he needs to use sink, can ask for help from co-worker.
Public bus Bus stops/ schedule Accessible bus	3 stops within 3 blocks. One stop across street from entrance. #10, 15, 43, at Oak St. & 5th—(every 20 mins.) #3, 8, 52 at 7th and Elm (every 20 mins.) #6, 9, 32, at 10th & Sycamore (every 20 mins.) #15, 8, 32 accessible.	Can take #15 bus by transferring downtown. Will require someone to meet him downtown.

(continued)

Appendix B. *(continued)*

Social integration	Staff are very friendly. 3 secretaries/office staff. All are female very nice/outgoing. 10 agents (7 male, 3 female)—also friendly.	Steve will enjoy friendly atmosphere. He likes working with women.
Grooming/ dress	Men wear coats/ties. Women dress-up. Person filling this job will not have to wear coat/tie (if male), but wear nice shirt, pants. Women can wear dressy slacks, but nice.	Will need to get D.V.R. to buy Steve new clothes and work closely with mother and him to keep them clean/neat.

(continued)

Appendix B. (*continued*)

TASK ANALYSIS MATCH

Task: <u>Photocopying</u>

Student: <u>Steve A.</u>

Codes:

1. Student can learn to perform independently.
2. Student can learn to perform independently if adaptations are made.
3. Student will not be able to perform independently.
4. Student could participate.

Major step	Description	Code	Difficulty/adaptation
1. Get original.	1. Jane keeps photo-copying on her desk.	2	1. Create in-basket for Steve to be kept in photo-copy room.
2. Remove clip/staple.	2. Most have both.	1 (clip) 3 (staple)	2. Steve can remove clip, but staple removal is hard. Will ask Jane to remove staples for him—this should take her very little time.
3. Determine number of copies to be made.	3. Agent tells Jane, she writes it on a post-it and puts on original.	2	3. We could make a photocopy order form that is easy to complete and interpret—have agents fill out or have Jane fill out for them.
4. Code machine—number of copies, collate.	4. Code panel on front of machine—easy to reach.	2	4. Probably need to color code collate button with piece of colored tape.

5. Put in originals.	5. Self-feeder machine.	2	5. Machine is on too high a table for Steve to easily feed. Put on lower table.
6. Push short button—remove copies/original.	6. Original comes out on top of machine, copies in bin at side.	2	6. Lower machine. Steve will need something to put copies in. He has previously used a paper collator in a box on his lap, which has worked well.
7. Staple/put clip back on.	7. There is a table to work on. They use a manual stapler.	2	7. Table is too low, so his chair won't fit. Get higher table, or put something under legs to raise slightly. Need an electric stapler and stapling jig that he uses.

Productivity demands: Just needs to be done by end of day. No work requiring a quick turnaround.

Quantity of work available: Always at least 1 hour of photocopying each day—Jane spends at least an hour on site.

Student productivity: Steve will be about 50% productive—will take him 2 hours to finish.

TOM

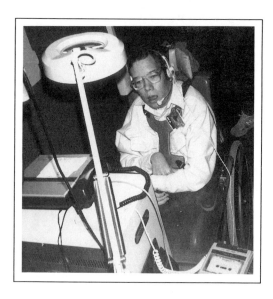

Tom is 20 years of age and is entering his last year of school eligibility. He uses a power wheelchair, but due to limited vision and poor motor control he requires significant assistance in doing so. He has almost no functional control of his hands. Due to the combination of his disabilities, Tom presented a particularly difficult challenge to staff to identify tasks that he could perform.

Computer-related tasks were attempted. Tom required a switch-scanning software program to enter information. He also required a program that enlarged the print on the screen. Unfortunately, these two programs cannot be operated simultaneously.

Tom is able to speak and enjoys activities that involve interaction with other persons. Playing off of his strength (speaking) and preference (social interaction), the school has focused on telephone-related tasks. He was first trained to answer phones for one office at his school. He used a head set like the one he is wearing in the photograph. A switch was used to activate and deactivate the phone and another to record messages on a tape recorder. Recently, Tom has been trained to call and remind members of different committees, task forces, and boards of meetings. Some of them are school groups and some are community service groups. Tom currently does his calling from the local Association for Retarded Citizens office, located in the downtown mall.

TOM
(continued)

A new adapted telephone system was devised so that Tom could do this job. A Freedom phone was purchased through the Southern Bell Telephone Company. This phone permits the user to "dial" numbers by simply saying a code number that corresponds to a telephone number stored in memory. The telephone also has speaker phone capacity. This phone was then modified for Tom by his school aide, who has a background in electrical engineering.

Tom uses a switch mounted at the side of his head, which activates five different functions. The first time he hits the switch, a tape recorder is turned on which says the name of the first person to be called and a number assigned that person. Tom hits the switch a second time which turns on the phone and he then says the person's memory number. The number is then displayed on a window at the top of the phone, part of the Freedom phone system. An Apollo camera has been placed over the window, which magnifies and broadcasts the number onto a monitor in front of Tom. After Tom verifies that the number is the one he wishes to call, he hits the switch again and the number is automatically dialed. When the person answers the phone, Tom introduces himself and reminds them of the date and time of the meeting. He hits the switch again, which activates a second tape recorder, on which he indicates if the person will be in attendance at the meeting.

The school is currently working with an adult service agency to begin looking for a possible paid position that Tom might be able to do using this phone system. A prime target area for job creation will be doctor's and dentist's offices, where he could call to remind patients of their appointments.

8 *Parent Involvement*

Clearly parents and families can play a critical role in the community-based employment of their sons or daughters (Schutz, 1986; Wehman, 1981). Parents typically make or greatly influence the decision between community and sheltered employment options for their child. Unless they understand the potential benefits and feasibility of community employment for their child, they may be unwilling to select it (Siegal & Loman, 1987). Consequently, school programs must attempt to provide parents with information about community employment, the contributions that it can make to their child's life, and the feasibility of it for their child given the new supported employment models.

Parents and families can also contribute to the success or failure of their children when placed in community employment (McDonnell, Hardman, & Hightower, 1990; McDonnell, Wilcox, Boles, & Bellamy, 1985; Schultz, 1986; Sowers, 1989). They can influence their child's general motivation to learn and perform the tasks and behaviors required by a job. Parents' willingness to assist their child in getting to work on time and wearing appropriate clothes can also determine job success. School programs should assist parents to understand the extent that their involvement and support is critical to the job success of their children and to use systematic strategies to gain this involvement and support.

The first purpose of this chapter is to describe a number of strategies that school programs can use to encourage parent involvement in and support of their child's vocational preparation activities. The second aim of the chapter is to identify a number of strategies that can be utilized to gain the parent support needed to enhance the success of a student at the time when she or he is placed on a paid community job.

STRATEGIES TO EDUCATE AND GAIN SUPPORT OF PARENTS DURING VOCATIONAL PREPARATION

Strategy 1:   Assist Parents to Understand the Importance of Employment for Their Child

Many parents may view employment as a low priority for their child. In part, this feeling may derive from the general belief that the major purpose of work is as a means to support oneself and one's family. Parents often are willing, with the assistance of public subsidies, to continue to provide financial support for their children as adults. Consequently, they may conclude that their child does not need to work. However, work has the potential of affording many other valuable benefits to the quality of a person's life, including the opportunity to demonstrate competence by performing work that is valued by a business, co-workers, and society at large. A job also provides the opportunity to socialize and make friends. It is the rare parent who is not genuinely interested in ensuring that his or her child has every possible opportunity to live as full and enriching a life as possible. Explaining the importance that work can play in their child's adult life will enhance the commitment that parents have to their child's vocational preparation.

Strategy 2:   Provide Parents with Information About the Vocational Options Available

Many parents may be naive regarding the vocational options and systems for persons who experience disabilities. Other parents may be aware only of sheltered employment and believe that this is the single option available for their child. Parents should be provided with a description of sheltered work as well as the emerging community-based, supported employment approaches. Parents should also be provided with a description of the extent to which each of these options provide opportunities to earn wages, interact with nondisabled persons, and perform meaningful work.

Strategy 3:   Provide Parents with Specific Information About Local Vocational Options

Information should be included about each of the local programs that provide vocational services to individuals with disabilities. See Figure 15 for the type of information that will be particularly helpful to parents in evaluating these programs. Parents should also be provided with information about the local adult service referral, eligibility, and funding systems.

Strategy 4:   Provide Parents with Illustrations of the Possibility of Community-Based Employment

Many parents may view community-based employment as a desired outcome, but have reservations about its feasibility for their child with physical and multi-

PROGRAM SERVICE DESCRIPTION

General Information

Program name: _____   Contact person: _____

Address: _____   Telephone: _____

Individuals served

Total number served last year:

Does program serve individuals with the following disabilities:

Severe/moderate mental retardation _____

Mild mental retardation _____

Vision impairments _____

Hearing impairments _____

Significant physical disabilities _____

Mental illness _____

Significant behavior difficulties _____

Other _____

Does the program "specialize" in serving individuals with certain types of disabilities or do the individuals currently in the program primarily experience one or two of these disabilities?

YES _____   NO _____

If the answer is yes, indicate the disabilities.

Work activity center (WAC)

Type of work performed:

Average annual salary earned:

Number of individuals who left WAC last year for sheltered workshop:

Number of individuals who left WAC last year for community job:

Number of individuals who left program and for what reasons:

Other types of activities individuals do as part of this program (e.g., recreational, academic):

Figure 15.   Program service description.

(continued)

Figure 15.   (*continued*)

Sheltered workshop (SW)

Type of work performed:

Average annual salary earned last year:

Number of individuals who left SW last year for WAC:

Number of individuals who left SW for community job:

Number of individuals who left program and for what reasons:

Other types of activities individuals do as part of this program (e.g., recreational, academic):

Community jobs program: Crews

Total number of individuals:

Total number in crews:

Annual wage earned (last year):

Description of disabilities
Experienced by individuals on crews:

Types of work performed:

How many individuals left crew (last year):

Where did they go, and why did they leave:

(*continued*)

Figure 15. (*continued*)

Community jobs program: Enclave

Total number in enclave group placement:

Annual wage earned (last year):

Description of disabilities
    Experienced by individuals in enclave:

    Types of work performed:

How many individuals left crew (last year), where did they go, and why did they leave:

Community jobs program: Individual placement

Total number in individual jobs:
Annual wage earned (last year):

Examples of types of jobs:

Description of disabilities
    Experienced by individuals on jobs:

How many individuals lost jobs last year and for what reasons:

Description of types of ongoing support and follow-up provided:

---

ple disabilities. Parents should be provided with examples and illustrations of individuals with disabilities similar to their child's who are successfully working in community-based jobs. If there are such individuals in the local community who are working, a description of these students and their employment situation should be provided to parents. Parents can also be provided with descriptions of individuals in other communities who are employed. Staff can obtain this information by developing contact with staff in other districts, by attending state and regional conferences, and by reading journals and newsletters that describe program demonstrations.

Strategy 5:   Arrange for Parents to Observe Their Child Working

After seeing other individuals with disabilities who are successfully employed, some parents may still have doubts about the ability of their own child to do so. To further assist them in overcoming these doubts, arrangements should be made for parents to observe their son or daughter at a work experience site. The sight of their child in a real business setting, working alongside with and being accepted by nondisabled persons as well as performing work competently, can serve as a powerful tool in opening the eyes of parents to the potential of their child, vocationally and otherwise.

Strategy 6:   Emphasize the Importance of Early and Ongoing Vocational Preparation

Parents may view work as important, but only at the time when the student is nearing or has graduated from high school. Students with multiple disabilities have a great number of instructional needs, including physical therapy, speech therapy, and mobility training, as well as important functional self-help skill training such as time management, social skills, money management, and perhaps academic skills. Finding time in a student's schedule for all of these activities will be difficult if not impossible. However, the importance of not waiting for a student to near graduation to initiate vocational preparation should be emphasized.

A great number of skills and behaviors can be taught as part of a student's vocational training activities. Mobility, time management, and social skills are only a few of these that are required in an employment setting and that a student can practice in that context. Parents will feel more comfortable agreeing to a substantial portion of their child's program being devoted to vocational activities if they understand this fact.

Strategy 7:   Ask Parents to Reinforce Their Child's Performance

Because parents can influence greatly the extent to which a student is motivated to perform vocationally, they should be encouraged to express interest in their child's work training and performance and to encourage him or her in this regard. One approach that can serve to enhance the probability that parents will remember to do this is to send home the Job Feedback Form that was described in Chapter 5. Parents can then review the information reported with their child, reinforce progress and good performance, and encourage him or her to try harder in other areas.

STRATEGIES TO ENHANCE
PARENT INVOLVEMENT AND SUPPORT AFTER
PLACEMENT IN COMMUNITY-BASED EMPLOYMENT

The importance of family support in the employment of persons with disabilities in community settings has been established (Kochany & Keller, 1981; Schultz, 1986; Wehman, 1981). For the most part, however, programs generally approach the issue of family involvement in an unsystematic fashion. They may tell parents how important their support is and then hope that parents will provide it. Given the critical importance of parent support, it is imperative that programs give as much attention and effort to developing a systematic intervention approach for gaining the support of families as is given to other program components. The following provides a description of seven strategies that can be utilized to increase the family's involvement in support of job placement and maintenance. The reader should also refer to Chapter 7 to gain additional information about the way in which school programs can and should include parents in the transition for school to paid employment.

Strategy 1:   Obtain Input from Parents About Their
Needs and Desires Related to Their Child's Employment

Families may have specific desires related to the hours when their child will work, the number of hours he or she will work, the type of job, the location of the job site, and so forth. Parents and families are also an excellent source of information about their sons and daughters and the types of situations in which they will most likely be successful.

One of the best strategies for obtaining input from parents regarding their desires related to their child's placement is through a structured interview approach (Schultz, 1986). The purpose of this approach is to provide a systematic yet flexible means to probe parents about their desires. The questions shown in Table 3 provide examples of those that might be included in the interview. It is important that they understand the issues facing them. For example, if parents indicated that they had no preferences regarding the hours when their daughter works, the interviewer should ask, "You wouldn't mind if she works at night?"

Also, a parent's initial response may be modified after discussion and clarification. For instance, parents may indicate that they do not want their child to work in the downtown area due to safety concerns. Program staff can explain that eliminating businesses in the downtown area will dramatically decrease the opportunities and increase the amount of time involved in locating an appropriate job. Staff may also provide examples of individuals whom they have placed downtown with no problems.

Through the structured interview, program staff will gain a clearer idea of the parents' desires related to their child's placement. This process also reinforces in the parents the importance of their involvement in their child's suc-

Table 3.   Parent interview questions

1. Do you have a strong preference regarding the type of work that your child will perform? Are there any jobs that you would be strongly opposed to your child performing?

2. Are there any jobs that you know that your child likes to perform? Are there any jobs that you know your child strongly dislikes?

3. Are there any areas of town where you would prefer your child to work? Are there any areas of town where you would be strongly opposed to your child working?

4. Do you think your child would prefer to work inside or outside?

5. Does your child work better at tasks that require moving around a lot or tasks that allow sitting or standing in one place?

6. Do you think your child will work better for a male or female supervisor, or does it matter?

7. Does your child like to work around a lot of other people, or does he or she work better alone?

8. What hours would you prefer that your child work? Are there any hours that you would definitely not want your child to work?

9. How many hours per week would you prefer that your child work? Would you be willing to consider a job for your child that had a different number of hours than your preference?

---

cessful employment. It also enhances their confidence that the program is interested in, and responsive to, their views.

Strategy 2:   Obtain Possible Job Leads from Parents and Family

The likelihood of obtaining a job in a company is greatly enhanced if the job seeker has a personal contact in the company. Parents and other family members typically have friends, relatives, and business contacts in numerous companies throughout a community that can be of great assistance in finding an appropriate job. In fact, Hasazi, Gordon, and Roe (1985) found that more than 80% of former special education students obtained employment through a family connection. Parents can be asked to identify any individuals who may be willing to advocate for the hiring of their child or other individuals with disabilities.

Strategy 3:   Keep Parents Informed of Placement Activities

In some cases it may take weeks or months to find a job for a person. In order to maintain parents' interest and motivation in the placement of their child during this period, it is useful to provide them with regular updates on job search efforts. This can be achieved by calling the parents to describe the companies that have been contacted and analyzed, the reasons why they did not work out as a placement, and those that are targeted for contact during upcoming weeks.

Strategy 4:   Review Details of a Potential Job with Parents Before Proceeding with Placement Activities

The fourth strategy occurs when a job has been located that may be a potential placement for a student. The program staff should meet with the individual's parents and describe all aspects of the job, including the tasks that will be performed, hours, pay, social environment, vacation policy, sick leave policy, and dress and grooming requirements. If there is more than one potential placement, then each should be described, and the parents should be given the opportunity to select the one that they prefer.

Parents often have certain responsibilities if they agree to the placement. Their commitment to fulfill them should be obtained. For example, if a job starts at 7:00 A.M., they will have to make a commitment to assist their child in getting up, getting dressed, and getting to the bus by 6:15 A.M. The parents may also need to make a commitment to assisting the individual to wear a clean uniform each day. Finally, because the company's policy directs that employees are not given time for doctor or dentist appointments, the parents will have to commit to making these appointments on their child's day off. Delineating these details and gaining the commitment of parents before a job is accepted and initiated will help ensure that difficulties related to parent cooperation do not arise later and, thus, jeopardize job success.

Strategy 5:   Give Parents Critical Information in Writing About Their Responsibilities

If parents do consent for their child to be placed into a particular job, the program can proceed in making the final arrangements with the employer regarding the placement. Before the individual begins the job, it is useful to provide parents with a Job Information Form (see Figure 16). This form provides a clear description of the critical information about their child's job. The purpose of this strategy, is to avoid difficulties that may arise due to a lack of parent understanding of the job. Program staff should go over the information on the form with the parents in order to make sure they understand it and to clarify any points of confusion.

Strategy 6:   Provide Specific Suggestions to Parents About How They Can Support and Reinforce Their Child's Job Performance

The family is probably the most powerful source of influence in the student's attitude, motivation, and behavior related to work. Program staff can provide parents with specific suggestions on how to reinforce and positively support their son or daughter for working and performing well at a job. Providing these

---

JOB INFORMATION FORM

1. Employment position _____
2. Employer's name _____
3. Employer's phone number and address _____
   _____
4. Hours worked _____   5. Days worked _____
6. Wages earned _____
7. When wages paid/how check received _____
   _____
8. Benefits _____
   _____
9. Vacations/Holidays _____
   _____
10. Starting date _____
11. Uniform/suggestions for uniform care _____
   _____
12. Transportation: To job _____
    From job _____
13. Meals _____
   _____
14. Doctor/dentist appointments _____
   _____
15. What to do if ill/late _____
   _____
16. Other relevant information _____
   _____

Figure 16.   Job information form.

suggestions in writing for parents is especially helpful. Table 4 provides an example of such a document. It identifies suggestions that can serve as a guide to parents for reinforcing their sons or daughters.

Staff can go over the suggestions with parents and emphasize the importance of following them as much as possible. It might be recommended that the document be posted in a location in the home where family members will see it and be reminded to do these things. During routine phone contacts with parents, staff can ask if they are doing these things and reinforce them for doing so. During the first few months of their child's job, the phone calls should be made on a weekly basis, after which they may occur monthly. It is useful to send a duplicate document to parents every month or two in case it has been misplaced or discarded, as a reminder of the importance of their support.

Table 4. How to reinforce and support your child's employment

1. Give your child a few words of encouragement before he or she leaves for work each day.
2. Talk with your child about how things went at work when he or she comes home each day.
3. Tell your child on a regular basis how proud you are that he or she has a real job.
4. In front of your son/daughter, tell your neighbors, relatives, friends about his/her job and how proud you are.
5. Be particularly enthusiastic each time your child brings home a paycheck.
6. Make depositing his/her check a particularly big event. Make a special trip to the bank. Make sure he/she understands that the money earned at work is going into the bank. Have your child get at least a small amount of cash when depositing the check to spend on something he/she would like, such as a record, tape, or article of clothing.
7. If a portion of your child's earnings are used to contribute to basic family expenses such as rent, food, and utilities, make sure that you and other family members reinforce him/her on a regular basis for the important contribution that he/she is making to the family.
8. Set aside a portion of your child's earnings to be spent on activities and items that he/she wants and provide him/her with the opportunity to purchase these items and to participate in these activities. The program staff will provide you with specific suggestions and assistance in doing this.

Strategy 7: Provide Ongoing Information to Parents About Their Child's Job Performance and Status

It is important to provide parents with ongoing information about how their child is doing on the job. The following are some of the types of information that should be shared with parents regarding their child's performance: 1) progress in learning assigned tasks, 2) social and survival skill performance, 3) progress learning to ride the bus to and from work, 4) co-worker relations, 5) changes that occur in the job (i.e., new co-workers, supervisors, task assignment change), 6) feedback from supervisors, and 7) how much their child seems to be enjoying the job.

This information can be shared with parents during the same phone calls used to prompt them about their role in reinforcing their son's or daughter's work performance. Progress reports can thus be used as the basis for the feedback that the parents provide to their child.

CONCLUSION

Involving parents in the education of their children can be a difficult and time consuming task for school staff. Goodall and Bruder (1985) have pointed out the fact that parents vary greatly in how much involvement they are able and willing to have and that staff should respect and work with these variations. However, staff should attempt to be creative in utilizing strategies that will allow parents to gain an understanding of the importance of vocational training and employment for their child and to gain their support of these activities.

REFERENCES

Goodall, P. & Bruder, M. (1985). Parent involvement in the transition process. In P. McCarthy, J. Everson, S. Moon, & M. Barcus (Eds.), *School-to-work transition for youth with severe disabilities*. Virginia Commonwealth University, Richmond, Va.

Hasazi, S., Gordon, L., & Roe, C. (1985). Factors associated with the employment status of handicapped youth exiting high school from 1979 to 1983. *Exceptional Children, 51*(6), 455–469.

Kochany, L., & Keller, J. (1981). An analysis and evaluation of the failures of severely disabled individuals in competitive employment. In P. Wehman (Ed.) *Competitive employment: New horizons for severely disabled individuals* (pp. 181–198). Baltimore: Paul H. Brookes Publishing Co.

McDonnell, J., Hardman, M. L., Hightower, J. (1989). Employment preparation for high school students with severe handicaps. *Mental Retardation, 27,* 396–405.

McDonnell, J., Wilcox, B., Boles, S. M., & Bellamy, G. T. (1985). Transition issues facing youth with severe handicaps: Parents' perspectives. *Journal of The Association for Persons with Severe Handicaps, 10,* 61–65.

Schultz, R. P. (1986). Establishing a parent-professional partnership to facilitate competitive employment. In F. R. Rusch (Ed.), *Competitive employment issues and strategies* (pp. 289–302). Baltimore: Paul H. Brookes Publishing Co.

Siegal, G., & Loman, L. (1987). Enhancing employment opportunities for persons who are developmentally disabled. *Journal of Job Placement,* Summer/Fall, 16–20.

Sowers, J. (1989). Critical parent roles in supported employment. In G. H. S. Singer & L. K. Irvin (Eds.), *Support for caregiving families: Enabling positive adaptation to disability* (pp. 269–282). Baltimore: Paul H. Brookes Publishing Co.

Wehman, P. (Ed.). (1981). *Competitive employment: New horizons for severely disabled individuals*. Baltimore: Paul H. Brookes Publishing Co.

DARCY

Darcy, who is 25 years of age, uses a power cart for mobility and has fairly good use of her hands. Darcy participated in a work experience program for several years, during which time she learned a variety of clerical tasks including simple computer data entry, filing, and photo-copying. During her last year of school, a job was created for Darcy at a bank as a microfilm specialist. The tellers were responsible for microfilm-ing all of the checks that came through the bank on a daily basis, but they were having difficulty keeping up with this task in addition to their other job duties. Consequently, the bank was very enthusiastic about creating a new position at the bank for Darcy as a microfilm specialist. Although microfilming is her major responsibility, she also does some photocopy-ing, supplies the customer area with deposit and withdrawal slips, does a simple filing task, and picks up mail from the officers' desks and delivers it to the mail room.

Darcy has been employed on a part-time basis for over 4 years. Her productivity is about 50%. However, the bank pays her a regular wage which is now $5 per hour. She also receives full employee benefits, which include vacation, health insurance, and a retirement plan.

Only a few job adaptations were needed for Darcy. The microfilm machine was moved to permit easier access to it, a table was put next to the machine for her to keep her work materials, and she uses a number

DARCY
(continued)

stamp in place of writing to record the code numbers of completed check batches.

Darcy's main task performance difficulties are remaining on task and keeping her rate of work up enough to complete all of the checks each day. Darcy and her supervisor talk for a few minutes at the end of each day, at which time the supervisor gives her feedback on how she did that day. The supervisor completes a simple job feedback form that Darcy keeps in a notebook and shows to her parents when she gets home.

9 Related Service Staff Roles

PL 94-142, the Education for All Handicapped Children Act of 1975, requires the provision of "related services," including physical, occupational, and speech therapy services to students with disabilities when it is deemed that a student requires these services to benefit educationally. In accordance with this law, therapists are involved in the educational programs of most students with physical and multiple disabilities (York, Rainforth, & Dunn, 1990). However, because these students have not typically been provided vocational training, little guidance is available regarding roles that therapists and other related staff should play in the vocational programs.

It is clear that therapists, given their expertise and knowledge, need to join teachers and vocational trainers in providing vocational preparation to students with physical and multiple disabilities. However, to make a meaningful contribution to this effort, many therapists will need to redefine their roles, as well as the basic service delivery beliefs and approaches in which they have been trained (Rainforth & York, 1987). In addition, administrative support will be required to support therapists in these roles.

This chapter describes the roles that occupational, physical, and speech therapists can and should play in preparing students with physical and multiple disabilities for the transition from school to work. A number of issues that must be considered and addressed in order to permit their involvement will be discussed. In addition, other types of related service expertise that may be needed when vocationally preparing and employing these students are addressed.

THERAPY MODELS: IMPLICATIONS FOR THERAPISTS' ROLES

Many therapists have been trained in traditional medical models of therapy and service delivery (York et al., 1990). These models focus on the underlying causes of disabilities, and they assume that a person's ability to learn and perform functional activities will be limited until these underlying causes can be remediated. The role of therapists in these models is primarily aimed at designing and delivering programs to improve the "causes" of a student's disability. These programs are typically delivered in therapy rooms or other isolated settings, and often do not include functional skills or activity instruction. Therapists operating in the traditional model also work autonomously rather than in collaboration with other staff.

A new model of related service delivery began to receive support in the late 1970s. This transdisciplinary model encourages therapists to work as a member of the educational team in teaching functional skills (Albano, Cox, York, & York, 1981; Campbell, 1987; Giangreco, 1987; Hart, 1977; Hutchinson, 1978; McCormick & Goldman, 1979; Orelove & Sobsey, 1987; Szymanski, HanleyMaxwell, & Parker, 1990). In this model of service delivery, therapy goals are not targeted and taught apart from other functional skills. Rather, goals are identified that have a clear and direct relationship to the ability of the student to perform a specified functional skill. The therapist works to achieve the therapy goal by teaching it as part of the functional skill, in the settings where the student will perform the skill. For example, in the traditional model a physical therapist might attempt to increase and maintain a student's range of motion during therapy sessions held in the classroom or therapy room, using prescribed exercises. In the new model, the therapist might work with the physical education teacher to identify ways that he or she can incorporate movements to improve the student's range of motion into the physical education activities planned for the class in which the student is mainstreamed. Therapists operating in this new model also provide consultation to other staff related to difficulties that students may have learning to perform a functional skill because of their physical or communication disability. For example, an occupational therapist may suggest the optimal seating for a student who is beginning to learn to use a computer.

Within the context of the new model of service delivery, occupational, physical, and speech therapists clearly have an important role to play in the vocational preparation and employment programs of students with physical and multiple disabilities (Rainforth & York, 1990; Sowers, Hall, & Rainforth, 1990; Wehman, Wood, Everson, Goodwyn, & Conley, 1988). One of their primary roles is to provide consultation to teachers and vocational trainers when a work experience site is being sought and established for a student. Information related to task and work-related skill performance issues that may be affected by a student's physical disability or communication difficulties should be discussed. In this role, the teacher or vocational trainer will take the lead responsibility for developing and implementing the task training, but they will utilize the specialized expertise of the therapist. Optimally, an occupational or physical therapist should accompany the teacher or vocational trainer to the site (including in-school work experiences for students in middle school) during the job and task analysis process, in order to get a first hand look at the physical characteristics of the site and the physical and communication requirements of the job. If the therapist is not able to do so, he or she should discuss specific details that the teacher or other vocational trainer should note during the analysis, which may be particularly relevant to the student. The therapists should then review the information gathered and provide input related to the extent to which the job is a feasible training or placement match for the student. If it is decided that the student will be placed at the site, the therapist should then suggest job design and adaptation strategies, including those pertaining to work-related issues that will enable him or her to function as independently and productively as possible. Some of these suggestions could be made without the therapist first seeing the site or job. However, the therapist should visit the site and observe the student working within a few days after he or she has started there. This will allow the therapist to more precisely identify the optimal positioning of the student and to identify additional task-design and adaptation strategies that may be needed, and to refine those that are in place. When special devices or jigs are needed, the therapists should take lead responsibility for ensuring that they are purchased or built and for setting them up at the site.

The amount of time that a therapist should devote to visiting a work site will depend on the needs of the student. For a student who faces significant physical challenges in performing a job, a therapist should be available to visit the site on a frequent basis (i.e., at least once a week), while for other students it may be sufficient, after the initial visits when the student first begins a work experience or job, for the therapist to visit the site no more than once a month.

It is probably not necessary for a speech therapist to accompany the teacher or vocational trainer during the site analysis. However, if a student has communication difficulties, the therapist should be available to discuss the communication demands of the job with the staff before the student begins at the site and to suggest communication strategies that can be used. If this involves buying or devising a special communication device, the speech therapist should take this responsibility and provide instruction to the teacher, aide, or vocational trainer regarding how to teach the student to use it.

A second role of therapists is to develop and implement programs that will assist students to become as independent as possible in performing work-related behaviors. The work-related behaviors identified in Chapter 3 often serve as barriers to employment for students with physical and multiple disabilities. These are bathroom use, eating and drinking, mobility, communication, and drooling. Because therapists have particular expertise related to these issues, it may be appropriate for them to take the lead in developing and implementing programs that will prepare students to function as independently as possible when placed in community work experience and employment sites. During students' elementary and middle school years occupational therapists should develop a bowel-and-bladder control management program for students who have difficulties in these areas. For students who are not able to transfer independently when using the bathroom, therapists should identify and train strategies that will enable them to do so as independently as possible. Eating and drinking programs should be devised and delivered by an occupational therapist, possibly in collaboration with a speech therapist. A physical therapist should focus on teaching students to ambulate or use a mobility device to move around buildings, sidewalks, and across streets, and when using public buses. The occupational therapist should design a program that will assist students to control their drooling. Finally, a speech therapist should identify a mode of communication that students can use most functionally and teach the student to use it.

In this discussion, the roles that physical and occupational therapists can play have not been differentiated. This is not meant to imply that the training or expertise of these two professions are the same (Sowers et al., 1990). Both occupational and physical therapists have in-depth knowledge of physically handicapping conditions and their potential impact on a student's functioning related to the dynamics of body positioning. However, the preservice training of occupational therapists typically prepares them to have a more functional-skill training orientation than physical therapists. For example, occupational therapists often learn basic instructional strategies such as task analysis, and in-depth information about adaptive strategies. However, many physical therapists have acquired a significant knowledge base in functional-skill training issues and adaptation strategies. In addition, physical therapists have particular expertise related to mobility issues.

Given the orientation and background of these two professions, it is likely that in most districts occupational therapists will play a more key role in the vocational preparation of students. They will assist in the analysis of job sites and tasks, and in identifying adaptation strategies. They will also identify and develop many of the strategies and programs to teach work-related skills, while a physical therapist will consult with the occupational therapist regarding positioning and will take the lead with mobility issues.

ENHANCING THERAPISTS'
VOCATIONAL PROGRAM INVOLVEMENT

The involvement of therapists in the vocational preparation and employment of students with physical and multiple disabilities as defined in this chapter represents a departure from the manner in which therapists function in many school districts. There are a number of things that must occur to enable therapists to fill these roles. First, and perhaps most importantly, there must be administrative support for these shifts (Wilcox & Bellamy, 1982; York et al., 1990). Related service staff scheduling must reflect the new model in order for therapists to be willing and able to implement it. Scheduling staff to work with individual students during brief and set times derives from the traditional model of service delivery. For staff to be able to visit work experience sites and to provide their assistance based on the changing needs of students at these sites, they will need much greater flexibility. Block scheduling has been suggested as a way to provide this flexibility (Rainforth & York, 1987; York, Rainforth, & Wiemann, 1988). Using block scheduling, staff are assigned to be available to work with a number of students for longer periods of time. For example, from Monday through Thursday a therapist might be assigned to visit four different schools where she or he will be available to work with all of the students at each school, while Fridays can be left unscheduled for providing additional assistance as needed to students as well as other duties (e.g., arranging for the purchase of devices or building jigs). This schedule provides the therapist the flexibility to provide more or less attention to students, depending on their needs at a specific time. For example, during the week when a new work experience site is being set-up for John, the therapist could devote several hours at the site to analyze it and the tasks that he will perform and to consult with the vocational trainer. After John is settled into the site, the therapist would devote less time to him and more to other students.

Many school districts assign therapists to work with students from all age groups. Yet, the focus of therapy intervention is clearly different for younger and older students (Wilcox & Bellamy, 1982). This is particularly true in relation to the amount of emphasis that is placed on vocational training. It may be more efficient and effective for districts to designate a number of therapy staff to specialize in, and focus on, the needs of secondary-aged students, while others focus on younger students.

Another implication of a service delivery model that intimately involves therapists in student vocational preparation is the need for therapists to become knowledgeable of "best-practice" vocational preparation strategies and supported employment. Many therapists received some preservice training related to employment and some have worked in adult service employment programs. However, it is likely that this training and experience reflected traditional employment models and approaches. School districts should provide therapists with training that will allow them to most effectively fill their new roles. District staff with vocational training and employment expertise can provide this training. Related service staff should also be provided with the opportunity to attend in-service training programs, workshops, and conferences related to vocational training and employment issues.

The success of therapists' involvement in vocational preparation programs will be influenced by their willingness to view themselves as members of a team as well as their ability to communicate their knowledge to other team members. There are specific things that therapists can do to foster team collaboration and increase the utility of information they provide to the team. First, they should avoid highly technical or medical language. Using terms that teachers, aides, and vocational trainers (as well as co-workers and employers) understand increases both the usefulness of the information being communicated and the sense of equality among the members of the team. Second, when teaching staff to use specific procedures with a student (e.g., bathroom transfers, positioning), therapists should write the procedures down, demonstrate them several times, and provide feedback while staff practice the procedures (York et al., 1990).

In most districts, related service staff carry large caseloads and thus the amount of time that can be devoted to individual students is limited. The block scheduling strategy should assist in allowing therapists to most effectively use the limited time they have (Lyon & Lyon, 1980). Role release is another strategy that can be used to allow therapists to use their expertise where it is most critical. Through role release, therapists proactively impart their knowledge and expertise to other staff and empower them to take on some of the roles that formally may have been designated only to such a therapist. Teachers and vocational staff can learn such things as basic positioning principles, what questions to ask and what things to look for when analyzing tasks and job sites, communication strategies, and how to adapt job sites and tasks. Therapists, as any specialized professional, will understandably be protective of the knowledge and expertise that they have spent many years gaining. The same is true for teachers and vocational staff. However, the delivery of services to students will be enhanced if all members of the team are willing to share their knowledge and to define their roles based on need of students and program effectiveness, rather than on tradition.

OTHER EXPERTISE NEEDED

The focus of the discussion to this point has been on the contributions that speech, occupational, and physical therapy can make to the vocational preparation of students with physical and multiple disabilities. Clearly, there are other areas of expertise that may be needed to achieve this objective. Many of these students also experience sensory disabilities, such as vision and hearing deficits. For these students, schools will need to gain the input of specialists in these areas. In Chapter 3, the need to consult with medical specialists for a student with bladder or bowel control difficulties was pointed out. Medical specialists will also be needed for student's who experience health problems that may affect their employment.

Job design, site modifications, and device design and building are important activities in the vocational preparation and employment of students with physical and multiple disabilities. Occupational therapists as well as teachers and vocational trainers will be able to take on most of the responsibility. However, on occasion they will need assistance from a person with rehabilitation engineering expertise. These are persons who have specific training in identifying, designing and building devices to increase the ability of persons with physical disabilities to perform functional tasks (Wehman et al., 1988). There are persons who have been formally trained through rehabilitation programs. However, in most cases, persons who identify themselves as rehabilitation engineers or technicians have some formal training in engineering or related fields, and through experience have gained expertise in applying their skills to persons with physical disabilities. Most school districts will not need or cannot afford to have such a person on staff. An attempt should be made to find one or more individuals who would be willing to work on an "as-needed" consultative basis. Hospitals, adult programs and vocational rehabilitation agency are places to seek names of persons with expertise in these areas.

In some cases, district staff may have the expertise to identify most job design needs and jigs that need to be built, but do not have the skills or time to actually construct them. A rehabilitation engineer or technician may not be needed in these situations—persons who have construction skills, such as shop teachers, may be willing to help out. The parents or relatives of students are also resources for this assistance. A staff person might also approach local civic organizations and ask if any of their members would provide assistance in building jigs and devices.

Jobs that include computer-related tasks are often ones that students with physical and multiple disabilities are trained to perform and into which they are placed (Everson et al., 1990; Wehman et al., 1988). Consequently, a person with expertise in computers and computer assistive devices is needed. It is likely that with the increasing use of computers in schools for students with disabilities (as well as those who do not have disabilities) that there will be staff in the district with this knowledge. Such persons should be consulted about relevant vocational and employment issues.

DEFINING STAFF ROLES

This chapter has provided a general discussion of the roles that related service staff can play in the vocational preparation of students with physical and multiple disabilities. The actual roles and duties of these staff, as well as those of teachers, teaching assistants, and vocational trainers, will vary from district to district. The availability of each of these staff and their individual expertise will determine the specific duties that they can assume in delivering vocational services to students. In addition, staff will need to take on different functions at different phases of a student's program (i.e., elementary school, middle school, high school, and transition). It is critical to the success of vocational programs that districts plan and clearly define the roles of staff during each phase. An example of how a district might define the roles that staff will play during different phases of a student's program is provided in Figure 17.

	Teacher	Vocational staff	Occupational therapist	Physical therapist	Speech therapist
Elementary school	• Identify and assign simple chores to students. • Organize projects that will provide students work opportunities. • Convey expectation that students can and will work as adults to students and parents. • Visit several work experience sites where middle and high school students work.	• Assist teacher to organize presentations by adults with disabilities to speak to class about their life and jobs. • Meet with teacher once a year to get information on what vocational activities he or she is doing, to make suggestions, and to become familiar with students.	• Assist teachers to identify task design and adaptation strategies that will allow students to perform chores and work projects. • Plan and implement eating, drinking, bathroom use, and drooling programs as needed. • Visit several work experience sites where middle and high school students work.	• Plan and implement functional mobility programs. • Provide input related to student positioning when performing work tasks.	• Plan and implement functional communication programs.
Middle school	• Recruit potential in-school work experience sites. • Conduct job and task analysis. • Train student or supervise classroom aide who provides training. • Continue to reinforce expectations for employment to students and parents.	• Communicate to teacher the types of tasks that are available in local job market. • Provide job analysis and work experience instruction to teachers and therapists. • Meet with teachers several times each year to provide input into their vocational	• Assist teacher in analysis of work experience sites and tasks. • Assist teacher to identify task design and adaptation strategies that will allow students to perform tasks at in-school work experience sites as independently as	• Plan and implement functional mobility programs and incorporate into work experience. • Provide input related to student positioning at in-school work experience sites.	• Plan and implement functional communication programs. • Identify specific strategies that students can use to most effectively communicate at work experience site.

Figure 17.   Examples of staff role definitions.

Middle school (con't)	• Visit several community work experience and employment sites where high school students work.	preparation programs and to track student progress.	possible. • Plan and implement eating, drinking, bathroom use, and drooling programs as needed, and incorporate into work experience. • Visit several community work experience and employment sites where high school students work.	
High school	• For students 16–17 years of age, take lead responsibility for providing community work experiences to them, including conducting job analysis, training or supervising classroom aide trainers at sites, and interfacing with site supervisors. • For students 18–20 years of age, provide input to vocational staff about types of tasks and sites around which work experience can best	• For students 16–17, recruit community work experience sites that will be conducted by teachers. Provide instruction and assistance to teachers and aides about how to set up and conduct work experience sites. • Recruit and conduct work experience sites for students 18–20 years of age. • Talk with teacher via telephone once a week about student progress.	• Assist teacher and vocational staff to conduct job site and task analysis. • Identify and implement job design strategies at site for student. • Identify and implement strategies that students can use related to eating, drinking, and using the bathroom. • After initial job analysis and design, visit site at least monthly to determine need for additional design	• Provide input to teacher, vocational staff, and occupational therapist regarding optimal positioning. Visit site if necessary to determine best positioning. • Identify the mode of mobility that students will use to get to and around work site. • Provide guidance to staff re-	• Based on teacher or vocational staff description of communication demands of site, identify best mode of communication for students to use. If needed, program electronic communication device or construct communication board that students will use

(continued)

Figure 17. *(continued)*

Teacher	Vocational staff	Occupational therapist	Physical therapist	Speech therapist
be established for students. • Talk with vocational staff via telephone once a week about student's program at site. • Along with vocational staff person, meet with parents at least twice annually. These meetings will include descriptions of adult system, their child's current work experience and work performance, and what they can do to become involved in and support their child's vocational program. • Provide practice on difficult steps in classroom. • Go over Job Feedback Form with student. • Visit site monthly. • Attend quarterly vocational team meetings to review student progress.	• Meet with teacher and parent. • Attend quarterly meeting to review student progress. • Send job feedback forms to teachers.	and adaptation strategies. • Attend quarterly meetings to review student progress.	lated to training strategies for mobility issues. • Attend quarterly meetings to review student progress.	at site. • Attend quarterly meetings to review student progress.

High school (con't)

Job placement/transition				
• Ensure that students are referred for services to local funding agencies. • Provide input to vocation staff about type of job to seek for students.	• Identify adult provider who will provide ongoing support to students. • Gain input from student and family about the type of work situation desired—location, hours, tasks, type of company. • Search for and place students into jobs. • Provide detailed information to adult provider about site, student, and support needs and strategies. • Introduce employer and co-workers to adult service provider. • Work with adult provider to arrange transportation to site if public buses are not available. • Introduce parent to adult provider.	• Assist in job site and task analysis. • Identify and implement job design and adaptation strategies at site for student. • Identify and implement strategies related to eating, drinking, using bathroom, and drooling. • Meet with adult providers and instruct them in issues around positioning of the student, adaptive strategies that the student will use to eat, drink, use the bathroom, and decrease drooling.	• Identify mode of mobility that student will use to get to and around work, and assist in training. • Provide input related to positioning as needed.	• Identify and design communication strategy for students to use at site; give demands there. • If needed, meet with co-workers and supervisors to help them to feel comfortable communicating with students.

It is suggested that districts bring staff together each year for a day or half a day to discuss and plan the vocational program. Of course, this meeting will include discussions of the vocational program provided to all students, not just those with physical and multiple disabilities. This meeting should be used to provide staff with general information and innovations in supported employment and vocational preparation. This may include descriptions of demonstration projects that have been successful in working with students and adults with difficult challenges (e.g., students with physical and multiple disabilities) and new vocational preparation best-practice strategies. Representatives from local employment funding and provider agencies can be asked to speak and discuss services that are available and how students can access them. These persons may also be asked to provide input and suggestions for what the school program can do differently to better prepare students for future employment, and to ease their transition to the adult program system. Information about the employment status of past graduates should also be presented as a basis for determining the need for program change. Finally, program activities and staff roles related to these roles have contributed to the effectiveness and efficiency of the program should be discussed. Descriptions of what activities at each level of the program and staff roles should occur, along with a critical analysis of what has and has not worked. Using all of this information, plans for how the program will be organized, including the roles that staff will play can then be made.

CONCLUSION

The roles and functions of related service staff have over the last decade begun to be redefined and to depart from those which they have traditionally practiced. This chapter has discussed how therapists' roles will be need to be further expanded as students with physical and multiple disabilities begin to be provided with vocational preparation and employment opportunities.

REFERENCES

Albano, M. L., Cox, B., York, J., & York, R. (1981). Educational teams for students with severe multiple handicaps. In R. York, W. Schofield, D. J. Donder, & D. L. Ryndak (Eds.), *The severely and profoundly handicapped child.* Chicago: Illinois State Board of Education.

Campbell, P. (1987). The integrated programming team: An approach for coordinating professionals of various disciplines in programs for students with severe and multiple handicaps. *Journal of The Association for Persons with Severe Handicaps, 12*(2), 107–116.

Everson, J., Callahan, M., Hollohan, J., Gradel, C., Cohen, R., Button, C., Franklin, K., & Brady, F. (1990). *Getting the job done: Supported employment for persons with severe physical disabilities.* Washington, DC: United Cerebral Palsy.

Giangreco, M. F. (1987). Delivery of therapeutic services in special education programs for learners with severe handicaps. *Physical and Occupational Therapy in Pediatrics, 6*(2), 5–15.

Hart, V. (1977). The use of many disciplines with the severely and profoundly handicapped. In E. Sontag, J. Smith, & N. Certo (Eds.), *Educational programming for the severely and profoundly handicapped*. Reston, VA: Council for Exceptional Children –Division of Mental Retardation.

Hutchinson, D. J. (1978). The transdisciplinary approach. In J. B. Curry & K. K. Peppe (Eds.), *Mental retardation: Nursing approaches to care*. St. Louis: C. V. Mosby.

Lyon, S., & Lyon, G. (1980). Team functioning and staff development: A role release approach to providing integrated educational services for severely handicapped students. *Journal of The Association for the Severely Handicapped, 5*(3), 250–263.

McCormick, L., & Goldman, R. (1979). The transdisciplinary model: Implications for service delivery and personnel preparation for the severely and profoundly handicapped. *AAESPH Review, 47*(2), 152–161.

Orelove, F. P., & Sobsey, D. (1987). Designing transdisciplinary services. In F. P. Orelove & D. Sobsey (Eds.), *Educating children with multiple disabilities: A transdisciplinary approach* (pp. 1–24). Baltimore: Paul H. Brookes Publishing Co.

Rainforth, B., & York, J. (1987). Integrating related services in community instruction. *Journal of The Association for Persons with Severe Handicaps, 12*(3) 190–198.

Sowers, J., Hall, S., & Rainforth, B. (in press). Related services personnel in supported employment: Roles and training needs. *Rehabilitation Education*.

Szymanski, E., Hanley-Maxwell, C., & Parker, R. M. (1990). Transdisciplinary service delivery. In F. R. Rusch (Ed.) *Supported employment: Models, methods and issues* (pp. 199–214). Sycamore, IL: Sycamore Publishing Co.

Wehman, P., Wood, W., Everson, J. M., Goodwyn, R., & Conley, S. (1988). *Vocational education for multihandicapped youth with cerebral palsy*. Baltimore: Paul H. Brookes Publishing Co.

Wilcox, B., & Bellamy, G. T. (1982). *Design of high school programs for severely handicapped students*. Baltimore: Paul H. Brookes Publishing Co.

York, J., Rainforth, B., & Dunn, W. (1990). Training needs of physical and occupational therapists who provide services to children and youth. In A. P. Kaiser & C. M. McWhorter (Eds.), *Preparing personnel to work with persons with severe disabilities* (pp. 153–179). Baltimore: Paul H. Brookes Publishing Co.

York, J., Rainforth, B., & Wiemann, G. (1988). An integrated approach to therapy for school-aged learners with developmental disabilities. *Totline, 14*(3), 36–40.

NATHAN

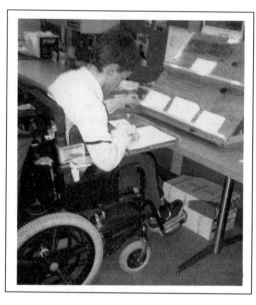

Nathan is 18 years old. He uses a power wheelchair for mobility and has limited functional use of one hand. He is unable to speak, but uses a symbol book to communicate. Nathan had his first opportunity to gain out-of-class work training and experience about a year ago. He had done some in-class computer data entry and benchwork-type task training, but had shown little interest and motivation to work in this setting. A work experience site was established for him at a city office. He goes to the site along with another student (who does not experience a physical disability) and a vocational assistant from the classroom. He works at the site three times a week for approximately 3 hours, doing three major tasks. He sorts information cards by area of the city (e.g., N.E., S.E.) that is typed at the top of the card. The jig shown in the picture was designed and constructed by the aide for Nathan to assist him to more easily perform this task. He also enters information from the cards into a computer database and participates in photocopying on a daily basis. A key-guard was made to fit the keyboard of the computer at the site. Nathan looks forward to going to work and the aide reports that he is highly motivated to do a quality job and to take on new tasks.

KRISTEN

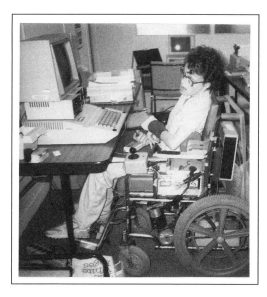

Kristen, who is 19 years of age, has limited functional use of her hands, uses a power wheelchair, and uses an electronic communication device.

Kristen had the opportunity to learn computer data entry through an in-school work experience, where she entered information for the library. This past year she went to a community site in an office, where she also did computer data entry, stapling, and photocopying tasks. Kristen worked at the site 2 hours a day, 3 days a week. A training assistant accompanied her to the site.

Kristen can gain access to a computer keyboard by using a keyguard. However, this is very slow and tiring for her. Thus, she was trained to use a switch scanning system. The switch is placed on a surface located on her lap. The location was identified as the easiest for her to use after trying several locations. To photocopy, the training assistant places the document on top of the machine then Kristen slides it into the feeder. She then pushes the number to be copied and the start button. For her to be able to do these steps independently required many weeks of training. She is currently learning to remove the copies from the machine.

Kristen uses a jig for stapling. The jig includes a paper collator, a paper guide (made from two boxes), and an electric stapler. She slides the papers to be copied into the guide and then pushes the papers forward into the stapler.

Index